Social Marketing and Public Health
Theory and Practice

Second Edition

Edited by

Jeff French

CEO Strategic Social Marketing, Visiting Professor, Brighton University Business School, and Fellow, King's College, University of London, UK

OXFORD
UNIVERSITY PRESS

OXFORD

UNIVERSITY PRESS

Great Clarendon Street, Oxford, OX2 6DP,
United Kingdom

Oxford University Press is a department of the University of Oxford.
It furthers the University's objective of excellence in research, scholarship,
and education by publishing worldwide. Oxford is a registered trade mark of
Oxford University Press in the UK and in certain other countries

Published in the United States of America by Oxford University Press
198 Madison Avenue, New York, NY 10016, United States of America

British Library Cataloguing in Publication Data

Data available

Library of Congress Control Number: 2016952282

ISBN 978–0–19–871769–0

Printed and bound by
CPI Group (UK) Ltd, Croydon, CR0 4YY

Oxford University Press makes no representation, express or implied, that the
drug dosages in this book are correct. Readers must therefore always check
the product information and clinical procedures with the most up-to-date
published product information and data sheets provided by the manufacturers
and the most recent codes of conduct and safety regulations. The authors and
the publishers do not accept responsibility or legal liability for any errors in the
text or for the misuse or misapplication of material in this work. Except where
otherwise stated, drug dosages and recommendations are for the non-pregnant
adult who is not breast-feeding

Links to third party websites are provided by Oxford in good faith and
for information only. Oxford disclaims any responsibility for the materials
contained in any third party website referenced in this work.

Social Marketing and Public Health

To Bob Willis, a true craftsman, much-missed father, husband, and friend.

Preface to the Second Edition

For governments across the world, understanding human behaviour sits at the heart of developing interventions to tackle social and health issues as diverse as HIV, obesity, smoking, drug misuse, and sanitation. What we know is that our current approaches to tackling many of these huge challenges (UN, 2015) are not working, or at least are not delivering results at a rate to achieve the scale of improvement necessary to slow, and in some cases ultimately reverse, problems such as health inequalities or the growing tide of chronic disease. This book makes the case and explores much of what is known about what governments, public sector organizations, and others can do to work with people to tackle these challenges. Specifically, this book sets out to explore and define what social marketing is and how it can help with the design, development, delivery, and evaluation of more effective and efficient public health programmes that seek to influence health-related behaviour.

The term 'social marketing' was used for the first time in 1971 by Philip Kotler and Gerald Zaltman, who defined it as follows:

> Social marketing is the design, implementation, and control of programs calculated to influence the acceptability of social ideas and involving considerations of product planning, pricing, communication, distribution, and marketing research.

Since the publication of this definition, a great deal of refinement of the concept of social marketing has occurred and much learning has been gained from field-level experience, which we explore in this book. In chapter two we discuss the defining principles and concepts of social marketing and discover that it not only draws upon theory, methodology, and techniques developed in the commercial sector, such as audience segmentation, but also draws on experience, theory, and techniques from the public and not-for-profit sectors. At its core, social marketing is focused on enabling, encouraging, and supporting behavioural change or on maintaining and re-engineering services and systems to support and facilitate positive health behaviour.

The Aim of this Book

The simple premise of this book is that those concerned with public health need to put a lot more effort into understanding why people act as they do and then ensure that this understanding is used in a systematic way to develop and deliver social improvement intervention programmes. We need to understand what people are prepared to buy into with their time, energy, beliefs, and values, and sometimes their money, if we are going to be able to make a significant impact on issues such as smoking or infection control. We need to enable and empower people so that their energy, understanding, and skills are harnessed as part of the solution to improving health. Social marketing is an approach that recognizes that if we are to be successful, it is not about doing things to people but about working with and for them.

The second key theme of this book is the need for public health programmes to be more rigorously researched, designed, developed, implemented, and evaluated. Too many public policy interventions have unclear or unrealistic aims, poor pre-testing and piloting, and often weak evaluation. A key feature and strength of social marketing is its obsession with systemic analysis and systematic programme development and implementation. Without clear measurable objectives and cogent implementation plans, it is probable that little will be achieved and little will be learned about how to help people that can be used to further refine new interventions.

This book also recognizes that social marketing, like every other multidisciplinary field of endeavour, is not static. It is a developing and dynamic concept. We have attempted in this second edition of the book to simultaneously update the discussion of social marketing theory and practice and take a more globally relevant stance so that the principles, techniques, and methodologies described are relevant to those working in both the developed and developing world.

This book is intended to give the reader a structured learning experience that results in a good understanding of social marketing principles and techniques, alongside examples of real interventions that have made a difference to people's lives. Each chapter starts with a brief overview and a set of learning objectives. Most chapters also include case studies to illustrate the concepts or techniques being described. The chapters are set out in such a way as to lead the reader through a logical sequence of understanding, but each is also capable of being read in isolation and it is anticipated that some readers will pick and mix the chapters and sections that they are interested in. It is our intention in this book to capture in a single volume an up-to-date picture of the theoretical principles and concepts that underpin social marketing as they apply to public health and to set them out in an accessible way. We hope that you enjoy this book and that you will play an active part in further developing and refining our collective understanding of social marketing within the public health field.

Jeff French
February 2017

References

Kotler, P., Zaltman, G. (1971). Social marketing: an approach to planned social change. *Journal of Marketing* 35(3): 3–12.

UN (2015). Sustainable Development Goals [website]. New York: United Nations http://www.un.org/sustainabledevelopment/sustainable-development-goals/

Acknowledgements

I would very much like to thank all the authors of chapters for this book and those colleagues at Population Services International who supplied many of the case studies featured. I would also like to thank all the staff at Oxford University Press for their support and encouragement in developing and completing this second edition.

Jeff French

Contents

Abbreviations

AASM	Australian Association of Social Marketing
ACT	artemisinin-based combination therapy
AMA	American Marketing Association
ASSIST	A Stop Smoking in Schools Trial
BIT	Behavioural Insight Team
BoP	base of the economic pyramid
CDC	Centers for Disease Control and Prevention (US)
CFW	Child and Family Wellness (franchise)
CoE	code of ethics
DALY	disability-adjusted life-year
DH	Department of Health
ECDC	European Centre for Disease Prevention and Control
ESMA	European Social Marketing Association
FHE	field health educator
FP	family planning
GP	general practitioners
HAM	Health Action Model
MRC	Medical Research Council
mRDT	rapid diagnostic test for malaria
MSI	Marie Stopes International
MWRA	married women of reproductive age
NGO	non-governmental organization
NICE	National Institute for Health and Care [formerly Clinical] Excellence
OC	oral contraceptives
PPP	public–private partnership
PSI	Population Services International
QALY	quality-adjusted life-year
RCT	randomized controlled trial
ROI	return on investment
SCT	Social Cognitive Theory
SF	social franchise
SFMWG	Social Franchising Metrics Working Group
SMART	specific, measurable, achievable, relevant, time-bound
SMC	Social Marketing Company
SQH	Sun Quality Health
STEPLE	social, technological, economic, political, legal, and environmental (factors)
SWOT	strengths, weaknesses, opportunities, and threats
TIB	Theory of Interpersonal Behaviour
TMA	total market approach
UV	ultraviolet
VMMC	voluntary medical male circumcision
WHO	World Health Organization
WRA	women of reproductive age

Contributors

Qaiser Jamshad Asghar
Marie Stopes Society Pakistan, Karachi, Pakistan

Asma Balal
Marie Stopes Society Pakistan, Karachi, Pakistan

Lauren Beek
The HealthStore Foundation®, MN, USA

Hana Bilak
PATH, Geneva, Switzerland

Melissa K. Blair
The Reputation Group, Melbourne, Australia

Nikki Charman
Population Services International, Nairobi, Kenya

Kumbirai Chatora
Population Services International, Harare, Zimbabwe

Socheat Chi
Population Services Khmer, Phnom Penh, Cambodia

Daniel Crapper
Population Services International/Myanmar, Yangon, Myanmar

Adam Crosier
Word of Mouth Research Ltd., Hampton, London, UK

Stephan Dahl
Hull University Business School, University of Hull, UK

Komal Daredia
Marie Stopes Society Pakistan, Karachi, Pakistan

Stephanie Dolan
Population Services International, Nairobi, Kenya

Lynne Eagle
College of Business, Law and Governance, James Cook University, Australia

Jeff French
Strategic Social Marketing Ltd., Conford, Liphook, Hampshire, UK, and Fellow, King's College, University of London, UK

Karin Hatzold
Population Services International, Harare, Zimbabwe

Han Win Htat
Population Services International/Myanmar, Yangon, Myanmar

Sotheary Khim
Population Services Khmer, Phnom Penh, Cambodia

Dianna Long
Population Services Khmer, Phom Penh, Cambodia

Kim Longfield
Population Services International, Washington, DC, USA

David Low
College of Business, Law and Governance, James Cook University, Australia

Cristina Lussiana
Population Services International, Nairobi, Kenya

Yasmin Madan
Population Services International, Washington, DC, USA

Munyaradzi Mapingure
Population Services International/Zimbabwe, Harare, Zimbabwe

Webster Mavhu
Centre for Sexual Health and HIV/AIDS
Research (CeSHHAR), Harare, Zimbabwe

Julie McBride
MSA Worldwide, Washington, DC, USA

Dominic McVey
Word of Mouth Research Ltd., Hampton,
London, UK

Dominic Montagu
Associate Professor of Epidemiology and
Biostatistics, University of California San
Francisco, San Francisco, CA, USA

Stephen Poyer
Population Services International,
Bristol, UK

Ashfaq Rahman
The Social Marketing Company, Dhaka,
Bangladesh

Rova Ratsimandisa
Population Services International/
Madagascar, Antananarivo,
Madagascar

Dana Sievers
Population Services International,
Washington, DC, USA

Greg Starbird
Starbird Consulting, Ashland,
OR, USA

Noah Taruberekera
Population Services International,
Johannesburg, South Africa

Manuela Tolmino
Population Services International,
Dhaka, Bangladesh

Chapter 1

The case for social marketing in public health

Jeff French

Social Marketing seeks to develop and integrate marketing concepts with other approaches to influence behaviour that benefits individuals and communities for the greater social good.

Social Marketing practice is guided by ethical principles. It seeks to integrate research, best practice, theory, audience and partnership insight, to inform the delivery of competition sensitive and segmented social change programmes that are effective, efficient, equitable and sustainable.

Global definition of social marketing endorsed by the Boards of the International Social Marketing Association, European Social Marketing Association, and Australian Association of Social Marketing, October 2013

Learning points

This chapter:

- reviews key macro societal drivers of change and development, together with the impetus these are adding to the application of social marketing by public health agencies and practitioners around the world;

- explores the need for a new citizen-focused approach to addressing health challenges and reviews the characteristics of effective practice;

- explores the rationale and arguments for why social marketing has become a key tool for public health agencies and professionals.

Introduction to the case for social marketing in public health

It is a fact that every big health challenge facing governments around the world contains significant behavioural elements. Infection control, family planning, drug misuse, sanitation, smoking, obesity, alcohol misuse, and infection control all involve the need for people to behave in ways that will promote or protect their health. In addition to influencing individuals' behaviour, most public health programmes aim to influence organizational and often professional behaviour. Influencing behaviour, as we will explore in chapter six, can be achieved in many different ways, but one thing is constant: the need for systematic planning and delivery based on the widest set of evidence and intelligence available.

The world has experienced unprecedented improvements in health over the last 50 years (UN, 2015) but there is much still to be done. In the developing world we face the ongoing threats of infectious disease and child mortality and new threats from the rise in chronic disease (WHO, 2015a) and climate change (Stern, 2007). We also face huge economic and social challenges associated with persistent and growing inequalities between regions and countries and within countries (WHO, 2008). At an individual level, a personal sense of self-worth and the search for meaning act on the mental and physical health of millions of people (WHO, 2010); these are both contributory factors to and consequences of this complex web of challenges (Australian Public Service Commission, 2007).

Despite these challenges it needs to be remembered that at a global population level a fantastic amount of progress is being made in improving health and well-being. In large part this success has been brought about through the application of more evidence-based practice (WHO, 2015b) and user insight-informed programmes about how to influence behaviour and how to construct, deliver, and evaluate public health programmes to influence behaviour.

In parallel with these developments, data shows that in many countries questions relating to the legitimacy of state intervention to influence people's lives are growing (Ipsos MORI, 2010), together with calls for state intervention to be limited because it often breeds dependence (Acemoglu and Robinson, 2012) and sometimes even encourages people to behave in ways that are not good for them or society as a whole (Murray, 2006).

Given the rapidly evolving health threats and opportunities faced by the world and the equally rapidly changing relationship between states and the people they seek to govern and protect, this chapter explores how and why social marketing is becoming regarded as a standard approach to public health practice. It argues that citizens' views and wants should be given more prominence in the selection, planning, and delivery of all public health programmes. Such a change means that governments and their public health agencies will increasingly look to enhance traditional public health tools to bring about behaviour change such as legislation, taxation, and information giving with other types and forms of intervention—see chapters five and six—that are focused more on encouraging, engaging, and enabling people to act to improve their own health and the well-being of others.

The growth of global paternalistic healthism

In most health policy over the last 20 years, the word 'health' denotes not merely the absence of disease but also well-being and social justice. Health has also been promoted as a fundamental 'human right' at least since the 1978 World Health Organization (WHO) Alma-Ata Declaration (WHO, 1978). WHO has argued that this 'right to health' can only be realized through the combined and coordinated action of all social and economic sectors. This is a reasonable proposition supported by a wealth of insights and evidence from many academic and practice fields.

Health has been described as an emergent capacity arising from the integrated effects of somatic, social, economic, and cultural activity. It is not something that can be attained solely from health sector-directed expenditure or attempts to get people to live healthy lives (Wilkinson and Marmot, 2003). If we accept that health is determined by such factors, the development of better health will need whole-system solutions (French and Gordon, 2015). Such solutions, however, depend on how the system is conceived and the role of state-sponsored public health within this. There are very different views about the answers to these questions among public health practitioners and between governments, the commercial sector, and citizens.

WHO and many public health practitioners have, for over 30 years, argued that prevention and treatment of disease should be viewed by all governments as their primary duty. In so doing, the avoidance and treatment of disease is positioned as the driving force and the ultimate goal of the world's economic and political systems. Smith et al. (2003) have advocated that health actually constitutes the most important form of 'global health good'. Conceived in this way public health represents a radical left-of-centre position, calling for no less than a global, political, and economic reorientation of society as proposed by Marmot (2008).

For those public health practitioners who hold such views, the main goal of society is not seen as the promotion of individual freedom, collective prosperity, or the accumulation of wealth and personal independence but medically defined health status. Many public health practitioners view markets and capitalism as a key part of the problem rather than part of the solution to improving health. This antagonism towards markets runs deep—for example, the refusal to tax high-sugar or fatty foods or the failure to restrict tobacco advertising by governments is often criticized by public health practitioners, even though such measures often have a disproportionate economic effect on the poorest in society. Politicians, on the other hand, often view with increased frustration the constant criticism from public health professionals and recommendations that they view as being at least partly ideologically motivated.

Public health conceived in this way has been criticized by Armstrong (1983; 1993; 1995), Fitzpatrick (2001), and others as representing the ever-expanding medicalization of life. Kurtz (1987) has also argued that health has become the 'new religion' and public health workers are the new puritanical priests offering punishment for the 'bad' life and rewards for the 'good' healthy life.

This 'collective paternalistic' stance stands in stark contrast to how health promotion is perceived by most governments. Minkler (1989) believes that health promotion and public health are predominantly viewed as being largely about protection from infectious diseases, encouraging behavioural change. Traditionally, governments use an intervention mix of law, education, and service provision to improve health. They are also responsible for developing regulated markets to act as an engine for collective and individual prosperity and increased well-being. This clear clash of ideological positions between most governments and the paternalistic collectivist stance supported by many public health professionals sits at the heart of the current theoretical and practical antagonism between public health advocates and many administrations. Kelly and Charlton (1995) agree with the proposition outlined above that public health has become a left-of-centre political campaign in which health is viewed as a moral right. Peterson and Lupton (1996) have further criticized public health as a source of moral regulation and consequent state-sponsored control of individual freedoms. Stevenson and Burke (1991) are also critical of health promotion, arguing that it seeks to weaken and depoliticize action for social equality by turning what is a political and economic struggle into a technical professionally led intervention.

It could be argued that public health then sits at a crossroads. It could continue to hold to a position that simultaneously emphasizes that health promotion and protection is the pre-eminent responsibility of the state and that public health practitioners hold the body of expertise and the moral authority that can deliver this goal. Alternatively, public health practitioners can assume a less ideological position and a more technically focused role based on what is known about how to influence health behaviour, drawn from a broad range of science and experience, and position public health through the application of social marketing principles as a field dedicated to working with and through citizens to achieve collectively agreed social objectives defined by citizens and their representatives.

Acknowledgement that governments cannot do it alone

Creating an environment of maximum choice for the majority requires the coordinated application of all policy tools to influence the behaviour of individuals, organizations, and markets. In this way, we can shift to a more balanced view of the locus of power, to what Rothschild (2001) calls the 'apparent power' of government to the 'actual power' of individuals. We need to recognize the fact that both governments and individuals have power and responsibilities; public health strategy must explicitly acknowledge this. In this regard, Kickbusch et al. (2005) have emphasized the need in public health for co-production of solutions to complex social issues and challenges.

Liberal democracy and regulated free market economies are generally recognized as forces for social good (Roberts, 1985; Fukuyama, 1992). These complex systems, with all their benefits, problems, and complexities, are the reality for many and an aspiration for more and more of the world's population. There is also increasing recognition that the power of civil society, the private sector, the non-governmental organization (NGO) sector, and the thousands of community groups and civil associations represents and has always represented the main bedrock of success in building better lives for people. Civil society provides more health and social care than the state, informs and educates more children and adults, creates more employment than the state, and provides the myriad of social networks that nurture and develop citizens. The well-being of society is intertwined then with the well-being of individuals, their social networks, cultures, and the confidence and resources they have to choose and create the kinds of lives they want, often using markets to drive prosperity and improved life chances. As we explore in chapter ten, the private sector and NGO sector have a vital part to play in tackling almost all of the big health challenges that the world faces. These sectors' reach, expertise, and deep understanding of people needs to be harnessed in a far more coordinated way (Box 1.1).

Box 1.1 Case study: evidence-based demand creation and advocacy interventions for voluntary medical male circumcision scale-up in Zimbabwe

Karin Hatzold, Kumbirai Chatora, Noah Taruberekera, Webster Mavhu, Munyaradzi Mapingure

Aims

Zimbabwe is among the countries most affected by HIV and AIDS. In 2015, HIV prevalence among adults was estimated at 15% (UNAIDS, 2013). The Government of Zimbabwe adopted voluntary medical male circumcision (VMMC) as an HIV prevention intervention in 2009 following WHO's recommendation that countries with generalized HIV epidemics and a low prevalence of male circumcision progressively expand access to safe VMMC (National AIDS Council, 2011; CSO and Macro International, 2007; WHO and UNAIDS, 2007).

Despite scale-up of service provision by Population Services International (PSI), uptake of VMMC was slow. By September 2013, only 170,000 men had been circumcised against a five-year target of 1.27 million (MOHCC, 2014). In 2013 PSI/Zimbabwe launched a campaign using mass media and interpersonal communication to generate greater demand for VMMC services.

Behavioural objectives and target group

The campaign targeted two groups of men, segmented by age: adolescents (15–24 years) and adults (25–49 years). Its objectives were to increase men's uptake of VMMC services by addressing barriers and dispelling myths and misconceptions about the procedure.

Customer orientation

Male circumcision prevalence prior to the start of the VMMC programme was one of the lowest in the Southern African region, at 10.3%, since only minority ethnic groups practice circumcision traditionally (CSO and Macro International, 2007). Thus, a priority of the social marketing campaign was to distinguish VMMC for HIV prevention and its health benefits from the traditional practice. PSI also needed to understand personal barriers and motivators for VMMC uptake among the target audiences.

Social offering

VMMC provides a range of health and social benefits to the individual. In addition to a 60% risk reduction in heterosexually acquired HIV infection (Auvert et al., 2005; Bailey et al., 2007; Gray et al., 2007), VMMC reduces the risk of sexually transmitted infection (Weiss et al., 2006) and penile cancer in men (Auvert et al., 2009), improves genital hygiene, and is believed by many to increase sexual appeal and performance (Bailey et al., 1999; Mattson et al., 2008) (Figure 1.1).

Furthermore, VMMC reduces the risk of human papillomavirus transmission and consequently the risk of cervical cancer in female partners of circumcised men (Auvert et al., 2009). Impact modelling demonstrated that Zimbabwe's VMMC programme could avert 212,000 new HIV infections by 2025 and save the country more than $1 billion in health expenditures related to HIV treatment (MOHCC, 2014; Njeuhmeli et al., 2011).

Target audience engagement and exchange

While HIV prevention is often cited as a reason for getting circumcised, men seem mainly motivated by non-HIV-related factors. To increase acceptance of the service, PSI positioned VMMC as a lifestyle choice rather than only for HIV prevention.

The campaign offered information about the procedure to address fears of experiencing pain, complications, and a difficult healing period. Because fear of receiving an HIV-positive test result especially prevented older, sexually active men from getting circumcised, the campaign also clarified that HIV testing was not a prerequisite for male circumcision (Hatzold et al., 2014; Mavhu et al., 2011; Westercamp and Bailey, 2007).

To address the issue of perceived threat to masculinity and to capitalize on the importance of social support, the campaign featured women. Since women are likely to influence their partners' decision to get circumcised, even if covertly (Lanham et al., 2012), testimonials were used. These featured women discussing how they had supported their partners and how they themselves had benefited from male circumcision. Messages also highlighted VMMC's role in improving men's hygiene and sexual appeal to women.

Another way the campaign leveraged the importance of social support was by tailoring messages for adolescents that presented VMMC as fashionable and leading to success, and as a lifestyle choice for 'smart' men. Peer groups also worked with youths to improve their attitudes towards VMMC.

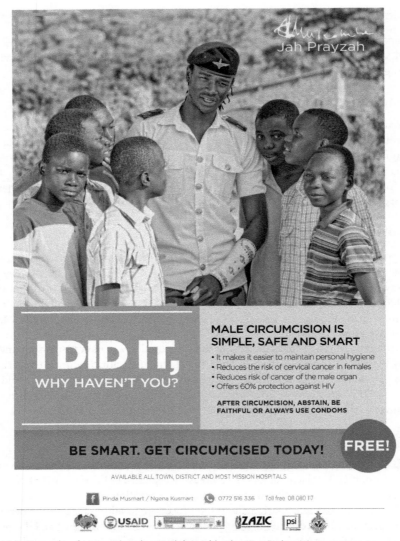

Figure 1.1 Example of promotional material used in the 'I'm Doing It' programme. Reproduced by kind permission of PSI Zimbabwe.

Competition analysis

VMMC is a one-time, highly effective intervention with substantial prevention against HIV. No other HIV intervention currently available provides this permanence of effect. Condoms, microbicides, pre-exposure prophylaxis, and HIV treatment all require considerable adherence to realize the desired effectiveness (Reed et al., 2012).

Audience insight and segmentation

PSI conducted quantitative and qualitative research to inform the VMMC communications and marketing strategy. It was clear from the data that the target age groups expressed strong attitudes towards VMMC and were motivated by different factors. Study findings suggested that demand-creation messages needed to be tailored for different age groups. Older men were motivated by the promise of improved hygiene, enhanced sexual performance, and the opportunity to set an example for the community. Younger men were influenced by peers' attitudes and behaviours and by role models, such as popular musicians who took up VMMC to advocate for the programme.

Integrated intervention mix

Campaigns were implemented during school holidays with intensified service delivery as well as community mobilization before and during breaks, combined with mass media. VMMC services were offered in clinics located close to schools and other places where young people congregate.

Longer media formats, such as radio and television programmes, were used to engage with the target audiences. Satisfied clients were featured and answered general questions, while doctors and nurses provided technical information about the procedure plus its associated health and HIV prevention benefits.

Community-level activities reinforced mass media messages. Younger and older men and women were trained at the community level to promote VMMC among peers through small group discussions and edutainment.

Systematic planning

The success of the campaign was based on intensive formative research, which guided the marketing planning process. Consistent messaging through multichannel mass media and interpersonal communication was supported by intensive advocacy featuring public celebrities and politicians who encouraged men to 'lead by example'. Intensified demand creation was coupled with VMMC service expansion and rapid scale-up.

Results and learning

Between 2011 and 2014, uptake of male circumcision among males more than quadrupled and the 'smart campaign' became a popular synonym for VMMC in Zimbabwe.

Marketing approaches to public health are becoming increasingly recognized as more effective strategies for translating knowledge and awareness in the population to action. Although many men may understand the benefits of VMMC, they require a different intervention to support their personal decision to get circumcised. Rather than a 'product-driven' or an 'expert-driven' programme, VMMC demand-generation strategies must address consumers' values and needs, their anxieties towards the service, and develop messaging that positions VMMC as responsive to consumers' emotive and functional needs (Lefebvre and Flora, 1988).

References

Auvert, B., Taljaard, D., Lagarde, E., Sobngwi-Tambekou, J., Sitta, R., Puren, A. (2005). Randomized, controlled intervention trial of male circumcision for reduction of HIV infection risk: the ANRS 1265 Trial. *PLoS Med* **2**(11):e298.

Auvert, B., Sobngwi-Tambekou, J., Cutler, E., Nieuwoudt, M., Lissouba, P., Puren, A., Taljaard, D. (2009). Effect of male circumcision on the prevalence of high-risk human papillomavirus in young men: results of a randomized controlled trial conducted in Orange Farm, South Africa. *Journal of Infectious Disease* **199**(1): 14–19.

Bailey, R.C., Neema, S., Othieno, R. (1999). Sexual behaviors and other HIV risk factors in circumcised and uncircumcised men in Uganda. *Journal of Acquired Immune Deficiency Syndrome* **22**(3): 294–301.

Bailey, R.C., Moses, S., Parker, C.B., Agot, K., Maclean, I., Krieger, J.N., Williams, C.F.M., Campbell, R.T., Ndinya-Achola, J.O. (2007). Male circumcision for HIV prevention in young men in Kisumu, Kenya: a randomised controlled trial. *Lancet* **369**(9562): 643–656.

CSO, Macro International. (2007). *Zimbabwe Demographic and Health Survey 2005–06.* Calverton, MD: Central Statistical Office Zimbabwe and Macro International Inc.

Gray, R.H., Kigozi, G., Serwadda, D., Makumbi, F., Watya, S., Nalugoda, F., Kiwanuka, N., Moulton, L.H., Chaudhary, M.A., Chen, M.Z., Sewankambo, N.K., Wabwire-mangen, F., Bacon, M.C., Williams, C.F.M., Opendi, P., Reynolds, S.J., Laeyendecker, O., Quinn, T.C., Wawer, M.J. (2007). Male circumcision for HIV prevention in men in Rakai, Uganda: a randomised trial. *Lancet* **369**(9562): 657–666.

Hatzold, K., Mavhu, W., Jasi, P., Chatora, K., Cowan, F.M., Taruberekera, N., Mugurungi, O., Ahanda, K., Njeuhmeli, E. (2014). Barriers and motivators to voluntary medical male circumcision uptake among different age groups of men in Zimbabwe: results from a mixed methods study. *PLoS ONE* **9**(5): e85051.

Lanham, M., L'Engle, K.L., Loolpapit, M., Oguma, I.O. (2012). Women's roles in voluntary medical male circumcision in Nyanza Province, Kenya. *PLoS One* **7**(9):e44825.

Lefebvre, R.C., Flora, J.A. (1988). Social marketing and public health intervention. *Health Education Quarterly* **15**(3):299–315.

Mattson, C.L., Campbell, R.T., Bailey, R.C., Agot, K., Ndinya-Achola, J.O., Moses, S. (2008). Risk compensation is not associated with male circumcision in Kisumu, Kenya: a multi-faceted assessment of men enrolled in a randomized controlled trial. *PLoS ONE* **3**(6): e2443.

Mavhu, W., Buzdugan, R., Langhaug, L.F., Hatzold, K., Benedikt, C., Sherman, J., Mundida, O., Woelk, G., Cowan, F.M. (2011). Prevalence and factors associated with knowledge of and willingness for male circumcision in rural Zimbabwe. *Tropical Medicine and International Health* **16**(5): 589–597.

MOHCC (2014). *Accelerated Strategic and Operational Plan 2014–2018: voluntary medical male circumcision.* Harare, Zimbabwe: Ministry of Health and Child Care.

National AIDS Council (2011). *Zimbabwe National HIV and AIDS Strategic Plan 2011–2015.* Harare, Zimbabwe: National AIDS Council of Zimbabwe.

Njeuhmeli, E., Forsythe, S., Reed, J., Opuni, M., Bollinger, L., Heard, N., Castor, D., Stover, J., Farley, T., Menon, V., Hankins, C. (2011). Voluntary medical male circumcision: modeling the impact and cost of expanding male circumcision for HIV prevention in eastern and southern Africa. *PLoS Med* **8**(11):e1001132.

Reed, J.B., Njeuhmeli, E., Thomas, A.G., Bacon, M.C., Bailey, R., Cherutich, P., Curran, K., Dickson, K., Farley, T., Hankins, C., Hatzold, K., Ridzon, R., Ryan, C., Bock, N. (2012). Voluntary medical male circumcision: an HIV prevention priority for PEPFAR. *Journal of Acquired Immune Deficiency Syndrome* **60**(suppl 3):S88–S95.

UNAIDS (2013). HIV and AIDS estimates (2013) [website]. Geneva: UNAIDS http://www.unaids.org/en/regionscountries/countries/zimbabwe, accessed 30 March 2015.

Weiss, H.S., Thomas, S.L., Munabi, S.K., Hayes, R.J. (2006). Male circumcision and risk of syphilis, chancroid, and genital herpes: a systematic review and meta-analysis. *Sexually Transmitted Infections* **82**(2):101–110.

Westercamp, N., Bailey, R.C. (2007). Acceptability of male circumcision for prevention of HIV/AIDS in sub-Saharan Africa: a review. *AIDS and Behavior* **11**(3): 341–355.

WHO, UNAIDS (2007). *New data on male circumcision and HIV prevention: policy and programme implications.* Geneva: World Health Organization.

The new citizen-informed public health model

There is always a tension when setting out the goals of social programmes between aiming high and being realistic about what can be achieved. However, it is the case that we have succeeded in many parts of the world in generating a belief and reality that people can make their own history. As Anthony Giddens (1991) has pointed out, in the developed world ours is the first mass generation to view life as other than just the playing-out of fate; we have become the lead actor in the film of our own lives and are able to determine what happens to us to a larger extent than has ever been possible before.

This shift in emphasis for an increasing number of people away from just a daily struggle to survive towards a situation where they are increasingly seeking higher levels of self-understanding, satisfaction, and happiness is a huge social triumph. A profound consequence of this achievement is that the notion that your fate is determined by structural or mystic forces outside your control is being increasingly seen as untrue and even offensive to more and more people. With regard to factors outside individuals' control, Corrigan (2004) has argued that there is a danger when public health becomes too focused on the macrosocial and economic determinants of health to the exclusion of other explanations. Corrigan argues that an over-focus on health determinants can attempt to explain too much and leaves no dialectic for the importance of individual agency. The concept that the determinants of health should be the principle focus of public health has to be reconsidered in the light of the fact that we now live in a world of consumption—a place where more people are able to have many more 'consumption experiences', or choices, than were available in previous eras. People enjoy consumption and the sense of being in control that it brings them. In these circumstances determining factors make a less powerful impact, and the concept of external determining factors is itself also less acceptable to many people. Public health cannot stand outside this world of consumption experience. As LeGrand (2007) argues, there are four basic factors that underpin any type of public services including public health services:

1. trust—where professionals are just trusted to deliver high-quality services;
2. targets and performance management—where workers are directed to deliver by a higher authority who sets the targets and measures performance;
3. voice—where users are given a chance to say what they think about the service;
4. the 'invisible hand' of choice and competition.

LeGrand further argues that although all of these factors have their strengths and weaknesses, approaches to public health service delivery that incorporate substantive elements of choice and competition have the best prospect of delivering services that make a positive contribution to people's lives. LeGrand sets out extensive evidence that systems driven by choice and competition are not only more efficient and responsive but also better at providing people who have less voice and economic advantage with better services. It is also true that poor people want choice just as much as the better off and stand to derive just as much if not more benefit from systems set up to emphasize these features. In short, there is a need for what Osborne and Gaebler (1992) argued for in their seminal work *Reinventing government*: 'customer-driven government'. This means services and interventions being informed by data about citizens' views and needs and by a desire to meet these needs, as opposed to aims and objectives identified by professional elites driving the system. As Halpern et al. (2004) state:

> Ultimately, this is not just about the government and its agencies learning a few extra techniques to 'make people eat their greens'. Rather it is about helping individuals and communities to help

themselves. A more sophisticated approach enables governments to do this in ways which command greater public engagement and therefore greater effectiveness.

In this situation, state approaches to behavioural change that emphasize telling people what to do, or restricting behaviour by the force of law, can be doomed to failure unless they have the popular support of the vast majority of citizens. People now need to be engaged, listened to, and helped to change—not just forced, nudged, or hectored into change. It is also worth noting that as people become more empowered they trust governments and state organizations less and become more resistant to what they perceive as interference by governments (OLR, 2002; Ipsos MORI, 2010). Halpern et al. (2004) have suggested that there is a case for moving towards what they call the 'full co-production' model, in which citizens are engaged in the design, implementation, and evaluation of policy and practice.

We do, of course, know that those with more power and resources can have more control over their experiences and also have more choices. These disparities in choice and control are some of the key reasons for health inequalities (Wilkinson and Marmot, 2003). However, less choice and less power are not the same as no choice and no power. It is also well understood that setting up choice or market systems is usually the most efficient way to distribute resources, provided they are set up in such a way to address the risk that those with more resources and capacity may seek to gain a disproportionate share or access to such resources or services (Giddens, 2003; Lent and Arend, 2004).

The fact of increasingly empowered citizens has huge implications for state-sponsored public health interventions intent on making the world a better place and improving health. It means that a focus on enabling and empowering people to do the right thing for themselves and others is increasingly a key part of the way forward. This requires services and interventions driven by a desire to meet citizens' needs and not needs defined solely by experts.

Many public health behavioural change interventions are based on evidence derived from published studies and analysis of demographic, service uptake, and epidemiological data. This information is vital but not always sufficient to develop effective behavioural interventions. In contrast, the commercial sector invests heavily in market research to understand people's motivations, needs, wants, fears, and aspirations about why they would purchase goods or services, or what goods and services they feel they need or would like. Public health and other forms of public sector interventions need to enhance their understanding of the target group's motivations if they are going to be able to develop more effective programmes. It should be remembered also that by target groups we mean not only individuals but also social groups, organizations, policy-makers, and politicians, all of whom may be the target of a social marketing-informed public health programme.

A key driver for a more user-focused approach to tackling population health behavioural challenges is essentially a public sector version of a switch from a product- or service-focused approach to a citizen-focused strategy. This switch in emphasis drives most successful for-profit organizations and many not-for-profit organizations that rely on user or donor support. An increasingly empowered and demanding citizenry represents a triumph rather than a problem for governments. This shift in power and expectation demands that governments and their institutions demonstrate that they are adding value to the lives of the people that they serve. Given this perception by the public, one of the challenges facing governments is to set out more clearly what value they are creating for the people they serve.

Moore (1995) and Kelly et al. (2002) have identified the concept of public value as having three dimensions: outcomes, the delivery of services, and trust. Kelly et al. (2002) also argue that public value only exists if people are willing to give something up in return for the service they get, such as granting coercive powers to the state in return for security and protection. This 'exchange' is a key feature of social marketing and requires reciprocal actions on the part of both the state and citizens; it is often called the 'social contract'. The state is required to understand citizens' perspectives on the nature and value of these trade-offs, and citizens are required to accept limitations on behaviour for the collective good. In a world where public value will be measured and used by citizens to assess government and public sector performance, we require new approaches to understand both citizens and what they are prepared to exchange for different behaviour and change programmes that make changing behaviour easy and, where possible, rewarding for people. This change in emphasis sits at the heart of this book and at the heart of social marketing.

There is a case then for governments and those concerned with promoting health to move away from a purely 'expert-defined', systems-focused, mechanistic 'product' approach to change and service delivery and towards a social marketing approach that places more emphasis on the citizen user and co-producer. The focus of such a new model is set out in Figure 1.2. In this new approach views, beliefs, and suggestions from citizens are key streams of intelligence that are used alongside epidemiology, demographics, and intervention evidence to inform public health policy and strategy development and programme delivery.

The development of such a citizen-informed model of service delivery and improvement in public health, through the rigorous application of social marketing, can result in public service organizations that are more motivated, progressive, ambitious, and constantly striving to improve services, not for the sake of managers or policy-makers but for the benefit of the service users.

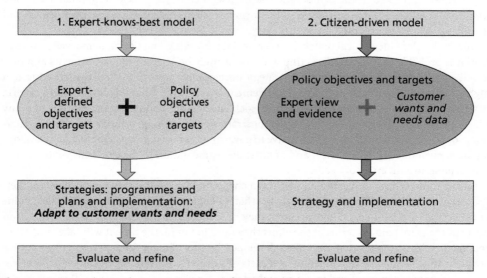

Figure 1.2 Expert-knows-best versus citizen-informed model.
Source: data from Moore MH. *Creating public value—strategic management in government.* Cambridge, MA: Harvard University Press, Copyright © 1995 by the President and Fellows of Harvard College; and Kelly G, Mulgan G, and Muers S. *Creating public value. An analytical framework for public sector reform.* London: Prime Ministers Strategy Unit, Cabinet Office, Copyright © 2002 Crown Copyright, http://webarchive.nationalarchives.gov.uk/20100416132449/http:/www.cabinetoffice.gov.uk/media/cabinetoffice/strategy/assets/public_value2.pdf, accessed 01 May 2016.

If such an approach was universally applied, it would soon become clear to citizens that the public health providers were seeking to provide them with the kinds of help they need and in ways that were most convenient for them. Health improvement interventions would be developed and delivered from a perspective of listening and understanding, and not telling and selling. Public health would be characterized by responsiveness and dedicated to satisfying people's health needs.

Social marketing adding value to a citizen-informed approach to public health

As argued so far in this chapter, most health issues stem from a combination of personal choice, environmental factors, cultural factors, and economic factors. Personal choices about issues such as healthy eating are played out against a background of many powerful influences on individual behaviour. As we will explore in chapter six, there is evidence from many disciplines that people do not always act in a logical way. This fact has led some to argue for an approach that uses non-rational appeals and design to influence health behaviour (Thaler and Sunstein, 2008), which is known as 'libertarian paternalism' (Sunstein and Thaler, 2003). Liberal paternalism seeks a middle ground between a state-dominated coercive paternalistic approach that appeals to logic to drive social change and a more liberal approach that emphasizes free choice and the power of the market.

Although social marketing employs a lot of what Thaler and Sunstein (2008) call 'nudges', it goes beyond nudges to include interventions that people value both cogitatively and emotionally—see chapters two and six for more on this issue. Social marketing is a set of principles and concepts that are largely ideologically neutral. It can be used to inform paternalistic policy, libertarian paternalism, and a laissez-faire approach to promoting health. Social marketing is, however, rooted in the democratic tradition as it constantly seeks a mandate for action from the target groups it aims to help in the form of insights gained from market research and the market testing of potential interventions.

Due to the close ideological match between social marketing and liberal democratic imperatives it is probable that social marketing will increasingly be selected by governments as a preferred public health intervention and strategy development approach. Social marketing is a highly systematic approach to health improvement that sets out unambiguous success criteria in terms of behaviour change. In this respect, social marketing stands in stark contrast to many health promotion interventions which demonstrate weak planning systems and poor evaluation. Social marketing will also be attractive to governments because of its emphasis on developing deep customer insight, choice, and population segmentation to develop interventions that can respond to a diversity of needs.

As mentioned above and explored further in chapter two, a central concept of social marketing is that of 'exchange'. Exchange recognizes that if people are going to change their behaviour or collectively work for social improvement they need to believe that the reward for such action is worth the price paid, in terms of the effort they need to put in, the time it will take, and other cost factors. This implies that any offers developed by those intent on assisting people to live healthier lives need to be developed on the basis of a deep understanding of the views, motivations, and barriers encountered by target audiences.

Does social marketing work?

Notwithstanding the very real issues of proving cause and effect that are explored in chapters four and five, over the last 40 years a growing and compelling body of evidence has been developing about the effectiveness of social marketing. This has been reviewed by organizations such as the Centers for Disease Control and Prevention in the USA (CDC, 2007; 2011) and the European Centre for Disease Prevention and Control (French and Apfel, 2014), both of which have endorsed the application of social marketing as an effective approach to delivering behavioural influence programmes. Social marketing has also been endorsed by a number of governments including the UK, Canada, America, Australia, India, and Bangladesh. There are also many social marketing conferences every year around the world, a number of academic institutions that teach and research in the field of social marketing, a growing number of academic journals such as *The Social Marketing Journal* and *Social Marketing Quarterly*, and a growing number of national and regional professional associations. Details of most of these developments and resources can be found at the International Social Marketing Association website: http://www.i-socialmarketing.org/.

Conclusion

Over many years public health has developed impressive data-gathering systems related to mortality, morbidity, and health sector utilization. However, we have invested much less time and effort in developing methodologies to generate deep understanding of the wants, fears, needs, motivations, and barriers people face that either enhance or detract from their ability to live healthy lives. In short, we are fantastic at counting the sick and the dead but much less adept at understanding the living. The fundamental shift set out in this chapter and the rest of this book is from an approach through which solutions are derived principally by public health specialists and policy experts utilizing limited forms of evidence and data towards a more inclusive model that is also influenced by a deep contextual understanding of what target audiences know, believe, value, and say will help them, supported by a deep understanding of the science, methodologies, and technologies that can be applied to develop deliver and evaluate more successful public health programmes.

This fundamental shift includes the coordinated use of all forms of intervention that will help and enable people to adopt and sustain health behaviours to prevent disease, promote wellness, and reduce the impact of both infectious and chronic diseases. This chapter has explored why social marketing is a natural fit with modern evidence and data-informed social policy. Social marketing's focus on measurable returns on investment and respectful co-production of solutions with citizens is an approach that many governments and public health organizations are trying to bring about. Social marketing is also attractive to governments and public health organizations because of its emphasis on deep citizen insight and population segmentation, enabling the development of interventions that can respond to a broad diversity of needs of specific subgroups within increasingly diverse communities in many countries.

At a time of declining trust in civic institutions, fragmentation of society, and rising consumerism, social marketing also offers a systematic and systemic approach for tackling many of the key health behavioural challenges faced by societies around the world. Social marketing offers a transparent methodology that embraces the reality of markets, choice, and mutual responsibility and balances the rights and responsibilities of individuals and of wider society. Authentic social marketing is not about telling people what to do or coercing them into doing it, but is the process of understanding what will help people make choices and take action that will lead them to healthier lives. In short, those who seek to serve the public and make the world a healthier place have to learn how to make positive life choices the easy and desired choices.

In the coming years, it is highly probable that social marketing will become part of the standard operating systems for governments and all public health organizations, and among for-profit and not-for-profit organizations concerned with promoting health, as advocated by WHO (2012) and the US Department of Health and Human Services (2010). This is because social marketing works, it can be shown to work, and it is a deeply democratic and empowering approach to health promotion and disease reduction. Social marketing as we have seen in this chapter is also well matched to the sophisticated cultural, social, and political environment of the twenty-first century. Public health specialists, health promoters and educators, and health policy planners will all need to invest time and effort in developing their understanding of social marketing's principles so that they can become champions for the communities they serve. It is our hope that this book makes a small contribution to bringing this about.

References

Acemoglu, D., Robinson, J. (2012). *Why nations fail: the origins of power, prosperity, and poverty.* London: Profile Books.

Armstrong, D. (1983). *The political anatomy of the body.* Cambridge: Cambridge University Press.

Armstrong, D. (1993). Public health spaces and fabrication of identity. *Sociology* 27(3): 393–410.

Armstrong, D. (1995). The rise of surveillance medicine. *Sociology of Health & Illness* 17(3): 393–404.

Australian Public Service Commission (2007). *Tackling wicked problems: a public policy perspective.* Barton: Australian Government Publishers Ltd.

CDC (2007). *CDCynergy Lite: social marketing made simple.* Atlanta, GA: Centers for Disease Control and Prevention http://www.cdc.gov/healthcommunication/cdcynergylite.html

CDC (2011). Gateway to social marketing and health communication [website]. Atlanta, GA: Centers for Disease Control and Prevention http://www.cdc.gov/healthcommunication/

Corrigan, P. (2004). *An evening with Paul Corrigan, Government Advisor on Health.* Coventry: Warwick Institute of Governance and Public Management, Warwick University.

Fitzpatrick, M. (2001). *The tyranny of health: doctors and the regulation of lifestyle.* London: Routledge.

French, J., Apfel, F. (2014). *Social marketing guide for public health programme managers and practitioners.* Stockholm: European Centre for Disease Prevention and Control http://ecdc.europa.eu/en/publications/Publications/social-marketing-guide-public-health.pdf

French, J., Gordon, R. (2015). *Strategic social marketing.* London: Sage.

Fukuyama, F. (1992). *The end of history and the last man.* London: Penguin.

Giddens, A. (1991). *Modernity and self-identity.* Cambridge: Polity Press.

Giddens, A. (2003). *Neoprogressivism: the progressive manifesto.* Cambridge: Polity Press.

Halpern, D., Bates, C., Mulgan, G., Aldridge, S., Beales, G., Heathfield, A. (2004). *Personal responsibility and changing behaviour: the state of knowledge and its implications for public policy.* London: Cabinet Office.

Ipsos MORI (2010). *National health? Citizens' views of health services around the world.* London: Ipsos MORI http://www.ipsos-mori.com/researchpublications/publications/1395/National-Health-Citizens

Kelly, G., Mulgan, G., Muers, S. (2002). *Creating public value: an analytical framework for public sector reform.* London: Prime Minister's Strategy Unit.

Kelly, M., Charlton, B. (1995). The sociology of health promotion. In: R. Bunton, S. Nettleton, R. Burrows (eds). *The sociology of health promotion: critical analysis of consumption, lifestyle and risk.* London: Routledge.

Kickbusch, I., Maag, D., Sann, H. (2005). Enabling healthy choices in modern health societies. Background paper for Parallel Forum F6 on 'healthy choices', presented at the 8th European Health Forum Gastein 2005 on Partnerships for Health, Bad Gastein, Austria, October 6, 2005.

Kurtz, I. (1987). Health educators—the new puritans. *Journal of Medical Ethics* 13(1): 40–41.

LeGrand, J. (2007). *The other invisible hand: delivering public service through choice and competition.* Princeton and Oxford: Princeton University Press.

Lent, A., Arend, N. (2004). *Making choices: how can choice improve local public services?* London: New Local Government Network.

Marmot, R. (2008). *Closing the gap in a generation: health equity through action on the social determinants of health.* Geneva: World Health Organization.

Minkler, M. (1989). Health education, health promotion and the open society: an historical perspective. *Health Education Quarterly* 16(1): 17–30.

Moore, M.H. (1995). *Creating public value—strategic management in government.* Cambridge, MA: Harvard University Press.

Murray, C. (2006). *In our hands.* Washington, DC: AEI Press.

OLR (2002). *It's a matter of trust: what society thinks and feels about trust.* London: Opinion Leader Research.

Osborne, D., Gaebler, T. (1992). *Reinventing government: how the entrepreneurial spirit is transforming the public sector.* Reading, MA: Addison-Wesley.

Peterson, A., Lupton, D. (1996). *The new public health.* London: Sage.

Roberts, J.M. (1985). *The triumph of the west.* Boston, MA: Little, Brown.

Rothschild, M. (2001). Ethical considerations in the use of marketing for the management of public health and social issues. In A. Andersen (ed). *Ethics in social marketing.* Washington, DC: Georgetown University Press.

Smith, R., Beaglehole, R., Woodward, D., Drager, N. (eds). (2003). *Global public goods for health.* Oxford: Oxford University Press.

Stern, N. (2007). *The economics of climate change: the Stern Review.* Cambridge: Cambridge University Press.

Stevenson, H., Burke, M. (1991). Bureaucratic logic in new social movement clothing: the limits of health promotion research. *Health Promotion International* 6(3): 281–289.

Sunstein, C., Thaler, R. (2003). Libertarian paternalism is not an oxymoron. *The University of Chicago Law Review* 70(4): Article 1.

Thaler, R., Sunstein C. (2008). Nudge: improving decisions about health, wealth and happiness. New Haven & London: Yale University Press.

UN (2015). *Millennium Development Goals report 2015.* New York: United Nations http://www.un.org/ millenniumgoals/news.shtml

US Department of Health and Human Services (2010). Healthy *people* 2020. Washington, DC: Office of Disease Prevention and Health Promotion.

WHO (1978). *Declaration of Alma-Ata: International Conference on Primary Health Care.* Geneva: World Health Organization.

WHO (2008). *Closing the gap in a generation: health equity through action on the social determinants of health.* Geneva: World Health Organization.

WHO (2010). *Mental health and development: targeting people with mental health conditions as a vulnerable group.* Geneva: World Health Organization.

WHO (2012). *Health 2020: the European policy for health and well-being.* Copenhagen: WHO Regional Office for Europe http://www.euro.who.int/en/what-we-do/health-topics/health-policy/health-2020

WHO (2015a). No communicable Diseases Country Profiles 2014. Geneva: World Health Organization.

WHO (2015b). Global Strategy for Women's, Children's and Adolescents' Health (2016–2030). Geneva: World Health Organization.

Wilkinson, R., Marmot, M. (2003). Social determinants of health: the solid facts, 2nd edition. Geneva: World Health Organization.

Chapter 2

Key principle, concepts, and techniques of social marketing

Jeff French

Nothing is as practical as a good theory.
> Kurt Lewin, 1945, The research center for group
> dynamics at Massachusetts Institute of Technology.
> *Sociometry*, Volume 8, pp. 126–135.

Learning points

This chapter:
- introduces the key principle, concepts, and techniques that distinguish social marketing from other approaches to developing, testing, implementing, and evaluating social programmes that seek to influence behaviour for social good.

Introduction to key principle, concepts, and techniques of social marketing

If social marketing is to develop both theoretically and in terms of its practice, an ongoing analysis focused on its nature is required. Like any modern multidisciplinary field of inquiry, social marketing is subject to a number of differing schools of thought (Wood, 2012) and debate (Tapp and Spotswood, 2013). To date there have been numerous attempts to define and codify the core components of social marketing and it is inevitable that this will be an ongoing process as more experience is gained, evidence is accumulated, and theory develops. Social marketing, like many other fields of study (Peters and Hirst, 1971), is what Gallie (1956) called an 'essentially contested concept'. What Gallie means is that fields of study that contain concepts contested by various commentators and practitioners because they are rooted in fundamental ideological, moral, and philosophical concepts—such as the nature of value and exchange, responsibility, mutuality, and relationships—will by their nature never reach a point of total agreement about their scope and focus. What is important is that such fields, including social marketing, need to engage in debate about their focus if they are to develop. This debate can be negatively characterized as one that leads to introspection, but viewed more positively the process can be seen as the means by which fields of study progress and become more robust.

The nature of social marketing

It has been argued by French and Gordon (2015) that social marketing seeks, through a critical and systemic approach, to bring together all understanding, data, and insights to assist in the development and implementation of effective, efficient, and ethical social programmes. In so doing it seeks to respond to some of the criticisms that are directed at singular approaches to behaviour change, such as the application of behavioural economics and social psychology (House of Lords Science and Technology Committee, 2011).

In order to differentiate social marketing contributions to influencing citizens' health behaviour, a number of sets of benchmark criteria have been developed to date, including by Andreasen (2002) and French and Blair-Stevens (2005). These attempts have sought to codify the core elements of social marketing practice as a distinct approach to behaviour change intended to bring about improved health. In particular, they have sought to distinguish social marketing from other forms of public health interventions such as behavioural change communication (O'Sullivan et al., 2003), mass communication (McQuail, 2009), and health promotion (Green and Tones, 2010). While social marketing principles or 'criteria' developed to date have been well received and globally applied, developments in marketing theory and practice over the past decade raise questions about the contemporary relevance of all the criteria identified to date (Vargo and Lusch, 2004; Bagozzi, 1975).

Developments in marketing theory and practice also question the relative importance of each of the principles of social marketing described so far, their completeness, and the nature of the principles or criteria themselves in terms of their equivalence. The very term 'criteria', which is commonly held to mean 'principle[s] or standard[s] by which something may be judged or decided',[1] implies that all the criteria are equally important in deciding whether an intervention can be described as social marketing. However, not all current criteria are seen by practitioners and academics to be of equal importance.[2]

As discussed in chapter one, since the inception of social marketing there has been a debate about its nature and scope (French, 2014). This debate has to some extent followed and reflected the debate within marketing about its nature and the contribution it makes to business activity and wider society (Shaw and Tamilia, 2001; Tadajewski, 2010). Some advocates portray social marketing as the application of the marketing mix offered by McCarthy (1960), while others advocate a conception of social marketing that reflects more recent marketing theory focused on exchange, value co-creation, and mutually beneficial relationships (Gordon, 2012; Domegan, 2008). So what are the core concepts of marketing and how are these reflected in the new, globally endorsed definition of social marketing? The current American Marketing Association (AMA) definition of marketing is:

> Marketing is the activity, set of institutions, and processes for creating, communicating, delivering, and exchanging offerings that have value for customers, clients, partners, and society at large.

> (AMA, 2013)

Inherent in this definition are the four concepts of offerings (goods, services, and ideas), value creation, systematic processes, and stakeholders. The definition of social marketing, endorsed by the European Social Marketing Association (ESMA), the Australian Association of Social Marketing (AASM), and the International Social Marketing Association (iSMA) is:

> Social Marketing seeks to develop and integrate marketing concepts with other approaches to influence behaviour that benefits individuals and communities for the greater Social good.

Social Marketing practice is guided by ethical principles. It seeks to integrate research, best practice, theory, audience and partnership insight, to inform the delivery of competition sensitive and seg-mented social change programmes that are effective, efficient, equitable and sustainable.

(iSMA, 2013)

This definition explicitly accepts that marketing concepts (offerings, value creation, systematic processes, and stakeholders) are central to social marketing and that they will be integrated with other approaches to delivering social progress.

It is possible to conclude from these two definitions that social marketing is based on and applies marketing concepts but is not confined to using only marketing concepts. Like market-ing, social marketing is essentially a practical, applied field of study and research. It is a process and approach that, through evidence collection, data analysis, theory building, systemic and systematic planning, and reflection, seeks to bring together everything that is known about how to influence behaviour to promote social good. Marketing and social marketing are not alone in this pursuit as many other fields of applied social policy also adopt such an eclectic and inclusive approach to analysis, intervention development, implementation, and evaluation.

The added value of social marketing in public health interventions

The added value of applying social marketing as an integral part of public health and health promotion interventions is the 'marketing' lens that it brings to social challenges. This lens is defined by a focus on the creation of social value through a process of exchange and the provi-sion of valued social offerings. These social offerings come in the form of ideas, understanding, systems, products, services, policies, and environments that are valued by citizens and have a positive social impact. The fundamental principle of using value-based exchange to create social value sits at the heart of social marketing theory and practice.

One of the central dilemmas when seeking to distinguish social marketing from other forms of social intervention is to decide how many and potentially what types of criteria are essential markers of its practice and which are desirable. There is also a need to be able to classify interventions as fully or partially applying a social marketing approach so that they can be included or excluded in reviews of evidence and practice. Finally, there are the twin practical needs to be able to construct education and training programmes that give participants a comprehensive understanding of the nature of social marketing and how to apply and evaluate its contribution to the quality, efficiency, and effectiveness of public health programmes.

Defining social marketing

Social marketing criteria developed to date contain a number of contradictions and ambiguities. Three key issues arise when assessing existing descriptive criteria of social marketing.

1. The issue of equivalence: currently identified criteria do not always appear to be of the same type—for example, some criteria appear to be principles of practice, others are more funda-mental essential concepts, and other criteria are descriptions of processes or techniques often but not always used in interventions labelled as social marketing.
2. The issue of relative importance: the question here is: are some criteria more important than others in classifying or assessing whether an intervention can be described as social marketing?

3. The issue of essentiality: a further question that needs to be addressed is: how many of the listed criteria need to be identifiable for an intervention to be classified as social marketing?

The criteria that are included in many existing descriptions of social marketing are assumed to be equal in value, potentially mutually exclusive, and collectively exhaustive. To date, authors have indicated a hierarchy of importance in relation to the criteria they set out, while not explicitly stating that a hierarchy exists. Both Andreasen (2002) and French and Blair-Stevens (2005) indicate by the ordering of the criteria they identify and through their accompanying commentaries that an order of importance does exists. For Andreasen the most important criteria are behavioural focus, research, and segmentation. For French and Blair-Stevens the most important criteria are customer orientation, behavioural focus, and the application of behavioural theory. One of the central problems that flows from current lists of criteria is that they have been developed for two distinct purposes: first for describing social marketing and second as checklists that can be used to identify projects as being social marketing interventions. The desire on the part of authors to be inclusive has resulted in comprehensive but unstructured lists of not necessarily similar potential elements of social marketing.

A hierarchical model of social marketing principle, concepts, and techniques

As proposed by French and Russell-Bennett (2015), social marketing can be best understood if its elements are separated out into three categories that can have a hierarchical relationship. These are:

1. principle
2. concepts
3. techniques.

The core principle of social marketing, proposed in Table 2.1, is social value creation through social exchange. This core principle, which is a unique feature of social marketing, is supported by essential concepts that reflect the globally endorsed definition of social marketing and constitute essential elements in any social marketing intervention. I propose that there are four such core concepts that flow from social marketing's marketing roots and support the delivery of the core social marketing principle:

1. social behavioural influence
2. citizen/customer/civic society-orientation focus
3. social offerings
4. relationship building.

The third category of criteria is techniques: these are a wide array of methods, models, and tactics that are often used in social marketing but are not exclusive to it.

The core social marketing principle

What makes social marketing distinct from other forms of social intervention is its focus, derived from marketing, on social value creation through the exchange of social offerings in the form of ideas, products, service, experience, environments, and systems. The core principle of value creation reflects the central feature of the consensus definition of social marketing developed by iSMA, ESMA, and AASM. The principle of value creation also sits at the heart of the AMA definition of marketing. Clearly questions arise about the fundamental

Table 2.1 The social marketing principle and four core concepts of social marketing

	Criterion	Descriptor
The key social marketing principle	Social value creation through the exchange of social offerings (ideas, products, service, experience, environments, systems)	The aim and objective of bringing about an increase in social value and/or the reduction of social problems through a reciprocal exchange of resources or assets at the individual, community, societal, or global level. Social policy, strategy, understanding, ideas, products, services, and experiences are developed that will enable and assist citizens to derive social benefits individually and collectively.
The four core social marketing concepts	1. Social behavioural influence	Behavioural analysis is undertaken to gather details of what influences behavioural patterns and trends. Interventions are developed that seek to influence specific behaviours and clusters of related behaviours. Specific actionable and measurable behavioural objectives and indicators are established. A broad range of behavioural theory is used to analyse, implement, and evaluate interventions. These behaviours could have a single or combined focus on upstream, midstream, or downstream factors.
	2. Citizen/civic society focus	Policy planning, delivery, and evaluation are focused on building understanding and interventions around citizen beliefs, attitudes, behaviours, needs, and wants. A range of different research analyses, combining qualitative and quantitative data gathering, is used and synthesized to plan, deliver, and review interventions that create value for citizens.
	3. Social offerings (idea, product, service, experience, etc.)	Citizens, policy-makers and/or other target groups are offered products, ideas, understanding, services, experiences, systems, and environments that provide them with value. In most cases such social offerings are positive in nature—for example, they provide protection or the promise of better health. However, these social offerings can also involve the imposition of restrictions on freedom that have collective support and result in benefits that are perceived to outweigh any restrictions on freedoms associated with them—for example, bans on smoking at work and speed limits on motorways.
	4. Relationship building	The establishment of collective responsibility and the collective right to well-being is developed through a process of engagement and exchange. Citizens, policy-makers, or stakeholders are engaged in the selection of priorities, and the development, design, implementation, and evaluation of interventions.

nature of value itself, such as who defines it, how is it measured, how is it created, and how does exchange (itself a contested concept) support such value creation? A full exploration of these deeper marketing questions is addressed in chapter one and chapter twelve. What makes social marketing unique is the interplay between this core marketing-derived principle and its four supportive, marketing-derived concepts. Social marketing also uses a wider range of techniques, such as segmentation and user insight, but these are also used by many other forms of social intervention such as health promotion and are therefore less important markers of social marketing practice.

Five supporting social marketing techniques

The remaining criteria that help to describe and identify social marketing practice are a cluster of marketing and business planning-derived techniques. This cluster of techniques contains common features of many but not all social marketing interventions. However, as stated above, these techniques also features in many other social programme interventions.

Social marketing techniques

The final cluster of characteristics of effective and efficient social marketing is that of social marketing techniques. These are not unique to social marketing as they are employed in many other types of social and commercial programmes and projects. The presence or absence of a particular social marketing technique is not critical in judging whether an intervention can be described as being 'social marketing'; nevertheless, they do indicate that an intervention has been well planned and based on sound analysis.

Five core techniques are commonly used but not universally applied in all social marketing interventions. Social marketing techniques, such as the application of a full mix of interventions or the use of insight-driven segmentation, are powerful tools. Five such techniques are set out in Table 2.2. These particular core techniques have been selected because they have been demonstrated to increase the efficacy and efficiency of social interventions, and because they are often applied in not-for-profit marketing programmes.

The three categories of criteria set out in Tables 2.1 and 2.2 are summarized in Figure 2.1. Within the clusters of concepts and techniques there is no obvious or logical way of delineating an order of importance of criteria of similar types. At this stage of the development of social marketing it is more important to distinguish and recognize the key hierarchical relationship between criteria of different kinds rather than the importance of hierarchies within clusters of similar criteria.

For an intervention or programme to be identified as a social marketing programme the core principle of social marketing must be identifiable; however, its presence alone is not enough to apply the classification of social marketing. For this to be the case an intervention should also be able to demonstrate that the entire next category—the four concepts—is being considered and applied. These four core concepts of social marketing indicate that planners and practitioners are applying best practice in marketing theory and practice and have accepted that the bottom line for social marketing success is a positive impact on observable behaviour.

The presence or absence of what are labelled in this chapter as 'techniques' is not critical to the identification of social marketing practice because they can and are applied in many other forms of intervention. For example, a social project applying a community engagement approach might segment residences in an area, while a health education intervention might use competition analysis to determine the impact of suppliers of counter-information. A further example is the application of systematic planning: most well-conceived social interventions seek to apply some form of rational planning and review—for example, in the field of health promotion models such as COMBI (WHO, 2002) and PRECEDE-PROCEED (Green and Kreuter, 2005) are often utilized.

The model depicted in Figure 2.1 indicates that the central bedrock and defining feature that all social marketing should be able to demonstrate is the clear aim of bringing about social good through a process of exchange and value creation. The exchange may be positive in nature and tangible, such as a payment or some other form of incentive for giving up smoking or taking up a vaccination. Exchanges may also be negative, such as fines or exclusions for negative social behaviour, where individuals give up rights or in some cases elements of

Table 2.2 Core social marketing techniques

Social marketing technique	Description
Systemic and systematic planning and evaluation and Integrated intervention mix	Interventions use proven strategy and planning theory and models to construct robust intervention plans that include formative research, pre-testing, situational analysis, monitoring, evaluation, and the implementation of learning strategies. Driven by target market insight data, segmentation analysis, competition analysis, and feasibility analysis to develop an effective mix of 'types' and 'forms' of interventions that are selected and coordinated to produce an effective and efficient programme to influence target group behaviours.
Competition analysis and action	Internal (e.g. internal psychological factors, pleasure, desire, risk taking, genetics, and addiction, etc.) and external (e.g. economic, social, cultural, and environmental influences) competition are assessed. Strategies are developed to reduce the impact of negative competition on the target behaviour.
Insight-driven segmentation	The aim is to develop 'actionable insights' and hypotheses about how to help citizens that are drawn from what target markets know, feel, believe, and do, and the environmental circumstances that influence them. Segmentation using demographic, observational data and psychographic data is used to identify groups that are similar and can be influenced in common ways. Segmentation leads to the development of an interventions mix directly tailored to specific target market needs, values, and circumstances.
Co-creation through social markets	Citizens, stakeholders, and other civic and commercial institutions are engaged in the selection, development, testing, delivery, and evaluation of interventions. Strategies are developed to maximize the contribution of partner and stakeholder coalitions in achieving targeted behaviours.

their freedom in exchange for safer and healthier communities—for example, by obeying speed limits while driving or not being allowed to attend school unless they have had required vaccinations.

The balancing of possible trade-offs between individually perceived benefits or losses and social benefits is one that requires interventions that are perceived to be fair and proportionate by a majority of citizens: both beneficiaries and those negatively affected. Exchanges may also be characterized as being rational, involving considered decisions, or may alternatively be brought about through appeals to unconscious motivators such as chance of reward or fear (French, 2011); see chapter six for a broader review of these issues. What all such social exchanges have in common is that they are driven by the aim of bringing about social and individual benefit rather than just economic advantage, they are informed by consideration of ethical standards, and they have the broad popular support of the majority of citizens.

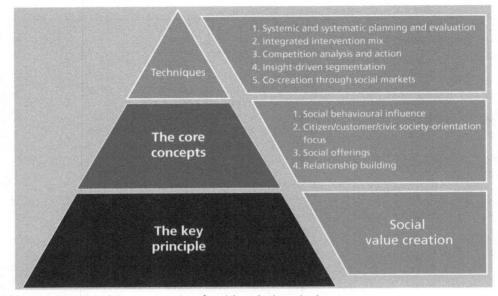

Figure 2.1 Model of three categories of social marketing criteria.

The core concepts that enable the successful creation of social value start with an explicit focus on influencing social behaviour. Influencing and being able to measure the impact on behaviour is a key marker of social marketing practice. Social marketing pursues its goals of creating social value by influencing behaviour through the development, promotion, and supply of social offerings in the form of ideas, tangible products, services, experience, systems, policies, campaigns, and environments. To optimize the impact of these social offerings social marketing interventions are based on citizen-centric planning and programme building. Such an approach includes a commitment to building meaningful and sustained relationships with citizens and stakeholders who can help foster beneficial social relationships that result in sustained, positive social benefit.

Conclusion

Up to this point in the development of social marketing's theoretical base authors have been content to set out descriptors of activities and actions, together with some concepts and principles of practice that have been observed to be associated with what practitioners and academics have called social marketing. Writers have described the features that they have observed and advocated as the basis of social marketing as 'criteria'. The word 'criteria' itself indicates an undifferentiated approach to describing and categorizing what makes up the essential elements of what can be described as social marketing practice. This essentially reflective, observational approach to analysis has helped focus debate about what social marketing is, but it has not assisted the field in more explicitly delineating the uniqueness of social marketing and its distinct contribution as a field of study and application.

This chapter has sought to describe the key elements of social marketing by making a reasoned case for the need to differentiate between principles, concepts, and techniques when seeking to describe social marketing. What is clear from social marketing practice described in the literature and observed in the field is that few interventions labelled as 'social marketing' meet all previously described generic criteria. To do so is obviously a considerable challenge given the policy, management, and marketing sophistication needed, and the time and resources required. To set up the assumption that it is necessary to apply all the criteria described is therefore potentially setting people up to fail, given that many social interventions are not managed by social marketing experts with large budgets and plenty of time to research and test interventions and sustain them over time. To many it might be perceived that it is very difficult to apply social marketing if they cannot meet most of the criteria generally accepted to constitute good practice. This means that many projects fall short of achieving all the criteria specified in the past as being markers of social marketing practice and are consequently screened out of reviews of practice and evidence of impact. However, what is equally clear is that if people only apply what has been called the 'social marketing mind-set' (French and Blair-Stevens, 2005) this can add value to social programme design, intervention, and evaluation. This is the essential practical implication of the hierarchical model of the social marketing principle, concepts, and techniques set out in this chapter. The social marketing mind-set is encapsulated within the core social marketing principle set out above, reflecting as it does the core principle that underpins contemporary marketing theory, together with the four core concepts of social marketing that also reflect the internationally developed consensus statement on social marketing practice. Matching this supportive set of concepts is a more realistic proposition for many people and one that can improve the relevance, efficiency, and effectiveness of public health programmes focused at influencing behaviour.

It is not suggested that the planning rigour associated with social marketing, the importance of competition analysis, or the benefits of segmenting audiences are not important elements in social interventions. In some contexts the rigour associated with a systematic approach to planning an intervention with an equally rigorous situational analysis will be the key to success or failure. However, the application of such techniques is not a unique marker of social marketing, as a similar response would be promoted by advocates of many other forms of social programme design and development. Social marketing is not defined by these techniques: what defines social marketing is its central focus on social value creation using exchange, relationship building, and the provision of social offerings to influence behaviour that will result in positive social change. To be classified as an intervention that is applying a social marketing approach, an intervention or programme should be able to demonstrate that it is informed by the core social marketing principle and the four key concepts of social marketing described in this chapter.

Self-review questions

1. Describe the core principle that underpins social marketing practice.
2. List the four core social marketing concepts and set out a short description of each one.
3. Describe at least two social marketing techniques and how they can add value to a social programme's design, delivery, and evaluation.

Notes

1. Oxford Dictionaries: http://www.oxforddictionaries.com/definition/english/criterion.
2. iSMA 2014, *International survey conducted by iSMA, ESMA and AASM 2013 of members in preparation for the development of the global consensus definition of social marketing.* Survey results available from iSMA.

References

AASM (2013). What is social marketing? [website]. Victoria: Australian Association of Social Marketing http://www.aasm.org.au/about-us/, accessed 17 December 2013.

AMA (2013). Archive [website]. Chicago, IL: American Marketing Association https://www.ama.org/AboutAMA/Pages/Definition-of-Marketing.aspx http://www.Marketingpower.com/Community/ARC/Pages/Additional/Definition/default.aspx

Andreasen, A.R. (2002). Marketing social marketing in the social change marketplace. *Journal of Public Policy Marketing* **21**(1): 3–13.

Bagozzi, R.P. (1975). Marketing as exchange. *Journal of Marketing* **39**(3): 32–39.

Domegan, C. (2008). Social marketing implications for contemporary marketing practices classification scheme. *Journal of Business and Industrial Marketing* **23**(2): 135–41.

French, J. (2011). Why nudging is not enough. *Journal of Social Marketing* **1**(2): 154–162.

French, J. (2014). The unfolding history of the social marketing concept. In: D.W. Stewart (ed). *Handbook of persuasion and social marketing*. Santa Barbara, CA: ABC-CLIO.

French, J., Blair-Stevens, C. (2005). *The big pocket guide to social marketing*, 1st edition. London: National Social Marketing Centre, The National Consumer Council.

French, J., Gordon, R. (2015). *Strategic social marketing*. London: Sage.

French, J., Russell-Bennett, R. (2015). A hierarchical model of social marketing. *Journal of Social Marketing* **5**(2): 139–159 http://www.emeraldinsight.com/doi/pdfplus/10.1108/JSOCM-06-2014-0042

Gallie, W. (1956). Essentially contested concepts. *Proceedings of the Aristotelian Society* **56**: 167–198.

Gordon, R. (2012). Re-thinking and re-tooling the social marketing mix. *The Australian Marketing Journal* **20**: 122–126.

Green J., Tones K. (2010). *Health promotion: planning and strategies*, 2nd edition. London: Sage.

Green, L., Kreuter, M. (2005). *Health program planning: An educational and ecological approach*, 4th edition. New York: McGraw-Hill.

House of Lords Science and Technology Select Committee (2011). *Behaviour change*. London: The Stationery Office http://www.publications.parliament.uk/pa/ld201012/ldselect/ldsctech/179/179.pdf

iSMA (2013). *Consensus definition of social marketing*. Bethesda, MD: iSMA http://isma.memberclicks.net/assets/social_marketing_definition.pdf, accessed 10 July 2014.

McCarthy, E.J. (1960). *Basic marketing: a managerial approach*. Homewood, IL: Richard D. Irwin.

McQuail, D. (2009). *Mass communication theory*, 5th edition. Thousand Oaks, CA: Sage.

O'Sullivan, G.A., Yonkler, J.A., Morgan, W., Merritt, A.P. (2003). *A field guide to designing a health communication strategy*. Baltimore, MD: Johns Hopkins Bloomberg School of Public Health/Centre for Communication Programs.

Peters, R.S., Hirst, P.H. (1971). *The logic of education*, 2nd edition. London: Routledge & Kegan Paul.

Shaw, E., Tamilia, R. (2001). Robert Bartels and the history of marketing thought. *Journal of Macro Marketing* **21**(2): 156–163.

Tadajewski, M. (2010). Towards a history of critical marketing studies. *Journal of Marketing Management* **26**(9/10): 773–824.

Tapp, A., Spotswood, F. (2013). From the 4Ps to COM-SM: reconfiguring the social marketing mix. *Journal of Social Marketing* **3**(3): 206–222.

Vargo, S., Lusch, R. (2004). Evolving to a new dominant logic for marketing author(s). *The Journal of Marketing* **68**(1): 1–17.

WHO (2002). Communication for behavioural impact (COMBI) in the prevention and control of TB. WHO Communicable Disease Surveillance (CDS)/Communicable Disease Prevention, Eradication and Control (CPE) Social Mobilization and Training Programme, original article available at: http://www.who.int/ihr/publications/combi_toolkit_fieldwkbk_outbreaks/en/

Wood, M. (2012). Marketing social marketing. *Journal of Social Marketing* **2**(2): 94–102.

Chapter 3

Social marketing planning

Jeff French

Plans are useless, but planning is indispensable.

Attributed to Dwight D. Eisenhower, in
Richard Nixon, *Six crises*, 1962

Learning points

This chapter:

- sets out the rationale and reasons for the application of systematic planning in the delivery of social marketing;
- introduces a number of social marketing planning tools and outlines how they can be applied;
- introduces the STELa social marketing planning framework and shows how it can be used to enhance the delivery of programmes that aim to influence health and social behaviour, describing the social marketing planning process, its four key component steps and ten key tasks.

Introduction to successful public health programme planning

Programmes aimed at influencing human beliefs, attitudes, and behaviour are complex in nature. While it is not possible to develop an exact formula that can be universally applied for delivering population-focused behaviour programmes that will result in success every time in every situation, there is an emerging set of principles that can aid us in the development and application of interventions.

A number of universal underlying health intervention planning principles have been shown to increase the likelihood of success irrespective of the health issue, target group, targeted behaviour, or country context (Schorr, 2003; Klassen, 2010). These characteristics include developing a long-term strategic approach based on a deep understanding of the causes of problems, how people affected by them view the issue, and their recommendations about how to tackle it. The development of clear programme objectives, the application of a logical planning system, targeting interventions to particular audience needs, developing strategies that address causal factors as well as reactions to them, and the development of systems to evaluate and track programme success and failure are all key characteristics of effective and efficient public health interventions.

The sources of evidence that identify good social programme intervention planning are considerable. Other sources come from reviews of good social intervention design, such as Halpen (2004), and generic social programme implementation such as the Australian Public Service Commission (2007), through to specific guidance in areas such as health improvement (French and Mayo, 2006), environmental interventions (Darnton et al., 2006; McKenzie-Mohr et al., 2012), and behavioural design (Institute of Government, 2009; New Economics Foundation, 2005). Movements are also now underway in many policy circles to develop more evidence and experimentation-informed social policy—for example, the 'What Works' consortium in the UK.[1]

A good summary of much of these planning and other social programme design considerations is encapsulated in the Medical Research Council (MRC) guidance on developing and evaluating complex interventions (MRC, 2010). This sets out a number of helpful questions that planners and researchers should address when seeking to set up such programmes. In the planning and early development stages of a programme the questions include the following:

1. Are you clear about what you are trying to do, what outcome you are aiming for, and how you will bring about change?
2. Does your intervention have a coherent theoretical basis?
3. Have you used this theory systematically to develop the intervention?
4. Can you describe the intervention fully, so that it can be implemented properly for the purposes of your evaluation, and replicated by others?
5. Does the existing evidence, ideally collated in a systematic review, suggest that it is likely to be effective or cost-effective?
6. Can it be implemented in a research setting, and is it likely to be widely implementable if the results are favourable?

The MRC paper recommends that if any of these questions cannot be fully answered further development work is needed before projects are initiated. With regard to piloting and feasibility studies, the guidance sets out six additional questions that need to be considered:

1. Have you done enough piloting and feasibility work to be confident that the intervention can be delivered as intended?
2. Can you make safe assumptions about effect sizes and variability and rates of recruitment and retention in the main evaluation study?
3. What design are you going to use, and why?
4. Is an experimental design preferable and if so, is it feasible?
5. If a conventional parallel group randomized controlled trial is not possible, have you considered alternatives such as cluster randomization or a stepped wedge design?
6. Have you set up procedures for monitoring delivery of the intervention and overseeing the conduct of the evaluation?

The National Institute for Health and Care Excellence (NICE) has also developed a planning guidance framework for behavioural interventions, making recommendations that cover much of the same ground as the MRC guidance (NICE, 2007). Specifically, NICE sets out three core actions related to generic planning and intervention design principles. First, interventions and programmes aimed at changing behaviour should be planned carefully, taking into account the local and national context and working in partnership with recipients. Second, it is important to ensure that practitioners have the necessary competencies and skills to support behaviour change. Finally, interventions and programmes should be evaluated. It is possible to add to this list a further common characteristic: the need for clarity of purpose. Programmes that seek to influence behaviour for social good require a set of clear measurable behavioural goals, aims, and objectives that are achievable within the timescales and resources available to the programme.

Systematic planning is a hallmark and one of the key added value characteristics of adopting a social marketing approach to public health intervention development, implementation, and evaluation. Many social marketing texts set out key planning elements (Kotler et al., 2002; Weinreich, 2011; McKenzie-Mohr and Smith, 2011; French et al., 2010; Lefebvre, 2013). A number of specific guides and checklists have also been developed for planning specific aspects of social marketing, such as how and when to use new media (Mays et al., 2011), engaging with corporate partners and stakeholders (Kotler and Lee, 2005), enabling community empowerment (Bracht et al., 1999), using advocacy programmes (Maylock et al., 2001), cultural change (Cabinet Office, 2008), and the use of mass media (Hornik, 2002).

As can be seen in the case study in Box 3.1, a fundamental principle for social marketing planning is the need to focus on developing a set of unambiguous aims and behavioural goals, together with the means to measure outcomes. Clear outcome targets that accurately measure behaviour and its social impacts are an essential element of any social marketing intervention.

Box 3.1 Case study: a total market approach for family planning in Cambodia

Dianna Long, Yasmin Madan, Sotheary Khim, Dana Sievers, Socheat Chi

Aims

In 2011, reduced donor funding for contraception resulted in a commodity crisis in Cambodia. In collaboration with the National Reproductive Health Programme and other partners, Population Services International (PSI) used the total market approach (TMA) to develop a vision for the market for family planning (FP).

TMA is an approach for strengthening markets, which includes determining the need for a product or service, identifying gaps and opportunities, and defining the role of different market players, with the end goal of increasing use as a proportion of need. It also strives towards efficient resource allocation and sustainable market growth.

Behavioural objectives and target group

PSI's target group was women of reproductive age (WRA) who wished to delay birth for at least two years (NIS et al., 2011). This group included current modern FP method users as well as non-users (women who either used traditional methods or reported an unmet need for FP).

The behavioural objective was to increase WRA's use of modern FP methods by improving access to and promoting modern methods, while ensuring women's ability to make an informed choice (Figure 3.1 and Figure 3.2).

Figure 3.1 Example of the promotional material used in the TMA for FP in Cambodia.
Reproduced by kind permission of Population Services Khmer.

Customer orientation

The fertility rate in Cambodia has steadily declined over the past decade, while the modern method contraceptive prevalence rate has increased (NIS et al., 2011). Despite this positive trend, the current contraceptive prevalence rate still falls short of the National Reproductive Health Programme target of 52% by 2016 (NIS et al., 2015).

When the TMA programme began, nearly 17% of married WRA reported an unmet need for FP and 16% reported traditional method use. Three out of four modern contraceptive users relied on short-term methods (oral and injectable contraceptives) (NIS et al., 2011) and 24% discontinued use of any method (DHS Program and USAID, 2015).

Social offering

Since 2002, PSI Cambodia[1] has socially marketed short-term and long-term FP methods and medical abortion and operated the Sun Quality Health Network, a social franchise network of 293 private providers offering reproductive health services.

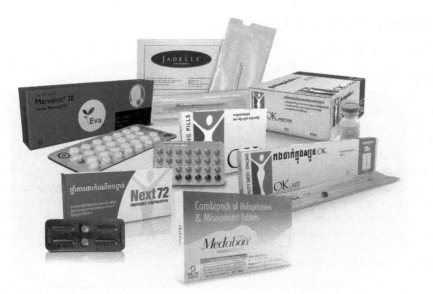

Figure 3.2 Examples of products and branding used in the TMA for FP in Cambodia.
Reproduced by kind permission of Population Services Khmer.

Target audience engagement and exchange

PSI reinforced the positive behaviour of current modern method users through outreach activities and follow-up through phone calls and home visits. Mass media behaviour change communications were targeted at non-users and traditional method users to correct misconceptions of modern methods, increase awareness of their relative effectiveness, and address barriers to use.

Competition analysis

The public sector distributed oral and injectable contraceptives, condoms, intrauterine devices, and implants free of charge. With donor assistance, other non-governmental organizations also promoted access to short-term and long-term methods.

Audience insight and segmentation

Data from 2010 revealed that women with unmet needs tended to have a lower socioeconomic status, live in rural areas, and report lower education levels; traditional method users had a higher socioeconomic status, lived in urban areas, and were more educated. Most WRA, even those in the highest wealth quintiles, relied on free and subsidized FP products, resulting in an inefficient use of subsidy (NIS et al., 2011).

Misunderstandings about menstruation, fertility, and the risk of pregnancy influenced women's decision not to use contraception, and perceived and real side effects prompted discontinuation of methods (Long and Khim, 2010; 2014). Despite high rates of unplanned pregnancy and abortion, users of traditional methods were confident in their effectiveness—they often attributed method failure to their own mistakes rather than the method itself (Long and Khim, 2014).

Integrated intervention mix

In addition to behaviour change for WRA, demand-side interventions included offering training and support to providers to improve services, and to outreach workers and national hotline counsellors to better target promotion efforts.

Supply-side interventions focused on pricing and cost-efficiency. Informed by results from a financial and marketing analysis, PSI moved all short-term methods to cost-recovery and set up a revolving fund for future purchases, which helped ensure commodity security and sustainability.

In 2012, PSI outsourced distribution of its entire portfolio to a national pharmaceutical company, which achieved significant cost savings and strengthened the capacity of the commercial sector. PSI also introduced two new products. The 'Next 72' emergency contraceptive pill was positioned as a gateway to promoting modern FP methods to consumers. 'Eva Marvelon', a mid-price-range oral contraceptive developed in partnership with Merck, addressed discontinuation and traditional method use among high quintile groups.

Co-creation through social markets

Collaborating with the public sector aligned FP targets and resources, while engaging the commercial sector increased coverage and access, introduced more product options, and improved overall market understanding. This multisector approach helped generate demand not only for PSI's social marketed products but also for FP in general.

Systematic planning

PSI worked closely with the National Reproductive Health Programme and Contraceptive Security Working Group and led a subgroup that would address the future of FP commodities. The subgroup developed a TMA commodity calculator to help stakeholders analyse and forecast market needs, allocate resources, and make evidence-based decisions.

To monitor progress, PSI conducted internal marketing planning and developed performance indicators.

Results and learning

Preliminary results are emerging, but lessons about the approach are already clear. The critical starting point for TMA implementation is gaining national support and ensuring government stewardship. PSI found that coordinating efforts with the public and commercial sectors helped expand and strengthen the entire market for FP. Another major lesson is the importance of having an integrated approach targeting providers and consumers. The investment in provider capacity building paired with behaviour change communication campaigns targeting WRA aligned behaviours on the supply and demand sides. The iterative nature of the total market approach necessitates that the programme apply these lessons to achieve continued impact.

References

DHS Program, USAID (2015). Cambodia, contraceptive discontinuation rates, all reasons. In: STATCompiler (online database). Rockville, MD: DHS Program http://statcompiler.com/, accessed 30 March 2015.

Long, D., Khim, S. (2010). *Cambodia (2010): Formative research among providers of long-term methods at Sun Quality Health clinics in Cambodia.* Phnom Penh: Population Services Khmer http://hdl:1902.1/N2QVY, accessed 30 March 2015.

Long, D., Khim, S. (2014). *Cambodia (2013): qualitative study among WRA segmenting the family planning market in Cambodia, phase 1.* Phnom Penh: Population Services Khmer http://dx.doi.org/10.7910/DVN/24478, accessed 30 March 2015.

NIS, DGH, ICF International (2015). *Cambodia demographic and health survey 2014: key indicators report.* Phnom Penh and Calverton, MD: National Institute of Statistics, Directorate-General for Health, and ICF International.

NIS, DGH, ICF Macro. (2011). *Cambodia demographic and health survey 2010.* Phnom Penh and Calverton, MD: National Institute of Statistics, Directorate-General for Health, and ICF Macro.

In 2013, PSI Cambodia became an independent PSI network member—Population Services Khmer. Since the activities of this programme began before the transition, we use PSI throughout the piece.

Based on the 2010 Cambodia demographic and health survey, 7.5% of married WRA reported unwanted pregnancies and 30.4% of married WRA reported having ever terminated a pregnancy in their lifetime (NIS et al., 2011).

Social marketing planning models

For a diminishing number of social marketers the 4Ps of marketing (product, price, place, promotion) are still used for social marketing planning (Kotler and Lee, 2009; Weinreich, 2011). This model is based on a somewhat outdated view of what the marketing process is. The 4Ps framework presents three other issues that go beyond promotional tactics that need to be considered by planners. However, many social marketers (Peattie and Peattie, 2011) continue to question the utility and theoretical basis of this model. In response to the identified limitations of the 4Ps model, a number of alternative social marketing planning models have been developed in recent years, based on more modern conceptions about the nature of marketing. Some of the best known are set out below.

The five-stage Total Process Planning model (French and Blair-Stevens, 2008); French et al., 2010a) promoted by the National Social Marketing Centre in the UK consists of five stages of planning (see Figure 3.3): scoping the issue, developing potential interventions and testing them, implementing the programme, evaluating it, and then following up, which includes feeding learning back into subsequent rounds of delivery. This model follows a simple logical approach to planning that is commonly found in most planning approaches.

The six-stage CDCynergy social marketing edition tool (CDC, 2007) (see Box 3.2) is similar in approach and stages. This model sets out six stages of planning and is accompanied by a large section of tools and reference material. In 2007, the US Centers for Disease Control and Prevention (CDC) produced a 'lite' version for smaller-scale projects.

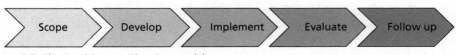

Figure 3.3 The Total Process Planning model.
Reproduced with permission from French J and Blair-Stevens C. *The total process planning framework for social marketing.* London: National Social Marketing Centre. Copyright © 2008 National Social Marketing Centre.

Box 3.2 CDCynergy social marketing planning model

- Phase one: describe the problem
- Phase two: conduct market research
- Phase three: create marketing strategy
- Phase four: plan the intervention
- Phase five: plan programme and evaluation
- Phase six: implement intervention and evaluate

Source: data from Centres for Disease Control and Prevention. *CDCynergy Lite: social marketing made simple.* Atlanta, GA: Centres for Disease Control and Prevention, available from: http://www.cdc.gov/healthcommunication/pdf/cdcynergylite.pdf, accessed 01 Mar. 2016.

The World Health Organization (WHO) COMBI planning model (WHO, 2012; see Figure 3.4) is another well-known and widely used planning model that is focused specifically on health issues and has been developed for application in developing world settings. Another useful eight step model called BEHAVE-based Marketing Plan is set out by Strand and Smith (2008).

There are numerous other models, from very simple plans contained in texts such as that of Hastings and Elliot (1993) to the ten-step approach advocated by Kotler and Lee (2009). In addition to these models many specialist social marketing companies and institutions have developed their own planning models and frameworks.

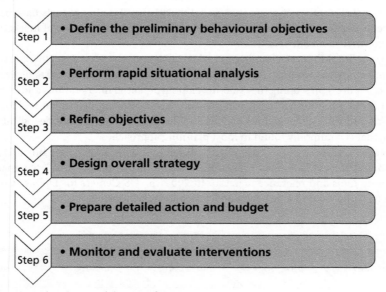

Step 1 • Define the preliminary behavioural objectives

Step 2 • Perform rapid situational analysis

Step 3 • Refine objectives

Step 4 • Design overall strategy

Step 5 • Prepare detailed action and budget

Step 6 • Monitor and evaluate interventions

Figure 3.4 Seven planning model steps of COMBI.
Adapted with permission from World Health Organization. *COMBI toolkit: field workbook for COMBI planning steps in outbreak response*, http://www.searo.who.int/entity/emerging_diseases/ebola/field_workbook_for_combi_planning_steps_in_outbreak_response.pdf, accessed 01 Apr. 2016. Copyright © 2012 WHO.

Each of these planning models sets out a number of steps that proceed from analysis through development into implementation and then evaluation. Each also has advantages and disadvantages. Some are very simple and easy to apply; others are more comprehensive and require more effort. Key issues to consider when selecting a social marketing planning model is the scale and complexity of the behaviour you are seeking to influence. Social marketing can be applied to small-scale local projects with little or no budget or to large-scale sustained international programmes. When a large-scale investment is being made in a social marketing programme it requires a more thorough planning approach and reporting process.

A practical guide to planning your own social marketing intervention

The STELa social marketing planning framework developed by French (20010b) is presented in Figure 3.5. This model will be used to illustrate the key steps, tasks, and activities that are required when planning, delivering, managing, and evaluating a social marketing intervention. STELa is available as an interactive web-based planning tool that includes planning tools aligned to each of its steps and tasks that can be accessed online at: http://ecdc.europa.eu/en/publications/publications/social-marketing-guide-public-health.pdf. An updated version of the STELa model was adopted by the European Centre for Disease Prevention and Control (ECDC) in 2014 as part of its first technical guidance on social marketing. A full version of STELa with an accompanying set of social marketing planning development tools can be downloaded for

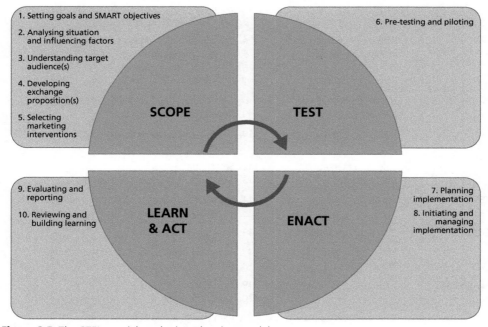

Figure 3.5 The STELa social marketing planning model.
Reproduced with permission from French J and Apfel F. *Social marketing planning guide for public health programme: managers and practitioners. European Centre for Disease Control. Technical Document.* Stockholm: ECDC, available from: http://ecdc.europa.eu/en/publications/Publications/social-marketing-guide-public-health.pdf, accessed 01 Nov. 2015.

free from the ECDC website at: http://ecdc.europa.eu/en/publications/publications/social-marketing-guide-public-health.pdf.

The principle that guided the design of the STELa planning framework was the need for a simple but robust planning framework based on modern marketing principles and the best evidence about what planning tasks lead to improved programme performance. STELa was developed as a response to the need for a planning model that can be applied by practitioners, those not trained in formal planning systems and procedures, and those new to social marketing. It was clear that practitioners needed easy access to specific planning tools to help them complete each step and task in the planning process, so STELa was designed with a set of in-built planning tools that can be simply pulled down and used when completing each task. The online tool prompts users to use these tools and the ECDC version has text links to each tool. STELa was developed following an extensive analysis of all previous social marketing planning tools and other generic planning approaches such as Log Frame planning. STELa reflects the characteristics of effective planning discussed earlier in this chapter.

Table 3.1 sets out in summary form the four planning steps, ten tasks, and 22 activities. The ten task areas within the four steps do not have to be undertaken in the sequence set out; some

Table 3.1 The social marketing actions framework steps, tasks, and activities

Steps	Tasks	Activities
SCOPE	1. Setting goals and SMART objectives	1. Explain what action is needed 2. Identify the target groups and behaviours you want to change 3. Set SMART objectives
	2. Analysing situation and influencing factors	4. Perform situation analysis 5. Perform competition analysis 6. Review evidence and data 7. Map and record assets
	3. Understanding target audience(s)	8. Gather target audience insights 9. Segment your audiences
	4. Developing exchange proposition(s)	10. Develop behaviour promotion strategy 11. Develop the value proposition
	5. Selecting marketing interventions	12. Select interventions 13. Design in cost–benefit analysis
TEST	6. Pre-testing and piloting	14. Test each potential intervention and hypothesis 15. Report on the impact of the pilot programme
ENACT	7. Planning implementation	16. Intervention plan
	8. Initiating and managing implementation	17. Manage partners, risk, and opportunities 18. Report on process
LEARN&ACT	9. Evaluating and reporting	19. Evaluate outcomes 20. Report findings
	10. Reviewing and building learning	21. Identify follow-up actions 22. Identify future implications

Reproduced with permission from French J and Apfel F. *Social marketing planning guide for public health programme: managers and practitioners. European Centre for Disease Control. Technical Document*. Stockholm: ECDC, available from: http://ecdc.europa.eu/en/publications/Publications/social-marketing-guide-public-health.pdf, accessed 01 Nov. 2015.

can be undertaken in parallel and in many cases there will be a need to revise early findings in one task area in the light of subsequent learning. Some tasks can be completed by simply reviewing existing evidence or analysis that an organization has access to. The STELa planning framework makes specific reference to a number of planning processes such as PESTLE (political, environmental, social, technological, legal, and ethical issues) and SWOT (strengths, weaknesses, opportunities, and threats): these tools can help the development of the social marketing interventions.

Though all four steps of social marketing planning are important, investing time in the scoping step is particularly critical. This helps to avoid a tendency to start generating and crafting solutions before a deep understanding and insight into the target audience and problem is achieved. Comprehensive scoping also ensures that a clear behavioural focus is identified from the start, and that relevant theory and ethical issues are considered early in the planning process. The understanding and insights gained during scoping are used to inform the development of working propositions about what will help bring about the desired behaviour in the target population and also the identification and selection of possible interventions that can be taken into the testing and development step. Some of the key advantages that accrue if time and resources are invested in scoping include:

- help to ensure that subsequent resources and time invested in addressing the challenge(s) can be used to greatest potential effect;
- provision of a valuable way to begin to engage and mobilize key partners and stakeholders, who (whatever interventions are selected) will be crucial to ongoing work;
- provision of important baseline understanding and insights on which all subsequent work can be based;
- help to grow the evidence base by setting out clear hypotheses and objectives that can subsequently be tested, evaluated, and reported on.

The four key steps, ten tasks and 22 activities of the STELa social marketing planning framework

Step 1. Scoping (five tasks)

Task 1. Setting behavioural goals and SMART objectives (three activities)

Activity 1. Explain why action is needed Set out why action is needed on the identified social issue. A useful approach is to identify a problem and look at its scale and its social, health, service, economic, and political consequences. The rationale and need for the intervention should be described in terms that all relevant stakeholders can understand.

Activity 2. Identify the target groups and behaviour goals This activity is about identifying the specific audience/s who will be the target of the interventions that will be put in place and the behaviours that are to be influenced. The key assumption made here is that influencing the behaviours of the intended target group will help solve the problem identified. In this task the behaviours that will be focused on need to be described—for example, stopping smoking through the use of nicotine replacement therapy.

Activity 3. Set objectives that can be measured This task is focused on the development of a set of SMART behavioural objectives. SMART stands for:

- specific: precise—not open to different interpretations
- measurable: objective measures can be observed and collected

- achievable: with the resources available
- relevant: to the issue and data can be gathered
- time-bound: measured within the time frame of the intervention.

Each behavioural goal should be underpinned by one or more SMART behavioural objectives.

Task 2. Analysing the situation and influencing factors (four activities)

Activity 4. Perform situation analysis Before initiating any intervention it is useful to identify key issues that may affect your proposed programme/campaign/action or on the receptivity of your target audiences to the intervention/s. This activity involves developing a list of factors which may influence the interventions. A SWOT analysis of current activity is one tool that can help identify potential new tactics. It is also useful to undertake a PESTLE (political, environmental, social, technological, legal, and ethical issues) analysis. Situational factors identified should be prioritized according to their likelihood and the level of impact they may have.

Activity 5. Perform competition analysis In addition to looking at situational issues it is useful to look at enabling factors and barriers to adopting the desired behaviour(s). You should analyse what or who may be influencing the target audience to act in the way that they currently do. Strategies and intervention plans can then be developed to address these influencing factors.

Activity 6. Review evidence and data Gather information about what is known about the issue(s) and how to tackle it/them from published and unpublished sources such as academic papers, meta-reviews, professional journals, case study reports, and interviews with people who have undertaken similar work. Ethical and risk considerations should also be identified and noted, and any preliminary action such as seeking of ethical approval should be started. If major risks are identified, plans to mitigate them should also be developed.

Activity 7. Map and record assets Identify all assets that can help you influence the behaviour among the target groups you are interested in. These assets may include: social networks, community, environmental factors, stakeholders, and health, education, and social care services. Other assets include all potential partner and stakeholder organizations, communities, and individuals that could help with research, implementation, or evaluation of the programme.

Task 3. Understanding target audiences (two activities)

Activity 8. Gather target audience insights Utilize qualitative and quantitative target audience research such as surveys, focus groups, and observational studies to gather intelligence on target audience knowledge, attitudes, and behaviours. Develop summaries of what is known, what people believe, feel, and currently do. You also need to make a note of what is unknown about the target audience as you may need to commission research to discover this.

Activity 9. Segment your audiences Segmentation is the division of an audience you intend to address into subgroups who share similar beliefs, attitudes and behavioural patterns. This approach goes beyond demographic, epidemiological, and service uptake data-based targeting to include data about people's beliefs, attitudes, understanding, and observed behavioural patterns. Target audiences are segmented using the data gathered into clusters of people sharing similar characteristics. Segmentation can also be used to describe the primary audience—i.e. the people you are seeking to influence—and secondary and tertiary audiences—i.e. the people who are influencing or could influence the primary audience. These can often be intermediaries such as parents if children are the primary audience.

Task 4. Developing exchange/value propositions (two activities)

Activity 10. Develop behaviour promotion strategy Based on target audience insight and understanding, set out how the proposed behaviour will be positioned and promoted with the target audience(s). In the case of a positive behaviour change, such as vaccination, uptake may be promoted by focusing on what emotional and physical benefits will be attained and how costs, such as inconvenient times, might be reduced. It is often useful to list the benefits associated with the behaviour and describe these in a way that is appealing to target audience preferences and beliefs. The core benefit associated with adopting or sustaining the targeted behaviour is the actual personally perceived value people get from it and not necessarily the value that you as a professional would ascribe to the behaviour. This is why it is important to have a deep understanding of what the target audience thinks are the positive attributes of the behaviour or service you are promoting so that these can be emphasized. It is also important to understand the negative feelings or views people have so that they can also be addressed and mitigated by your interventions.

Activity 11. Develop the value proposition Based on the target audience insight and data you have gathered, set out for each audience segment you will be seeking to influence how the benefits of compliance with the desired behaviour you are interested in would maximize what they value and minimize costs and barriers they perceive. This is the value proposition that will guide all your intervention selection choices and promotional tactics. If behaviour is being influenced by factors other than logically considered decisions you will also need to set out how systems, policies, rewards, punishments, or environmental design could be used to encourage compliance.

Task 5. Selecting social marketing interventions (two activities)

Activity 12. Select intervention 'forms' and 'types' This activity is focused on selecting which combination of intervention 'types' and 'forms' will be used to promote the adoption of the behaviours that you want to influence. 'Types' of intervention (see Figure 3.6) include controls,

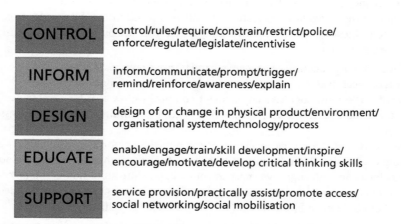

Figure 3.6 The five deCIDES intervention 'types'.
Reproduced with permission from French J and Apfel F. *Social Marketing planning guide for public health programme: Managers and practitioners. European Centre for Disease Control. Technical Document.* Stockholm: ECDC, available from: http://ecdc.europa.eu/en/publications/Publications/social-marketing-guide-public-health.pdf, accessed 01 Nov. 2015.

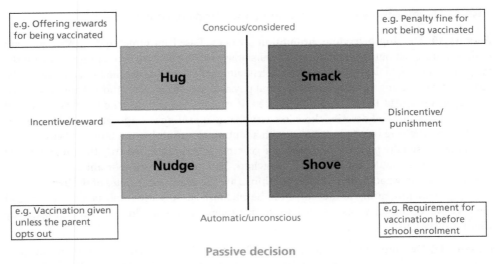

Figure 3.7 The four 'forms' of intervention.
Reproduced with permission from *French J* and *Apfel F. Social Marketing planning guide for public health programme: Managers and practitioners. European Centre for Disease Control. Technical Document.* Stockholm: ECDC, available from: http://ecdc.europa.eu/en/publications/Publications/social-marketing-guide-public-health.pdf, accessed 01 Nov. 2015.

laws, and regulations; information; environmental or system design changes; and educational and support services. 'Forms' of intervention (see Figure 3.7) focus on use of incentives and penalties to influence behaviour, recognizing that some behaviours are the result of considered logical decision-making but many others are the result of little cognitive engagement and based on gut feelings or internal biases.

The four 'forms' of intervention 'Forms' of intervention are defined by two main factors: first, whether the intervention uses rewards or punishment to encourage a particular behaviour; second, whether the approach seeks to influence cognitive or unconscious decision-making. The combination of these two factors creates four different possibilities: 'hug' and 'nudge' that use incentives to influence behaviour; 'shove' and 'smack' that use punishments and disincentives to influence behaviours.

♦ Hugs focus on high cognitive engagement and positive rewards for compliance—e.g. offering rewards or incentives such as money, feelings of satisfaction, or esteem.
♦ Nudges focus on low cognitive engagement and positive rewards for compliance—e.g. setting up a default scheme where vaccination is given to children in schools unless a parent opts out.
♦ Shoves focus on low cognitive engagement and punishment for non-compliance—e.g. traffic calming road design that uses bumps in the road to slow down those who drive too fast.
♦ Smacks focus on high cognitive engagement and punishment for non-compliance—e.g. if a person chooses to continue to smoke in the workplace despite having been informed that this is not allowed they can be fined or ultimately dismissed from their job.

All these 'forms' of intervention are legitimate public health strategies. Often a combination of such approaches is required. The selection of combination of interventions will depend on what the literature and target audience research show are effective, acceptable, practical, financially feasible, and sustainable approaches. This activity is finalized by setting out which combination of the intervention 'types' and 'forms' will be used and how they will be applied.

Activity 13. Design in cost–benefit analysis When you develop intervention plans, you will also need to consider what 'types' and 'forms' of intervention give the best value for money and return on investment in terms of the lowest cost for the biggest behavioural response. Building sustainable programmes requires an understanding of how resources can be best allocated and decisions about allocations based on return-on-investment and value-for-money analyses. This is especially important when implementing a new or novel intervention that has not been rigorously evaluated previously.

Step 2. **Testing (one task)**

The test step involves developing prototype interventions and testing them. It culminates in a report recommending what mix of interventions should be developed into a full implementation plan. Methods of collecting and analysing data for evaluation purposes can also be tested and developed during this step.

Task 6. Pre-testing and piloting (two activities)

Activity 14. Test each potential intervention Test each potential intervention that you have developed for each target group segment. This should include the development of an experimental design that is appropriate to the target group, issue, and methods being used. It is also important at this stage to consider any ethical issues and the gathering of any permission required to complete a pilot test. The exact evaluation method will depend on the 'type' and/or 'form' of intervention, scale of the target population, time scale, and budget. If possible, independent researchers should be engaged to assist with the study design and evaluating the pilot as this will add additional rigour to the process.

Activity 15. Report on the impact of the pilot programme Reports should include information on the immediate impact of the interventions on issues such as awareness, knowledge gain, attitude, and beliefs. They should also measure impact on short-term behaviours and systems acceptability and efficiency, such as the cost of generating interest in the programme and costs of different methods of generating contact with the intervention or short-term behavioural actions such as calls to a helpline.

Step 3. **Enacting (two tasks)**

This step is focused on implementing and managing an intervention plan based on the findings of the scoping and testing steps. At the beginning of this step a full social marketing implementation plan will be produced, together with a clear budget and evaluation strategy that will include details about how the programme will be managed, how it will report, and how it will manage risks and opportunities that arise. The plan will outline the ways the programme will be monitored for its impact and efficiency, how it will be evaluated, and how it will report back to funders, sponsors, and stakeholder and target groups.

Task 7. Planning implementation (one activity)

Activity 16. Intervention plan Building on the outcomes of the pilot project and the scoping findings, this task focuses on developing a full social marketing implementation plan. This plan should be made available to all stakeholders and partners and include the following elements:

1. a statement of the problem;
2. situation analysis and competition analysis;
3. what is known and what is unknown about how to influence the behaviour that is the focus of the programme, including theory, research, and case study data;
4. the intended target audience and any segmentation used;

5. clear behavioural goals and SMART objectives for each target group;

6. details of the mix of the 'types' and 'forms' of intervention that will be used;

7. consideration of any ethical issues and other risks and how they will be managed;

8. the anticipated impact and outcomes on each selected target audiences;

9. how the programme will be managed and how it will report;

10. the assets that will be used to bring about change;

11. the budget and how it will be used to achieve the agreed objectives of the intervention;

12. the evaluation strategy, including measures of the short-term change (impact evaluation), the efficiency of interventions (process evaluation), and the desired behaviour (outcome evaluation).

Task 8. Initiating and managing implementation (two activities)

Activity 17. Manage partners, risk, and opportunities It will be necessary to measure whether each partner has delivered on what they promised and record how well they have engaged with the programme. It is also necessary to set out a plan to review and manage any risks associated with the project. Careful tracking and management of the intervention budget is also required, ensuring that there are no significant cost overruns or underspends and that the intervention is being delivered in the most cost-effective way possible. Finally, a system for opportunity spotting, horizon scanning, and programme adjustment that can feed into the day-to-day management of the programme will need to be established.

Activity 18. Report on process Gather process and short-term impact data. Record progress and setbacks, analyse this data, and report to all relevant stakeholders and partners on a regular basis as the project proceeds. Programme staff should use this tracking data to adjust and refine interventions as the programme continues.

Step 4. Learning and acting (two tasks)

This step in the social marketing process is focused on gathering and disseminating the final findings about the efficiency, value for money, impact, and outcome of the programme. It also seeks to help practitioners and organizations learn about what worked well and what did not. This information can be used to inform future decision-making related to subsequent follow-on or new programmes.

Task 9. Evaluating and reporting (two activities)

Activity 19. Evaluate outcomes Utilize the SMART objectives developed in Task 1, Activity 3 as the basis for this evaluation. Record the outcomes from the individual 'forms' and 'types' of interventions used and the overall programme impact. The contribution of different stakeholders and partners to the achievement of specific interventions and overall programme goals should also be assessed.

Activity 20. Report findings The key focus of this activity is to report to stakeholders and partners, staff involved in delivering the programme, and target audiences the findings of your evaluation and tracking data and observations.

Task 10. Reviewing and building learning (two activities)

Activity 21. Identify follow-up actions Set out recommendations for action that should be taken by policy-makers, planners, professional staff, community groups, and other stakeholders and partners, based on your evaluation. Identify ways to disseminate the results and recommendations that you have developed to wider audiences through such actions as publications, presentations at conferences, etc.

Activity 22. Identify future implications Set out an agreed plan for how your organization and other partners and stakeholders can adapt and improve future action focused on influencing the behaviours you have targeted, informed by the learning and evaluation of the programme. Reassess and update your SWOT, competition and PESTLE analyses in the light of findings from your evaluation and make recommendations that result from any implications of this analysis for future implementation.

Conclusion

The focus of this chapter has been on setting out the rationale and key features associated with planning and implementing a social marketing programme. There is no one correct way to plan a social marketing intervention; therefore, practitioners will need to consider which model or approach to adopt. Regardless of the model adopted, there should always be a written plan that is capable of being interrogated by those who are the recipients of an intervention, those supporting the delivery, and those sponsoring it.

The literature concerned with social behavioural change planning and management provides a reasonably tight consensus on the importance of the application of planning principles. The setting out of clear goals and objectives, a development phase that includes reviewing and applying relevant theory, the need to interrogate data about the problem, clear identification and understanding of target audiences, piloting, pre-testing, programme refinement, and robust management, monitoring, and evaluation of programme implementation are all key.

However, the existence of planning templates or checklists is not sufficient to ensure the delivery of effective and efficient programmes. Other factors such as the need for appropriate leadership, well-trained and supported staff, and systems for learning and review are also important. Taken together with the planning steps, tasks, and activities set out in this chapter, these principles can be used to create a planning and performance culture which can lead to more efficient and effective social marketing programme performance and ultimately better social policy outcomes.

It is clear that despite there being a number of logical well-constructed planning models within the social marketing field there is a need to encourage a more comprehensive application of these models in practice. This is necessary not only for reasons of more efficient and effective delivery but also because it will help to improve the capture and dissemination of learning about what works and what does not. There a need for more training in the use of planning models and a need to develop simpler, more user-friendly starter models such as STELa and CDCynergy Lite to encourage the adoption of more systematic planning.

Self-review questions

1. List the four main stages of the social marketing planning process and some of the key tasks within each stage.
2. Why is it important to focus time and effort on the scoping stage of any social marketing project or programme?
3. Discus why testing, piloting, and prototyping are key elements in the social marketing process.
4. List some of the key tasks that are associated with managing a social marketing project when it gets to the enacting stage.

Note

1. See: https://www.gov.uk/government/publications/what-works-evidence-centres-for-social-policy.

References

Australian Public Service Commission (2007). *Changing behaviour: a public policy perspective.* Barton: Australian Government Publishers Ltd.

Bracht, N., Kingsbury, L., Rissel, C. (1999). A five stage community organisation model for health promotion. In: N. Bracht (ed). *Health promotion at the community level: new advances.* Thousand Oaks, CA: Sage.

Cabinet Office (2008). Cultural change: a policy framework. London: Cabinet Office.

CDC (2007). *CDCynergy Lite: social marketing made simple.* Atlanta, GA: Centers for Disease Control and Prevention http://www.cdc.gov/healthcommunication/cdcynergylite.html

Darnton, A., Elster-Jones, K., Lucas B., Brooks, M. (2006). *Promoting pro-environmental behaviour: existing evidence to inform better policy making.* London: Department for Environment, Food and Rural Affairs.

French, J. (2010a). Commissioning social marketing. In: J. French, C. Blair-Stevens, D. McVey, R. Merritt (eds). *Social marketing and public health: theory and practice*, 1st edition. Oxford: Oxford University Press.

French, J. (2010b). STELa social marketing planning model [website]. Available online at: http://ecomeu. info/wp-content/uploads/2015/11/STELa-tool.pdf

French, J., Apfel, F. (2014). *Social marketing guide for public health programme managers and practitioners.* Stockholm: European Centre for Disease Prevention and Control http://ecdc.europa.eu/en/publications/Publications/social-marketing-guide-public-health.pdf

French, J., Blair-Stevens, C. (2008). *The total process planning framework for social marketing.* London: National Social Marketing Centre.

French, J., Mayo, E. (2006). *It's our health: national review of social marketing.* London: National Consumer Council.

French, J., Blair-Stevens, C., McVey, D., Merritt, R. (eds). (2010). *Social marketing and public health: theory and practice*, 1st edition. Oxford: Oxford University Press.

Hastings, G., Elliot, B. (2013). Social marketing practice in traffic safety. In: *Marketing of traffic safety*, chapter III, pp. 35–55. Paris: OECD.

Halpen, D. (2004). *Personal responsibility and changing behaviour: the state of knowledge and its implications for public policy.* London: Prime Minister's Strategy Unit.

Hornik, R. (ed). (2002). *Public health communication: evidence for behaviour change.* Mahwah, NJ: Lawrence Erlbaum Associates.

Institute of Government (2009). *Mindspace: influencing behaviour through public policy.* London: Cabinet Office.

Klassen, A. (2010). Performance measurement and improvement framework in health, education and Social services: a systematic review. *International Journal for Quality of Health Care* **22**(1): 44–69.

Kotler, P., Lee, N. (2005). *Corporate social responsibility: doing the most good for your company and your cause.* Hoboken, NJ: John Wiley & Sons Inc.

Kotler, P., Lee, N. (2009). *Up and out of poverty: the social marketing solution.* Upper Saddle River, NJ: Prentice Hall.

Kotler, P., Roberto, W., Lee, N. (2002). *Social marketing: improving the quality of life*, 2nd edition. New York: Sage.

Lefebvre, C. (2013). *Social marketing and social change.* San Francisco, CA: Jossey-Bass.

Maylock, B., Howat, P., Slevin, T. (2001). A decision-making model for health promotion advocacy. *Promotion and Education* **8**(2): 59–64.

Mays, D., James, B., Weaver, I., Rernhart, J. (2011). New media in social marketing. In: G. Hastings, K. Angus, C. Bryant (eds). *The Sage handbook of social marketing*. London: Sage.

McKenzie-Mohr, D., Smith, W. (2011). *Fostering sustainable behaviour: an introduction to community-based social marketing*, 3rd edition. Gabriola Island: New Society Publishers.

McKenzie-Mohr, D., Lee, N., Wesley Schultz, P., Kotler, P. (2012). *Social marketing to protect the environment: what works*. Thousand Oaks, CA: Sage.

MRC (2010). *Developing and evaluating complex interventions*. London: Medical Research Council http://www.mrc.ac.uk/complexinterventionsguidance

NICE (2007). *Behaviour change at population, community and individual levels: reference guide*. London: National Institute for Health and Care Excellence.

New Economics Foundation (2005). *Behavioural economics: seven principles for policy-makers*. London: New Economics Foundation.

Peattie, K., Peattie, S. (2011). The social marketing mix: a critical review. In: G. Hastings, K. Angus, C. Bryant (eds). *The Sage handbook of social marketing*. London: Sage.

Schorr L.B. (2003). Determining 'what works' in social programs and social policies: towards a more inclusive knowledge base. Washington, DC: The Brookings Institution.

Stand, J., Smith, W. (2008). *Social marketing/behaviour. A practical resource for social change professionals*. Washington: AED.

Weinreich, N. (2011). *Hands-on social marketing: a step by step guide to designing change for good*, 2nd edition. Thousand Oaks, CA: Sage.

WHO (2012). *Communication for behavioural impact (COMBI): a toolkit for behavioural and social communication in outbreak response*. Geneva: World Health Organization http://www.who.int/ihr/publications/combi_toolkit_outbreaks/en/

Chapter 4

Evaluation of social marketing programmes

Adam Crosier and Dominic McVey

We do not learn from experience. We learn from reflecting on experience.
John Dewey, *How we think: a restatement of the relation of reflective thinking to the educative process*, 1933

Learning points

This chapter:

- explains why evaluation is important to social marketing;
- outlines the different research methods;
- explains the different stages of evaluation that can be carried out on a social marketing projects;
- provides case studies of evaluation in practice.

Introduction to evaluating social marketing programmes

A central consideration of evaluation is that of accountability. Evaluation can be thought of as a 'critical friend', questioning the claims of programme managers at times, and providing the evidence for claims at others.

Evaluation is the action of valuing or appraising. In addition to accountability it is also concerned with learning and improvement. In social programmes—including social marketing and behaviour change interventions—evaluation has a number of roles to play. It is the means by which to:

1. develop ideas that inform interventions (formative evaluation);
2. assess progress of a project or programme in order to improve it as it develops (process evaluation);
3. learn whether the programme has been effective (impact or summative evaluation);
4. determine whether one programme or intervention is worth investing in, by comparison with an alternative programme or the status quo, depending on the resources and level of change achieved (cost-effectiveness or economic evaluation).

An important and often overlooked role of evaluation is to consider whether the intervention has any unintended outcomes—either positive or negative—on those who were targeted, or on those who were not targeted but were caught up in the intervention. While the distinction between evaluation approaches is sometimes overstated, it is useful to think of evaluation as having these related, but distinct, phases or elements.

Because the notion of evaluation is so broad, the way that evaluation is understood in practice often depends on who is asking the question. For a body like the National Institute for Health and Care Excellence (NICE), which is responsible for assessing whether clinical or public health treatments or interventions are worth paying for from the public purse, it is unsurprising that their definition focuses on the summative aspect of the concept.

> Evaluation: an assessment of an intervention (for example, a treatment, service, project, or programme) to see whether it achieves its aims.
>
> (NICE, 2015)

However, evaluation is concerned just as much with understanding the process by which an intervention operates as it is with whether it achieves its intended goals.

Evaluation is everywhere

> Friend to Groucho Marx: 'Life is hard . . .'
> Groucho Marx to friend: 'Compared to what?'

Evaluation is concerned with comparison. Who would book a holiday or purchase a kitchen appliance without reflecting on the ratings and reviews of independent experts on the one hand, and of like-minded peers and 'people like us' on the other?

This focus on measurement and scoring is part of a broader 'performance management' culture of which evaluation is a component. Inspired by the work of management gurus like Peter Drucker, the 'what gets measured gets managed' approach to business and social policy programmes involves the setting of targets, and assessment against these as a means of improving productivity. As a result, audits and inspections form an integral part of just about every aspect of life—from nurseries and schools to hospitals and retirement homes. All are subject to evaluation by independent agencies, and increasingly by consumer feedback.

Moreover, the scoring and rating system that is part of the public sphere has entered our consciousness as citizens and private individuals, both in employment contexts and in the private realm. Performance appraisals and reviews are a standard requirement for employment purposes. Beyond this, the application of scoring and review extends elsewhere to our choices about what to see at the cinema or theatre, which restaurants to eat at, what books to read, and increasingly who we choose as partners.

Evaluation in the dock

> *I find it difficult to think of a major social policy area in the UK where you can say 'we're doing [it] this way because a randomised control trial told us that worked and something else didn't', which is fundamentally rather depressing.*
> Jonathan Portes, *Director of the National Institute of Economic and Social Research* (Rutter, 2012)

Despite the growth in the use of evaluation tools to improve the quality of everyday life, evaluation itself is a hot topic in social policy—not just social marketing and behaviour change programmes. For several years there has been growing unease at the apparent failure of successive political administrations—with their varying remedies—to tackle the more intractable social problems. Evaluation research has been implicated in this failure. Some commentators allege that evaluation research has not been used enough, others that when it has been used, researchers have used inappropriate research designs. But the end result is that we continue to struggle with finding answers to important questions that, in theory at least, are capable of being answered through research. And the presumption is that evaluation is in some way responsible for this failure.

When it comes to answering questions such as 'does prison work?' or 'do programmes designed to relieve social disadvantage work?' time and again, experts who review the evidence are stumped by conflicting narratives and a lack of good-quality evidence on which to base a judgement. A report by the Institute for Government, a policy 'think tank', on the role of evaluation research in policy-making came to the depressing conclusion that there was a serious weakness in the relationship between evidence and policy-making. It found that, despite huge investment in university-based research to evaluate policy, the evaluators were unable to translate the learning from past activities into future policy.

Demands for more and better evaluation

The lack of good-quality evidence is a persistent theme that informs debates about evaluation of social interventions, including social marketing and behaviour change programmes.

> We spent billions on research . . . we got really high quality papers but it was always felt they were answering yesterday's question tomorrow.
>
> Senior civil servant, Institute for Government (Rutter, 2012)

In the UK, a report by the House of Lords Science and Technology Select Committee (2011) published the findings of a two-year inquiry into behaviour change and made precisely this criticism. The inquiry was conducted to examine how government actions influence people's behaviour in relation to a whole range of social policies from crime prevention to health improvement.

It explored the way in which social marketing and other actions that seek to influence the 'choice architecture', and so influence behaviour, have been used and evaluated alongside regulatory methods (such as legislation). A key finding was the lack of adequate evaluation programmes to determine whether government behaviour change interventions achieve their goals.

The following elements were identified as not being considered adequately by those designing and implementing programmes that aim to bring about behaviour change:

◆ building evaluation into a policy design from the outset;
◆ good outcome measures;
◆ longitudinal data;
◆ the use of controls wherever possible;
◆ sufficient funding for evaluation;
◆ data on cost-effectiveness.

Experimental evaluation in the real world

Meanwhile, there are emerging examples of how evaluation can be used to improve the quality of policy. The Behavioural Insight Team (BIT) has successfully argued for more effective evaluation of policy and has implemented evaluation studies of new policies, using experimental research designs. BIT, formerly part of the UK civil service, earned the nickname the 'Nudge' unit because of its indebtedness to the work of Cass Sunstein and Richard Thaler, authors of a book of the same name (Sunstein and Thaler, 2009). They also coined the term 'choice architecture', which has been characterized as 'soft paternalism'. Much of BIT's work tests 'nudge' approaches to behaviour change. The unit's work is important because it demonstrates that it is possible to subject new policy initiatives to rigorous testing in a way that in the past was often thought impossible for 'real-life' situations (BIT, 2015).

Most famously, among several studies, BIT has shown that by introducing an aspect of social norms to tax collection—specifically by including in tax demand letters a message stating that most people pay their tax on time—it is possible to increase significantly the payment rate of income tax paid by citizens. Other examples include testing the effectiveness of policies that rely on citizen inertia or 'harnessing the power of default', as BIT describes it. Increasing enrolment onto work-based pension schemes by making enrolment the default option is a good example of this.

In all its work, which is well documented, BIT adopts an experimental evaluation design. The critical features of the experimental design are simple enough—that people with similar attributes should be allocated to either an intervention or a control/comparison group, and measurements of the impact of the intervention should be taken before and after exposure to it. Where possible, the two groups should be allocated randomly to either the intervention or control group because the process of randomization mitigates the possibility of bias.

While BIT's results are impressive, the unit itself acknowledges that, to date, much of its work has focused on relatively simple and straightforward aspects of behaviour change design, including 'one-off' behaviours. Ensuring that computer systems are set to have a default that has the intended outcome—and then relying on human inertia to avoid switching to the 'unwanted' outcome—is impressive. Similarly, improving the quality of messaging on official forms that appeals to social norms is both simple to implement and requires little effort on the behalf of the citizen to realize the desired behaviour change.

Indeed, randomized controlled trials in particular are well designed to cope with simple interventions where only a small number of variables may be responsible for observed outcomes. However, for more ingrained problems human behaviour is frequently much more complex. And the challenge is to find ways of subjecting complex interventions to similarly rigorous evaluation designs.

Alternative models: are they more realistic?

> Not everything that can be counted counts, and not everything that counts can be counted.
>
> Albert Einstein

Some commentators have sought to develop alternative approaches to evaluation research that reflect the need for good-quality evidence of the type provided by clinical trials while at the same time acknowledging that clinical trials are incapable of answering complex social questions. Pawson and Tilley (1997) pioneered work in this area with their concept of 'realistic evaluation'.

Realistic evaluation is centred on finding not only what outcomes are produced from interventions but also 'how they are produced, and what is significant about the varying conditions in which the interventions take place'. Pawson and Tilley were critical of quasi-experimental models of evaluation and felt they failed to identify effectively why interventions worked differently across different contexts. The realistic evaluation approach is sometimes shorthanded to the formula:

$$context + mechanism = outcome$$

In essence, the approach sets out to find the contextual conditions that make interventions effective, thereby developing lessons about how they produce outcomes to inform policy decisions. The key to the realistic evaluation approach is an understanding of the relationship between context, mechanism, and outcome. The following are summary definitions of each of these terms:

- Context: what conditions are needed for a measure to trigger mechanisms to produce particular outcome patterns?
- Mechanism: what is it about a measure which may lead it to have a particular outcome in a given context?
- Outcome patterns: what are the practical effects produced by causal mechanisms being triggered in a given context?

The role of evaluation research as part of social marketing and behaviour change programmes

Different forms of evaluation research serve different purposes. To be of most value, evaluation should be an integral part of the programme from the outset. This means understanding and integrating the evaluation design into every part of the planning process. A vital consideration is ensuring that evaluation is thought about at the planning stage of an intervention, and not left until the project is underway or near completion.

Step 1. Engage stakeholders

Stakeholders are people with an interest in a programme and the future use of its evaluation. They may include:

- participants: the intended target group(s) or beneficiaries of the programme;
- implementers: those involved in delivering the programme;
- partners and influencers: those who actively support the programme or who will have an interest in the findings of the evaluation.

Step 2. Describe or plan the programme

This involves reviewing the target audience, the context of the intervention, and the intended outcomes. As part of this, a theory or logic model should be developed to describe how the intervention is likely to bring about the intended outcomes (Funnell and Rogers, 2011).

A logic model is a theory to explain how change occurs. Many competing social and psychological theories that have been developed to explain how behaviour occurs and can be modified. Some of the better known include the Health Belief Model, the Social Learning Theory (Bandura, 1963), the Diffusion of Innovations Theory, the Theory of Planned Behaviour, and more recent iterations including the Behaviour Change Wheel (Michie et al., 2014).

Step 3. Focus the evaluation's remit

It is important to reflect on why the evaluation is being conducted. Frequently, stakeholders have a range of competing demands of evaluation. For example, some stakeholders may wish to know what impact the intervention has, in order to obtain additional funding; others may wish to know how the intervention was received by users. While both sets of questions are valid, it may be that the evaluation resources cannot address all the questions and prioritizing of demands may be required. Focusing on the most important—and realistic—goals is essential if the evaluation is to produce a worthwhile investment.

Step 4. **Develop an appropriate research design**

Once the aims of the evaluation are agreed, the research team must next develop a research design that is capable of answering the questions posed of it. For instance, if the focus is to assess impact (e.g. 'did the intervention lead to an in/decrease in the target group's identified behaviour?'), the best method is to seek an experimental design (see the 'summative evaluation' section below), as this is likely to provide the best evidence that any observed changes that occur during the course of the intervention can be attributed to the intervention—and not to some other factor. In this instance, a quantitative design would also be appropriate because the evaluation question implies a numerical outcome.

Alternatively, if the aim of the evaluation is to understand how the intervention is received from the point of view of the target group(s), an experimental design may not be necessary. A before/after design may be useful, with a qualitative research method to explore experiences.

Triangulation

An important consideration in developing an appropriate research design is to consider using a range of approaches. Triangulation is the process of combining data from a range of sources in order to answer a question. Using other data sources to cross-validate study findings provides another objective measure of performance and lends more strength to the research conclusions.

Rather than relying solely on the reported impact on the intended beneficiaries, an evaluation study may seek evidence of impact on both those involved in delivering the intervention and the social and physical environment, as well as checking for any unintended consequences. In these situations, a multimethod approach is employed to capture what has happened. Reported changes in a knowledge, attitude, belief, and practice survey can be triangulated with increases in helpline calls and changes in media coverage with each independent measure validating the other—or not.

Similarly, reported behaviours may be triangulated with sales data. For example, trends in reported condom use can be compared to industry data on condom sales to see if peaks in reported use coincide with peaks in sales (Goodrich et al., 1998). Likewise, trends in sexual health clinic attendance and test data can be compared with behavioural trend data. Behavioural reports of increases in attempts to stop smoking can be compared with data on attendance at stop smoking services, calls to helplines, use of online support services, sales of products designed to assist quitting, and even cigarette sales data.

However, caution is required in interpreting comparative data of this type. For instance, smuggled and counterfeit tobacco is estimated to account for around 10% of all tobacco sold in the UK, and is not captured by retail audit data. Similarly, disruptive technologies such as e-cigarettes, which are now widely used as a means of harm reduction as well as quitting, have an impact on sales data of other stop smoking aids.

Step 5. **Identify indicators**

As part of the evaluation design phase, the research team must identify indicators of outcomes. Indicators are simply factors (sometimes referred to as proxy measures) that signpost whether the outcomes are being achieved. Here, it is important to review the theory or logic model that identifies how and why the proposed intervention is capable of bringing about the intended outcomes among the identified target group(s).

Indicators of change in specific behaviours (for instance, stopping smoking) may include—among smokers: knowledge of the harms caused by smoking, perceptions of personal salience (whether the smoker feels they are personally at risk/vulnerable) to harm, intentions to stop smoking, calls to a helpline, use of stop smoking services, or the purchase or use of products designed to assist with stopping smoking. In the case of policy-makers, indicators of behaviour change may also be both cognitive (changes in knowledge and understanding of an issue) and psychological (attitudes to that topic), as well as more behavioural. For example, policy-makers' oral and written statements on a given topic may be considered an indicator of their intentions to change policy.

Examples of routinely collected data

As part of the development of indicators, evaluators should explore the potential of routinely collected data to assist with providing evidence of the impact of an intervention—or indeed of the needs of a target group.

Examples of routinely collected data are many and varied, and will often only come to light through consultation with stakeholders, particularly those closest to the topic. They include:

- data relating to the intervention in question—e.g. records and reviews of patients treated for a given condition;
- routine surveys of customers/patients/service users;
- complaints and other customer feedback;
- sales data;
- media analysis: the extent of coverage and whether it was positive or negative;
- document analysis, reviews of printed material, policy documents records, and similar;
- case studies;
- observations.

Step 6. **Data collection**

Having identified an appropriate research design, the next step is to collect relevant data to measure changes in the indicators and the outcomes. The choice of method for data collection will evolve inevitably from the research design. For instance, a programme that seeks to promote the use of clean needles and syringes among injecting drug users, in order to minimize the risk of bloodborne infections, may involve a number of data collection methods including:

- surveys of injecting drug users with questions about use of clean needles and syringes;
- reports of the number of new needles and syringes distributed by needle exchange facilities and pharmacies;
- reports of bloodborne infections among injecting drug users by health care services.

Quantitative research methods: face-to-face, telephone, postal, and online surveys

The most common survey methods involve face-to-face, telephone, postal, or online interviewing. It is important to consider the most appropriate method for the specific task, taking account of resources. Each method has its strengths and weaknesses. Online surveys, for instance, typically involve either convenience samples or panels of registered respondents. Panels are useful because they can be recruited in large numbers, enabling large quotas to be drawn. However, participants on panel surveys risk becoming 'experts' in responding to research studies and so become atypical of the population. Postal surveys, on the other hand, tend to have a poor response rate, and respondents tend to be those with more time and interest in the subject. Any method that relies on literacy skills (reading/writing and computer skills) is likely to lead to under-representation of disadvantaged groups, older groups, and some minority ethnic communities.

Considerations when developing data collection tools

Sampling methods are classified as either *probability* or *non-probability*. In probability samples, each member of the population has a known non-zero probability of being selected. In non-probability sampling, members are selected from the population in some non-random manner. These include convenience sampling, quota sampling, and snowball sampling. The advantage of probability sampling is that sampling error—the degree to which a sample might differ from the population—can be calculated. In non-probability sampling, the degree to which the sample differs from the population remains unknown.

Examples of sampling methodologies used in surveys of the public

Random sampling

Random sampling is the purest form of probability sampling. Each member of the population has an equal and known chance of being selected. This is the approach used in most government surveys because it ensures that the findings are representative and generalizable. Unfortunately, random sampling is also the most costly method of survey research.

Quota sampling

Quota sampling is a form of non-random sampling and involves identifying the strata and their proportions as they are represented in the population. Then convenience or judgement sampling is used to select the required number of subjects from each stratum. In many instances, quota sampling is used as a cost-effective substitute for random sampling. However, it is not an equivalent.

Snowball sampling

Snowball sampling is a special non-probability method used when the desired sample characteristic is rare. It may be extremely difficult or cost-prohibitive to locate respondents in these situations. Snowball sampling relies on referrals from initial subjects to generate additional subjects. While this technique can dramatically lower search costs, it comes at the expense of introducing bias because the technique itself reduces the likelihood that the sample will represent a good cross-section of the population. This method has been used to good effect in studies of stigmatized—and private—behaviours, including studies of injecting drug users and sex workers, where individuals are unlikely to be recorded on official lists. For each sampling approach, consideration has to be given to how the data is collected (Box 4.1).

Qualitative research methods: focus groups and individual interviews

As with survey research, careful consideration should be given to the sampling methodology of qualitative research. While the goal is clearly not statistical representativeness, it is important that respondents are broadly representative of the groups targeted by the intervention and of those involved in the delivery of the programme.

Focus group discussions have become a mainstay of qualitative research. Their strength is that the group dynamic tends to generate lively debate and discussion—and leads to a quality of data that is not matched by individual interviews. Again, careful planning is required in the

Box 4.1 Case study: SunSmart Victoria

Cancer Council Victoria and the Victorian Health Promotion Foundation first funded SunSmart in 1988 in Victoria, Australia. Today SunSmart is a multifaceted programme recognized for providing leadership and innovation in ultraviolet (UV) radiation protection. Programmes operate in each state and territory of Australia by respective cancer councils, all using common principles but tailored to jurisdictional priorities. The sun protection message has expanded to 'Slip! Slop! Slap! Seek! Slide!' (Figure 4.1).

Slip   **Slop**   **Slap**   **Seek**   **Slide**

Protect yourself in five ways from skin cancer

Figure 4.1 Cancer Council Victoria's SunSmart initiative.
Reproduced with permission from *Cancer Council NSW*, http://www.cancercouncil.com.au/72190/cancer-prevention/sun-protection/local-government-workplace/sun-protection-in-the-workplace/skin-cancer-and-outdoor-workers/, Copyright © 2015 Cancer Council NSW.

Almost 30 years of commitment and partnerships with the Victorian Health Promotion Foundation, government, key partners, and community agencies have seen huge changes in social norms and health.

◆ SunSmart has a proven track record in preventing cancer and saving lives—preventing more than 103,000 skin cancers in Victoria between 1988 and 2003, resulting in more than 1,000 deaths being averted.

◆ While melanoma incidence in Victoria continues to rise, there are now falling incidence rates in men and women younger than 40 years, consistent with a positive effect of the SunSmart programme on behaviour change.

◆ In contrast to the pre-SunSmart 'baby boomers', the number of basal and squamous cell carcinoma skin cancer treatments among those aged under 45 years is also decreasing, relative to population growth.

◆ SunSmart is extremely cost-effective, with a $2.30 net saving for every dollar spent, and is one of a handful of Australian public health interventions assessed as being 'excellent value for money'.

◆ Victoria was one of the first states in Australia to legislate against solariums in 2008, and more recently to ban solariums entirely. Since 1 January 2015, commercial tanning units have been banned in the state, saving lives.

◆ Of all Victorian primary schools, 90% are registered SunSmart schools, reaching 430,000 children. This is the highest participation rate across all Australian states, and the highest participation rate for any public health intervention in Australia. Compared with 17% in 1993, 89% of all Victorian primary schools now have a sun protection policy.

◆ In 1988, 2% of Victorian preschools reported that hats were available at preschool—this has now increased to 91%. The programme reaches approximately 194,000 Victorian children.

◆ Between 2009 and 2013, 491 workplace education sessions were conducted at more than 150 workplaces, reaching almost 8,000 participants.

◆ The SunSmart app has been downloaded by over 80,000 people. In summer 2010–11, 40% of Victorian adults reported recently using UV alerts or sun protection times to make decisions about sun protection—up from 26% in 2009.

To find out more, go to Cancer Council Victoria's web page: http://www.cancervic.org.au/research/behavioural/cbrc-skin

planning of the composition of the group to ensure that members are broadly similar. The goal is to encourage participants to feel confident to express their views without fear of being ostracized because other participants hold different attitudes based on their age, social class, or level of education—or indeed any other factor.

Individual interviews and paired interviews are valuable when research subjects may be unavailable for group discussions or where the topic is particularly sensitive and the participant feels uncomfortable discussing it in a group setting. Friendship pairs are a useful method for engaging young people in particular, to address subjects that they may feel uncomfortable discussing in larger groups.

Formative evaluation

Formative evaluation is the 'front end' element of evaluation. It is generally any evaluation that takes place before or during a project's implementation, with the aim of improving the project's design and performance. It includes:

◆ finding out the needs of the target group(s);
◆ testing elements of the intervention prior to implementation;
◆ helping establish programme goals and aims;
◆ identifying barriers and facilitators that may impede or enable the intervention to succeed;
◆ identifying indicators of success that can be measured in an impact evaluation.

It may also include reviewing existing evaluations or reviews of different approaches with the target group in question. It is used to find out what will be effective in motivating the target audience, and to ensure that the intervention will be accessible, understandable, and sustainable. Formative evaluation is also the means by which to determine the precise details of the intervention, including the marketing mix—all of which should emerge from the assessment of needs. Formative evaluation involves the testing of factors that are likely to be effective for a successful social marketing 'exchange'. It is essential for trying to understand why and how a programme works, and what other contextual factors may affect the programme over the course of its implementation.

Reasons to conduct a formative evaluation

Formative evaluation should be viewed as a valuable investment that improves the likelihood of achieving a successful outcome through better programme design. Without it, you may be embarking on a project that may not meet a real need, or one that may be constrained by external factors that you cannot control.

Formative evaluation is especially important in community engagement and behaviour change projects, as such interventions are often complex and require careful monitoring of processes in order to respond to conflicting priorities and any unexpected outcomes. Neglecting formative evaluation may mean that you are not able to observe and capture feedback that may improve the implementation of a project and therefore its chance of successfully achieving the desired outcomes.

Once designed—or as part of the design process—an intervention should be pre-tested. Formative evaluation is the place to do this. Pre-testing a social marketing intervention is the equivalent of road-testing a new car. It involves the same kind of thought processes. For instance, evaluators should ask some basic questions. How will the target audience find out about the product, through which channels? What will they think and feel about the product? Does it meet their needs? What is good/bad about it? Where are the gaps? Does it work better or worse with some audiences? How can it be improved? How does it compare to the competition?

Process evaluation

A process evaluation is concerned with how the intervention was implemented and functioned. It is a vital element of the programme because without it social marketers could measure outcomes without knowing how and why they were achieved.

Many evaluations do not include an adequate process evaluation, and some do not have one at all, making it very difficult to understand why an intervention has succeeded or failed. Hamilton et al. (1977) in their book *Beyond the numbers game*, make the case for process evaluation: 'It's rather like a critic who reviews a production on the basis of the script and the applause meter readings, having missed the performance.' The key components of a process evaluation are context, reach, and delivery.

Context

An intervention can be affected positively or negatively by the wider social, cultural, political, and economic environment in which it operates. For example, in England the smoking prevalence among all adults is approximately 19%, so the societal norm is non-smoking (Health and Social Care Information Centre, 2015). However, in certain areas of the UK the smoking prevalence is much higher, and in these areas smoking is frequently regarded to be the norm. The effectiveness of a smoking intervention in such communities will clearly be influenced by the social context, and this should be taken into account in the planning of interventions and the interpretation of the evaluation findings.

Reach

Although awareness should not be the primary measure of effectiveness, it is important to measure it. If the target group is not aware of the initiative then there is not much hope of anything else changing.

Dose delivered and dose received

There needs to be some estimate of the amount and intensity of the intervention you expect the target groups to receive. For example, if as part of a campaign you expect to deliver a mass media component, you should have a clear idea of how many times you expect the target group to see or hear your campaign over a specified period of time (known as the 'opportunities to see' figure). This is media space that is paid for, and is an estimate of the dose delivered. The dose received (the number of times the target groups claim they saw your campaigns) should tally approximately with the dose delivered. If they are very different, this indicates that there are problems with the delivery of the campaign. This could be due to an inappropriate mix of marketing channels—e.g. using press advertisements when radio would be more appropriate, or using radio but placing the ads in the wrong radio programmes, with poor listening figures for your target audience. Learning from marketing mix errors can help get it right next time. Another reason for a low dose response could be that the audience is not responding to a poorly constructed message—one that has no resonance with them and is easily forgotten.

Was the intervention delivered as planned?

Social marketing interventions are built on the work of a wide range of professional stake-holders: researchers, programme managers, advertising agencies, media and public relations agencies, outreach workers, and other professionals relating to the social objectives of the pro-gramme. These people work to their own professional standards, which means that strong proj-ect management is essential to keep the original objectives on course and to minimize 'project drift'. With complex interventions involving many players, projects will drift from the agreed objectives to some degree. As an evaluator, it is important to assess this. Many good ideas are judged to be ineffective and discarded when in effect the evaluation has assessed something which drifted considerably from the original good idea.

For example, an intervention may aim to provide a customer-friendly and accessible advice service to teenagers looking for advice on matters such as sexual health or drugs. The service should open at appropriate times and provide a safe, enjoyable space to which teenagers feel they can return if they need to. In this typical example, numerous agencies become involved and tinker with the original idea until the project drifts off course. The resulting service will not resemble the original vision and will, unsurprisingly, evaluate poorly. If the process evaluation makes the distinction between the planned and actual intervention, it will ensure that the ambi-tions of the original idea are not discarded nor deemed a failure.

Even when projects remain on course it is important to assess which elements have worked well and explain which have not worked so well. Some of the areas for investigation include:

◆ failure to take account of the context within which the intervention operates;
◆ an inability to fulfil the implementation objectives and deliver the correct mix of approaches;
◆ management and leadership problems;
◆ an inability to achieve enough stakeholder buy-in;
◆ poor translation into practice of the theories underpinning the intervention;
◆ poor use of the scoping research, resulting in poor project design and prioritization of target groups;
◆ unforeseen positive and negative consequences of the intervention.

As discussed earlier in this chapter, there are many research methods which can be employed to build a good process evaluation and a rich description of what has occurred (Box 4.2).

Summative evaluation

Summative evaluation looks at the impact of an intervention on the target group—and on oth-ers who are not intended as the target group. This type of evaluation is arguably what is most often considered to be 'evaluation' by project staff and funding bodies: that is, finding out what the project achieved.

Summative evaluation is often associated with more objective, quantitative methods of data collection. It is linked to the evaluation drivers of accountability. Using a balance of both quan-titative and qualitative methods is recommended in order to get a better understanding of

Box 4.2 Example: process evaluation of World AIDS Day campaign

Campaign goals: to raise awareness of HIV prevention and to promote positive social attitudes to those affected by HIV, including tackling of stigma.

Marketing mix: national, regional, and local promotion via traditional media (print and broadcast) and social media, involving the use of health experts and people living with HIV. Channels to include specialist media serving key identified groups (e.g. minority ethnic groups, gay men).

Evaluation methods

1. Traditional media (print and broadcast) analysis

Survey research should be conducted among identified audiences (e.g. general public, key subgroups) to track indicators of knowledge and attitudes towards HIV, including stigma.

Media analysis: this involves collation and review of coverage of HIV-related issues before and after World AIDS Day in a range of media. Indicators should include quantity, impact (position in newspaper/ website/broadcast), and tone and nature of coverage (e.g. whether the content is positive, negative, or neutral towards the campaign objective).

Key influencers analysis: journalists and commentators who have most impact (positive and negative) should be identified and qualitative research conducted to explore their views about campaign goals and what can be done to win over/increase their support in future.

2. Social media analysis

This should measure:

♦ awareness, metrics that explore volume, reach, exposure, and amplification to establish how far the message is spreading;

♦ engagement, metrics around retweets and reposts, comments, replies, and participants to establish how many people are participating, how often, and in what forms;

♦ the share of voice, metrics that can be used to track volume relative to the closest competitors.

Source: data from Health Education Authority (1999) *World Aids Day campaign evaluation*. London: Health Education Authority. Unpublished.

what the project has achieved, and how or why this has occurred. Using qualitative methods of data collection can also provide good insight into unintended consequences and lessons for improvement.

It is important to distinguish outcome from output. Summative evaluation is not concerned with demonstrating the number of people reached by an intervention or the number of events held to publicize a given issue: these would be classified as outputs or process measures. Rather, summative evaluation is concerned with changes that result from the intervention, such as increased knowledge or increased uptake of a service: these are the outcomes.

Why undertake a summative evaluation?

Key reasons you should undertake a summative evaluation include the following.

◆ Summative evaluation provides a means to find out whether your project has achieved its goals and outcomes.
◆ It allows you to quantify the changes in resource use attributable to your project so that you can track its impact.
◆ It allows you to compare the impact of different projects and make results-based decisions on future spending allocations (taking into account unintended consequences).
◆ It allows you to develop a better understanding of the process of change, finding out what works, what does not, and why. This allows you to gather the knowledge to learn and improve future project designs and implementation.

Summative evaluation research designs

There are a range of evaluation methodologies and research designs that can be used to determine whether an intervention is effective. Researchers have devised a hierarchy of evidence to help address the question of how to rank the quality of evidence produced by different types of studies (see Table 4.1).

Hierarchies of evidence

The hierarchy indicates the relative weight that can be attributed to a particular study design. Generally, the higher up a methodology is ranked, the more robust it is assumed to be. The top ranked *meta-analysis*, for example, involves the synthesizing of results from a number of similar

Table 4.1 Rank and definition of evidence type

Rank	Methodology	Description
1	Systematic reviews and meta-analyses	A systematic review is a review of a body of data that uses explicit methods to locate primary studies and criteria to assess their quality. Meta-analysis is a statistical analysis that combines or integrates the results of several independent trials. The appeal of meta-analysis is that it, in effect, combines all the research on one topic into one large study with many participants.
2	Randomized controlled trials	Individuals are randomly allocated either to a 'test' group that receives a specific intervention or to a 'control' group that receives no intervention. Both groups are interviewed (assessed) before and after the test intervention.
3	Cohort studies	Groups of people are selected on the basis of their exposure to a particular agent and followed up for specific outcomes.
4	Case-control studies	'Cases' with the condition are matched with 'controls' without, and a retrospective analysis is used to look for differences between the two groups.
5	Cross-sectional surveys	Quantitative surveys of a sample of the population of interest are conducted before an intervention and a similar sample is interviewed after the intervention.
6	Case reports	A report is based on a few patients or subjects; sometimes several reports are collected together into a short series.
7	Expert opinion	These include opinions from respected authorities and experts, based on clinical evidence, descriptive studies, or reports from committees.

trials to produce a result of higher statistical power. Meanwhile, *case reports* are considered to offer a much weaker level of evidence.

Randomized controlled trials

Experimental research is widely considered to be the best means of determining whether a given intervention works. Among the various types of experimental research design, the randomized controlled trial (RCT) is the gold standard (see example in Box 4.3).

An RCT is a study that involves a similar number of people or groups (schools or communities) randomly assigned to two (or more) groups to test a specific intervention. One group (the experimental group) receives the intervention being tested; the other (the comparison or control group) receives an alternative, a dummy (placebo), or no intervention at all. The groups are followed up to see how effective the experimental intervention was. Outcomes are measured at specific times and any difference in response between the groups is assessed statistically. This method is also used to reduce bias.

RCTs were developed as a means of comparing the effectiveness of different medicines in the late 1940s, and for much of the time since then they have been regarded as very much a clinical form of evaluation. As a research method the RCT offers several distinct advantages. Each unit (person) has an equal chance of being or not being in the experimental group. Assignment to the experiment or control group on the basis of randomization eliminates any potential bias. Over the past couple of decades there has been a call to make more use of RCTs to assess social—as opposed to clinical—interventions. Table 4.2 describes some of the challenges in applying a RCT design to a social marketing intervention aimed at large populations outside a clinical setting.

Box 4.3 Summative evaluation example: smoking prevention in schools

There is only a single example of a successfully completed controlled trial of a school-based smoking prevention intervention in the UK. This is the ASSIST trial (A Stop Smoking in Schools Trial) (Campbell et al., 2008), conducted between 2001 and 2005. It was an RCT of the effectiveness of a school-based, peer-led smoking intervention.

This large-scale effectiveness trial was funded by a grant of £1.5m from the Medical Research Council. The project aimed to test the effectiveness of the intervention using a cluster randomized trial design. The trial involved 10,730 students aged 12–13 years in 59 schools in south-east Wales and the west of England. Half were randomly allocated either to continue with their normal smoking education programme, or to do so with the additional peer supporter programme.

Students were followed up for two years to assess whether smoking prevalence in the intervention schools was lower than that in the schools which did not receive the programme. In addition, the study involved a substantial component of process evaluation and an economic evaluation to assess the gains of the intervention against the costs of achieving them.

The ASSIST trial is important in demonstrating that it is possible to conduct RCTs of complex interventions in real-world settings. However, it is also significant that it is the only published study of an RCT in this area of public health, despite the fact that other approaches to smoking prevention that have been developed since the ASSIST trial may be more effective.

Table 4.2 Differences between clinical trials and social marketing interventions

Clinical trials	Social marketing/health promotion interventions
Participants are usually seeking a cure.	Participants are currently well and may not perceive themselves as needing help. Interventions are likely to be preventive, not curing.
Clinical trials often have a simpler biological basis (e.g. drugs, surgery) and are easier to control.	Social marketing interventions are generally multifaceted and diffuse into the population to achieve behavioural change at the individual or societal level. There is a lot of extraneous 'noise' to control.
The unit of randomization is usually individuals or clusters.	The unit of randomization may be individuals, schools, workplaces, communities, or regions.
Internal validity (a measure of the extent to which the findings are real and not the result of bias) is not a problem with RCTs, as this can be achieved using control groups who receive a placebo. 'Double blind' (when neither the individuals nor the researchers know who belongs to the control group and the experimental group) and 'triple blind' (when multiple investigators are all blinded to the protocol) are also possible.	It is often very difficult to devise a placebo for a community development intervention and to 'blind' people to the fact that they have received the intervention.
Exposure of the control group to the intervention is more easily controlled.	There is a high risk that the control group (e.g. a neighbouring community) may be exposed to the intervention.

Quasi-experimental research designs

For many situations, while it may be desirable, it may be impossible to conduct a RCT in a non-clinical setting. In such circumstances, there are a range of research designs—grouped under the heading of 'quasi-experimental research designs'—that retain the critical aspect of the experiment (i.e. an intervention and a control group with a before and after measure) but do not employ more difficult-to-implement aspects such as random allocation of subjects to each group.

Matching the groups on the basis of key features may be a pragmatic means of retaining the experimental nature of the trial, without the cost and difficulty of having to randomize allocation (Box 4.4).

Value for money and economic evaluation in social marketing

> *Economics is a science which studies human behaviour as a relationship between ends and scarce means which have alternative uses.*
> (Lionel Robbins, *An Essay on the Nature and Science of Economics*, 1932)

In financially straitened times, stakeholders are increasingly concerned with evidence of both effectiveness (did the intervention work?) and value (how much did it cost to achieve the identified outcomes?). An important issue for any evaluation of a social marketing intervention,

Box 4.4 Case study: testing the impact of music—CD with Hepatitis C prevention messages for young offenders in custody

Aim

As part of the prison health service's programme to prevent the transmission of bloodborne diseases in prisons, a quasi-experimental study was undertaken. This assessed the impact on young offenders (aged 15–19) in custody, of prevention messages provided on a freely distributed music CD (including music and interviews with rap and hip hop artists), on which Hepatitis C was discussed and prevention information provided (McVey et al., 2006).

Method

Eight prisons in England were selected—four intervention and four controls. The prisons were selected on the basis of key known characteristics, including region, age, and sex of inmates, and category of institution. A random sample of inmates were selected for interview in each setting.

In the intervention sites, music CDs were provided to all young offenders. In the control settings, normal practice was maintained. Pre- and post-intervention interviews were undertaken with inmates and staff in all eight prisons. Interviews included questions about knowledge, attitudes, and risk behaviours (including sexual, drug-taking, and tattooing behaviours).

Challenges

There were practical difficulties in conducting the quantitative parts of the evaluation owing to the high rate of turnover of young offenders in institutions and the problem of gaining access to inmates. The scale of the task (400 interviews before and 200 interviews after the intervention) proved wildly optimistic.

In several establishments there were an insufficient number of suitable respondents. Only people with at least three months to serve at the time of the first interview were eligible, as they would need to be re-interviewed after exposure to the CD. However, sentence length for detainees varied between institutions and young offenders moved prisons during the course of their sentence.

There were other problems. Inmates had to be escorted to and from interviews, and this change in prison routine relied on the goodwill of prison staff. Sometimes disturbances and miscounted roll calls meant that prisoners were prevented from moving around the prison. All this had an inevitable impact on the numbers of interviews that could be conducted. In the end, the study fell short of the intended number of interviews, achieving 250 interviews before and 150 interviews after the intervention.

Findings

The study was difficult to implement because of the nature of the penal setting. However, with perseverance, it was possible to conduct the study and there were statistically significant increases on all relevant indicators in the intervention group. Although sample sizes were smaller than had been expected, the evaluation was able to give an indication of what the intervention had achieved: it showed that project managers had underestimated the change in relevant indicators that could be achieved with this approach and provided valuable information for further developing the intervention.

Reference

McVey, D., Crosier, A., Wellings, K. *An evaluation of Music4Messages: Hepatitis C prevention project. Report to Department of Health.* London: London School of Hygiene and Tropical Medicine.

therefore, is to demonstrate not simply that the intervention can produce the desired outcome(s) but also that the cost of achieving the outcomes is lower through the proposed intervention than through some alternative approach. This is where economic evaluation is relevant.

The application of economic evaluation techniques to social marketing interventions is complex, and the process of identifying models and methods to provide useful insights is still in its infancy. Most of the knowledge in this area is drawn from health economics, where models have been developed based on clinical interventions and—in many cases—categorical health outcomes (for example, life or death). Even within clinical health, determining value is more art than science. Health economists have sought to identify simple methods to calculate the value of medicines and clinical procedures. The QALY (quality-adjusted life-year) is an example of this. The premise of the QALY is that health is a function of length of life and quality of life. It assumes that a year of life lived in perfect health is worth 1 QALY (1 year of life × 1 utility value = 1 QALY) and that a year of life lived in a state of less than this perfect health is worth less than 1. By giving a value to different aspects of a person's quality of life—for example loss of a limb, loss of a sense, being bed-ridden—a 'utility value' is calculated; in turn, it is then possible to calculate the cost of an intervention in terms of the cost (in monetary terms) per QALY. While this method works reasonably well for definitive outcomes (loss of a limb, life/death, etc.) it is not so useful for more subjective outcomes, including pain, or for chronic conditions, where experience is less uniform. While the QALY remains the indicator of choice, it is even more problematic for public health and social care interventions, the benefits of which may not arise uniformly and may not become apparent for many years.

A vital and basic requirement, which is often overlooked by evaluators of social marketing interventions in the planning phase, is to consider the costs of the intervention and the costs and savings it may produce. It is important that the true costs of an intervention are calculated so that its true impact can be measured. Producing data relating to the cost-effectiveness of interventions and providing some estimate of the return on investment can make a compelling case for continued funding.

Conclusion

Determining the effectiveness of a social marketing intervention is always a challenge for evaluators. Attributing effects to complex multifaceted interventions requires the use of a range of qualitative and quantitative techniques which, where possible, should be triangulated with existing data sources.

Using the model of behavioural change adopted by the intervention can help construct the logic model and focus the evaluation effort on the key indicators of effectiveness. However, as well as measuring the hard quantitative outcomes, it is essential to conduct a process evaluation to build up a rich description of what has occurred during the intervention—scanning the environment for unforeseen negative and positive events and looking to see what the competition is doing. Using some of the emerging insights from the process evaluation can keep the key stakeholders and user groups involved and stimulated by the research, and ensure the findings are used to fine-tune the intervention. Stakeholders' involvement should, however, be balanced by having in place adequate research governance to ensure that the evaluators maintain a degree of independence and objectivity in the design, collection, and reporting of the findings.

Policy-makers and programme-planners learn from successful and unsuccessful interventions. Good-quality data on the effectiveness of an intervention should be shared, regardless of the outcome. It is therefore important to share findings in the public domain of evaluations that indicate successful and unsuccessful outcomes, in order to help build an evidence base that others may learn from.

Self-review questions

1. List the six main steps in developing a sound evaluation plan.
2. What are the three main forms of evaluation and what is the role of each?
3. Discuss some of the key tasks and decisions that need to be made when developing a health-focused social marketing evaluation.

References

Bandura, A. (1963). *Social learning and personality development.* New York: Holt, Rinehart, and Winston.

BIT (2015). *Behavioural insights team: update report 2013–2015.* London: Behavioural Insights Team.

Campbell, R., Starkey F., Holliday, J., Audrey, S., Bloor, M., Parry-Langdon, N. et al. (2008). An informal school-based peer-led intervention for smoking prevention in adolescence (ASSIST): a cluster randomised controlled trial. *The Lancet* **371**(9624):1595–1602 http://www.thelancet.com/journals/lancet/article/PIIS0140673608606923/abstract

Funnell, S., Rogers, P. (2011). *Purposeful program theory: effective use of theories of change and logic models.* San Francisco, CA: John Wiley & Sons.

Goodrich, J., Wellings, K., McVey, D. (1998). Using condom data to assess the impact of HIV/AIDS preventive interventions. *Health Education Research* **13**(2):267–274.

Hamilton, D., Jenkins, D., King, C., MacDonald, B., Parlett, M. (eds) (1977). *Beyond the numbers game: a reader in educational evaluation.* Basingstoke: Macmillan.

Health and Social Care Information Centre (2015). Statistics on smoking. Leeds: Health and Social Care Information Centre http://www.hscic.gov.uk/catalogue/PUB17526/stat-smok-eng-2015-rep.pdf

House of Lords Science and Technology Select Committee (2011). *Behaviour change.* London: The Stationery Office http://www.publications.parliament.uk/pa/ld201012/ldselect/ldsctech/179/179.pdf

Michie, S., Atkins, L., West, R. (2014). *The behaviour change wheel.* London: Silverback Publishing.

NICE (2015). Glossary [website]. London: National Institute for Health and Care Excellence https://www.nice.org.uk/Glossary?letter=E

Pawson, R., Tilley, N. (1997). *Realistic evaluation.* London: Sage.

Rutter, J. (2012). *Evidence and evaluation in policy making.* London: Institute for Government.

Sunstein, C., Thaler, R. (2009). *Nudge: improving decisions about health, wealth and happiness.* London: Penguin Books.

Chapter 5

Social marketing and public health strategy

Jeff French

The essence of strategy is that you must set limits on what you're trying to accomplish.

Porter, M. (1998) On Competition, Boston:
Harvard Business School, 1998.

Learning points

This chapter:

- develops understanding of the differences between operational and strategic applications of social marketing and how these can help public health programme development and implementation;

- helps readers appreciate how social marketing can be used to inform the strategic development of public health interventions that aim to influence attitudes and behaviours;

- builds understanding of how social marketing can add value to public health strategy development.

Introduction to social marketing and public health strategy

As reviewed in chapter six, over recent years there has been significant growth in knowledge about what works and what does not in the field of health behaviour change and how to plan, deliver, and evaluate public health interventions (French and Apfel, 2014; CDC, 2016). However, this knowledge is not always used to shape public health interventions. Worse still is the practice followed by some governments and public health organizations of running social advertising and social media dominated programmes that they know will have little impact other than to create a sense that something is being done. In this situation, governments and their public health officials and agencies seem to be trapped in a situation in which they all know that what is being delivered has little chance of success, but they still invest time, money, and effort in it. This is often the case in times when pandemic events occur. In such situations a great deal of political and media pressure to 'be seen to be acting' is rapidly exerted on public health officials and politicians. This often means that broadcast information-dominated media promotions are seen as a quick way of demonstrating that action is being taken. This situation has been described as a 'conspiracy of passive failure' (French, 2011a): it is not driven by a wish for programmes to fail or as a way to fool the public but more often by rather more positive and understandable motivators, such as a desire to do something and do it quickly, or a genuine belief that people need encouragement and information.

Clearly, media promotions, social advertising, and social media can be essential parts of an effective mix of interventions (Lannon, 2008; Hornik, 2002). The point, however, is that such interventions should be used as part of a planned and coordinated marketing strategy based on thorough strategic analysis and target audience research, rather than as an immediate default reaction. This is why strategic social marketing planning and analysis are required in the development, implementation, and evaluation of public health programmes aimed at influencing behaviour. However, before the full potential of social marketing can be realized in the development and implementation of public health programmes and other forms of social policy, it needs to be acknowledged that there is still a major under-utilization and misinterpretation of marketing and social marketing by many governments and public health institutions. Social marketing is often viewed as a second-order task in many public sector policy and strategy development circles (ECOM, 2016). So before social marketing can bring value to the public health policy and strategy table it is necessary to consider how it can best be embedded into the policy-making and strategy development process.

The nature of strategic social marketing

The real added value of applying social marketing in a strategic as well as operational way to the selection of public health programmes flows from the application of marketing principles to inform the development of an organization's overall mission and goals, reviewing its operating core and operating environment, and subsequently selecting the right mix of interventions to bring about positive health improvement. The application of what French and Gordon (2015) have called 'strategic social marketing' is the citizen-focused and whole-system analysis of health challenges and how they can be influenced. Conceived in this way, strategic social marketing can be defined as 'the systemic, critical and reflexive application of social marketing principles to enhance social policy selection, objective setting, planning and operational delivery' (French and Gordon, 2015). As can be inferred from this definition, strategic social marketing is concerned with informing policy selection, development, and strategic goal setting; selecting effective interventions; assisting with the process of determining how success will be measured; and ensuring that the mix of interventions selected are managed and coordinated.

Social marketing also has a critical role to play in ensuring that understanding and insights about the beliefs, values, and needs of target groups for any social intervention—such as citizens, community leaders, politicians, and professionals—are captured, analysed, and fed into the policy selection and development process. The added value of applying a social market to public health policy selection and strategy development is directly related to its:

1. strategic and operational focus on creating social value for communities and individuals, based on respect and a willingness to engage in the co-creation and delivery of solutions;
2. focus on mutuality, exchange, and reciprocity as positive social goods in their own right and as key enablers of social development and more effective and efficient social programme delivery;
3. reflexive learning orientation that encompasses both logical positivism and social reflexivity and takes account of social, economic, cultural, and environmental influences on the human condition and behaviour.

It is helpful to think about social marketing influencing policy, strategy, tactics, and operational delivery levels of social programmes, as depicted in Figure 5.1.

Figure 5.1 Added value of social marketing at the four levels of public health programme selection, development, management, and delivery.

Strategic policy selection

Adding value at this policy level relates to informing decisions about what specific attitudes and behaviours should be influenced, what needs to be achieved, and how success in terms of influencing behaviour and shifting attitudes will be defined and measured.

Environmental diagnosis and strategy selection

The second level is focused on analysing internal capability and external factors, alongside evidence, data, and trends related to the selected health challenge. The outcome of this strategic level analysis is the development and selection of the optimum mix of interventions that together form a credible array capable of having measurable impact on the health challenge selected.

Strategic coordination and management

At this third level the key tasks are to ensure that all those responsible for delivering and evaluating the selected mix of interventions are clear about their responsibilities and contribution, and that they have the capability and capacity—including all necessary resources—to deliver their part of the strategy. Attention is also focused on ensuring that robust managerial and reporting mechanisms are in place.

Operational and tactical delivery and evaluation

The focus at this level is on the effective implementation, risk management, coordination, and tracking of the impact of the selected interventions in support of the overall mission, aims, and goals of a programme.

How social marketing can add value to public health policy selection and implementation

One of the key weaknesses of many public health policies is the lack of clear insights about what the citizens who are the intended target of a programme know, feel, and believe. This is combined with a lack of understanding about what factors influence behaviour, which often results in a lack of clear measurable objectives and congruent evaluation targets. Social marketing can assist with the collection and analysis of citizen understanding, views, needs, and behaviour, and through this process with the development of achievable behavioural objectives using behavioural modelling and completion analysis based on theory, insight data, situational analysis, evidence, and assessments of existing practice. Social marketing can also help policy-makers with the development of targeted and segmented intervention strategies consisting of the optimum mix of interventions. It does this though a process of testing potential intervention strategies against intended target audience preferences, knowledge, and values. Social marketing also has a role to play in assisting with ongoing policy and strategy development through impact evaluation and return on social investment analysis.

Any social policy seeking to influence citizen behaviours that does not have the broad support of the public and does not meet the needs of the target audiences is unlikely to be successful. There is a need, then, if successful public health programmes are to be developed, to engender a sense of ownership among intended recipients in the solutions that are developed and implemented. Delivering any social policy also needs the involvement of the widest possible coalition of interests if a sense of ownership is to be created and if all available expertise and resources are to be used to inform the development and delivery of the policy (see chapter ten for a more detailed examination of how to build and sustained delivery coalitions).

Social marketing can also help politicians and public officials to test potential policies and refine them through a process of target audience engagement and consultation, as well as through a process of market research. The use of focus groups, surveys, interviews, observational studies, and other forms of gathering citizens' views can be powerful tools for ensuring that a policy or strategy is developed in such a way that it will be supported and taken up by those whom it is designed to help. However, such policy/strategy/intervention testing is still comparatively rare in many countries, despite the obvious advantages to policy-makers of testing and refining potential interventions using marketing research and principles to engage and gather citizens' views. The application of this kind of citizen-focused approach to the development and testing of policy and strategy will need to be use more often by governments and political parties to help them develop manifestos and social programmes that carry popular support and are feasible (Box 5.1).

Box 5.1 Case study: a business model to achieve financial sustainability through cross-subsidization: experience from the Social Marketing Company (SMC) in Bangladesh

Ashfaq Rahman and Manuela Tolmino

Aims

SMC started as a family planning (FP) project in 1974 under an agreement between Population Services International, the Government of Bangladesh, and USAID. Its strategic mission was to address rapid population growth in Bangladesh by social marketing oral contraceptives (OCs), and condoms. Over the past 30 years, SMC activities have expanded into other areas, such as reproductive and child health, hygiene, and nutrition.

Since becoming a 'company' in 1990, SMC has deployed a cross-subsidization strategy to make its operations financially sustainable and decrease reliance on donor funds. In cross-subsidization, losses incurred by subsidized products are fully or partially recovered by higher-priced profitable products. Cross-subsidization helps ensure that low-income populations have access to affordable health products, but that other wealthier segments pay more for theirs.

Behavioural objectives and target group

SMC addresses unmet FP need by improving access to quality and affordable products and services through private sector channels. By using a 'multitiered' pricing strategy, SMC targets women of reproductive age (WRA) and eligible couples. This strategy aims to make the private sector responsive to the different population segments' needs and shift subsidies where they are most needed.

Customer orientation

SMC addresses common barriers to modern contraceptive use, like lack of access to products and correct information. Just over half of WRA (52%) use modern contraception, with the majority (92%) using short-term methods, like OCs and injectables (NIPORT et al., 2011). Such an over-reliance on short-term methods cannot support a sustained fertility decline in Bangladesh (Streatfield and Kamal, 2013). As a result, SMC also aims to shift WRA from short-term methods to long-acting reversible contraception, which is a priority of the Government of Bangladesh.

Social offering

SMC markets a full range of contraceptives that includes three brands of combined OCs, a progestogen-only pill, an emergency contraceptive pill, six condom brands, a three-month injectable, an intrauterine device, and a two-rod implant (Figure 5.2). The price range of the products (in Bangladeshi taka) is:

- OCs: 18–40 Tk per cycle;
- condoms: from 1.50 Tk per piece to 70 Tk for a pack of three pieces;
- injectable: 35 Tk;
- intrauterine device: 30 Tk;
- implant: 200 Tk.

Target audience engagement and exchange

SMC conducts market research to gain consumer insight on behaviours and factors associated with contraceptive use. Results are used to position FP brands in the market and to design promotional campaigns.

Competition analysis

Bangladesh's contraceptive prevalence rate increased from 39.9% to 61.2% over the course of the last 20 years, and the total fertility rate declined to 2.3 births per woman (NIPORT et al., 2011).

In 2011, 48% of all modern contraception users obtained their methods from the private sector. SMC is the most dominant private sector player with 60% of national market share for condoms, 38% for OCs, and 20% for injectables. SMC contributes to just over 30% of the national contraceptive prevalence rate for modern methods (NIPORT et al., 2011). SMC's product distribution network reaches more than 100,000 pharmacies, 130,000 non-pharmacies, and 50 institutions and non-governmental organizations annually.

Figure 5.2 Examples of condom brands used by SMC.
Reproduced by kind permission of The Social Marketing Company, Bangladesh. Copyright © 2016 The Social
Marketing Company.

For service delivery, SMC supports a network of 6,000 non-formal health providers who
provide injectables, and more than 550 private sector doctors specially trained in intrauterine devices and implants.

Audience insight and segmentation

The product pricing categories include:

1. for-profit products, which are self-financed and net a positive margin after recovering all
   direct costs, including the product, advertising and promotion, and packaging;
2. breakeven products, which are self-financed but net little to no margin after recovering
   all direct costs;
3. subsidized products, which are donated and sold at highly subsidized prices.

Integrated intervention mix

Using targeted communication, SMC aims to increase awareness and effective use of modern contraception. Through cross-subsidy, revenues from sales of for-profit products help
sustain the market created through sales of subsidized products. As revenues increase from
non-subsidized operations, SMC is able to recover more of the losses from subsidized commodities, and ultimately generate an overall surplus, which is then used to diversify and
expand programme activities.

Co-creation through social markets

SMC is a significant partner of the Government of Bangladesh in the National FP Programme. By marketing affordable, high-quality FP products in the private sector, SMC has created an alternative market for WRA who rely on the public sector and are able to pay for affordable FP products.

Systematic planning

Supported by USAID and with the assistance of key consultants and partners, SMC's subsidization strategy was designed and implemented according to the following principles.

◆ Create brand equity for donated products through over-branding and promotion. Doing so will ensure that products can remain on the market with minimum volume loss even if the donor discontinues supply.

◆ Invest company resources to market for-profit products, even outside of FP. SMC created a branded oral rehydration solution, which generates high revenue and is used to subsidize other products, including FP methods.

◆ Introduce and build a number of health products through independent financing, but use donor funds to temporarily support marketing costs and increase brand volume.

Results and learning

SMC has demonstrated that it is possible to grow and maintain services to low-income clients. SMC is the major source for condoms among users from all the five wealth quintiles and 25% of OC users from the poorest quintile use SMC oral pills (Karim et al., 2007).

In 2014, over 4.3 million couples protected themselves from unplanned pregnancy with SMC-supplied contraceptives, 22% of whom used low-priced subsidized brands. In the same year, SMC recovered 6% surplus over its total cost for self-financed operations (Figure 5.3).

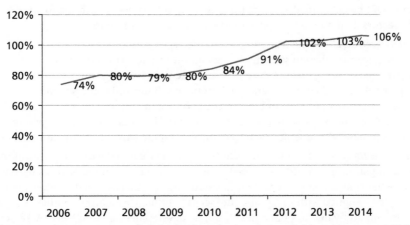

Figure 5.3 SMC's percentage surplus: funds generated over costs achieved between 2006 and 2014.
Reproduced by kind permission of The Social Marketing Company, Bangladesh. Copyright © 2015 The Social Marketing Company.

In 2014, the growth of profitable products led to the formation of a for-profit fully-owned subsidiary company called SMC Enterprise. Profits from SMC Enterprise in the form of dividends are being used by SMC to innovate, grow, and expand its programme portfolio.

For such a cross-subsidization strategy to be successful, several conditions must be met, especially the existence of a robust private sector, donor commitment to sustainability, and flexible government policies that allow pricing and over-branding for donated commodities. It is also essential to take a long-term strategic approach. Programmes must ensure that income and expenditures from self-financed activities are tracked separately from donor-funded programmes to gauge actual progress towards sustainability and multiple revenue streams. In SMC's case, the oral rehydration solution provides 60% of the company's revenue, which permits subsidization across other health products.

References

Karim, A.M., Sarley, D., Hudgins, A.A. (2007). *Bangladesh: family planning market segmentation—update of the 2003 analysis*. Arlington, VA: USAID.

NIPORT, Mitra and Associates, ICF International (2013). *Bangladesh demographic and health survey 2011*. Dhaka and Calverton, MD: National Institute of Population Research and Training, Mitra and Associates, and ICF International.

Streatfield, P., Kamal, N. (2013). Population and family planning in Bangladesh. *Journal of Pakistan Medical Association* 63(4): 73–81.

Adopting a strategic approach to influencing health behaviour

There are many reasons that organizations tend to avoid or at least not fully adopt a strategic approach to defining their priorities, understanding their operating environment, and developing coherent integrated interventions to deliver their identified organizational or social goals. Bowman (1990) has identified seven reasons that organizations in both the for-profit and not-for-profit sectors do not tend to apply strategic thinking and analysis:

1. lack of awareness about the true situation of the organization;
2. senior management deluding themselves about the organization's position;
3. some managers having vested interests in sticking with the status quo;
4. managers getting locked into operational problem solving and management;
5. past success making people blind to current or future threats and opportunities;
6. changing direction being seen as an admission that what was done before was a mistake;
7. lack of awareness within senior management about quite why the organization is successful.

All of these reasons can individually or collectively conspire to reduce strategic thinking, management, and planning. To address these barriers a strategic social marketing approach starts from the belief that a comprehensive understanding of citizens' needs, beliefs, values, and circumstances—aligned with a response that seeks to influence identified audience segments—can inform and add value to public health policy development and delivery. A key challenge for social marketing, then, is to focus on supporting both individuals and communities to adopt health behaviours but also to focus 'upstream' to influence policy and environmental factors that affect people's behaviour, such as fiscal policy, food policy, and transport policy (Gordon, 2013).

Any public health strategy should seek to set out clear objectives, time frames, and the resources that will be applied in the delivery of the strategy. The strategy will be delivered through a series of action and intervention programmes within which there will be specific projects. It is also essential to ensure that this simple set of management processes is well understood if the policy is to have any chance of achieving its aims. As discussed above, there is often a short-term political driver in developing public health policy to jump from policy-making directly into the establishment of pilot projects or even full-scale intervention programmes without having fully developed a long-term strategy that includes an evaluation approach capable of capturing both process and outcome data. The development of effective policy requires that each of these planning stages is addressed systematically.

One of the most famous marketing papers, called 'Marketing myopia', was written by Theodore Levitt in 1960. Levitt argued that marketing strategy is not about starting from an analysis of your products and services and how they can be improved and sold to the public; instead, the key is to focus on understanding what business you are in and what the needs of your customers are. Levitt uses the example of the American railroad operators to illustrate the mistake they made of assuming they were in the railroad business rather than the transportation business.

In public health the myopic mistake is viewing a social marketing strategy as being about fixing an expert-defined health problem rather than providing a solution to people's perceived and actual needs. Public health planners who apply social marketing principles need to keep a clear focus on meeting the needs of citizens rather than on just meeting the policy goals of politicians and public health experts. As shown in Figure 5.4, people's views, beliefs, and needs need to be factored into policy selection, strategy development, and the operational delivery of programmes of action. In free democratic societies, policy goals have usually been informed by a process of dialogue with the electorate. In this situation, the political process is based on the views of citizens; however, it is possible for governments to lose touch with their electorate. Adopting a social marketing approach can help maintain this link between the policy goals and people's preferences and needs, as social marketing involves the continuous collection of research insights about citizens' beliefs, needs, and wants.

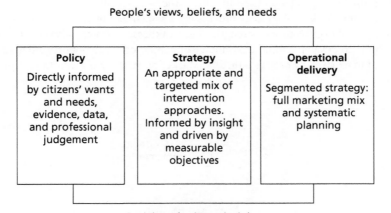

Figure 5.4 Factoring people's views, beliefs, and needs into policy.
Reproduced with permission from French J. Business as unusual. The contribution of social marketing to government policy making and strategy development. In: Hastings G, Angus K, and Bryant C. (Eds.) *The Sage handbook of social marketing*. London: Sage, Copyright © 2011 SAGE Publications.

The components of strategy

There is, unsurprisingly, no one universally accepted definition of marketing strategy. Strategy is a contested concept but it is mainly viewed (Wensley, 2005) as a process focused on agreeing a clear mission and set of objectives for an organization, which is then, via a set of analytical steps, developed into a short-, medium-, and long-term intervention plan informed by evidence and data. Strategy typically consists of three main clusters of actions and decisions, as depicted in Figure 5.5.

First is the process of strategic analysis to understand the operating environment and internal capabilities and goals of the organization. Next comes a set of choice processes to select the most appropriate strategic approach. Finally, strategy implementation involves the development, execution, coordination, and review of the strategy. All three of these tasks are iterative in nature rather than being undertaken in a simple mechanistic linear fashion.

In terms of implementation, strategy can also be seen as the process of developing a detailed plan for achieving the stated goals of the organization. In a public health programme context this might be the eradication of a disease or a prompt to change behaviour. Strategy can also be viewed as a stream of significant decisions taken over time that are focused on the development of a consistent approach to achieving organizational or social objectives.

As Kotler and Armstrong (2008) state, strategic planning sets the stage for the rest of planning:

> We define strategic planning as the process of developing and maintaining a strategic fit between the organisation's goals and capabilities and its changing opportunities. It relies on developing a clear company mission, supporting objectives, a sound business portfolio and coordinated functional strategies.

Marketing strategy starts with articulating the business's and/or in the case of social programmes the social mission and goals that are to be achieved. Critically, this involves decisions about what business to be in or, when focused on social issues, what social issues to focus on.

In the case of a health challenge, strategic choice involves decisions about which aspect of a health problem is capable of being influenced and to what extent effective, sustainable, and affordable interventions exist. The next stage in the strategy process is the generation and selection of the optimal mix of interventions to achieve the overall goal.

A key part of the marketing strategy process is an assessment of external environments and trends, and internal organizational strengths and weaknesses. Strategy also considers an organization's ability to develop and take advantage of market or social opportunities and its ability to respond to existing or probable threats. Marketing strategy is a continuous process, but

Figure 5.5 The three key strategy processes.

Box 5.2 The seven strategic processes

1. Determine the mission, aims, and objectives of the social programme.

2. Analyse the current intervention strategy and assess its strengths and weaknesses.

3. Assess current and future external and internal threats and opportunities.

4. Generate new options; analyse each against conclusions from internal and external analysis and mission goals and objectives.

5. Agree criteria and apply them to the selection of any new strategy.

6. Summarize the results of analysis and conclusions and articulate the new strategy.

7. Plan and deliver the new strategy through selected operational and tactical approaches.

Source: data from Thompson A and Stickland A. *Strategic management: concepts and cases.* Des Moines, IA: Business Publications Inc., Copyright © 1987 Business Publications Inc.

it is also influenced by and influences short- and medium-term planning and delivery cycles. Marketing strategy in the commercial sector is essentially about ensuring continued competitive advantage; in the social and health sector marketing strategy is about ensuring optimal impact and return on investment.

Strategy is the coordinated application of all of an organization's resources to achieve its goals. As discussed above, it is not the same as operational social marketing planning: it involves strategic analysis, strategic choice, and strategic implementation, and these three tasks are iterative in nature. Strategy is focused on both how an organization, service, or department is structured and operates, and how it develops specific plans and applies its resources to achieve specific goals. The development of marketing strategy consists of the seven sets of actions depicted in Box 5.2.

As stated above, strategy is a continuous process rooted in the gathering and feedback of data about the success or failure of the mix of interventions deployed to achieve the goal. The seven sets of actions outlined in Box 5.2 can also be thought of as a cyclical process involving feedback and iterative development.

When analysing each possible component of a strategy, a number of issues need to be considered. These should be used to assess and filter strategic options. It can help to think of two kinds of criteria when assessing strategic options. The first set of criteria can be described as essential or critical criteria. These will always be specific to the issue and context but might include the need for the strategy to be, in the first instance, ethical, non-discriminatory, and deliverable. Strategic options that meet the first set of essential criteria can then be subject to secondary criteria that might include issues such as comparative costs and sustainability. Figure 5.6 sets out the first set of criteria that are often used to assess strategic options.

The need for programmes of action

As discussed throughout this book, many social marketing programmes need to be sustained over time to bring about measurable change. The term 'programme' is significant in that it indicates the need for sustained action over time rather than short-term interventions, projects, or even campaigns. Realistic time frames and sufficient budgets both create the possibility of achieving programme goals and allow for appropriate evaluation to be completed. This in turn facilitates the opportunity to use the learning that flows from the evaluation to develop more

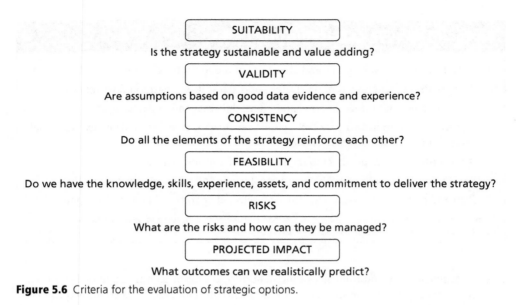

Figure 5.6 Criteria for the evaluation of strategic options.

effective subsequent programmes of action. In addition to long-term programmes of action, we also know that significant investment is often required, not just to sustain a programme over time but also to fund it to a level at which it can have a measurable effect. Many behavioural programmes are ineffective, not because they are poorly researched, designed, or executed but because they are simply not funded to a level that allows them to have an impact. The scale of investment required is dependent on the issue and what other assets can be mobilized to address it. Any examination of commercial sector marketing programmes reveals that they have far greater budgets than most public sector interventions. Yet the commercial sector is often working to achieve small percentage shifts in customer behaviour. In comparison, public sector interventions often have highly ambitious behavioural targets to address issues such as smoking or obesity, with much smaller budgets.

The intervention tool box

As discussed above, applying a social marketing approach means recognizing that in any given situation there are a range of interventional options that could be used to achieve a particular goal with different segments of people. Single interventions are probably going to be less effective than a coordinated multilevel and multicomponent strategy. The challenge is to make transparent and reasoned judgements about the selected mix of interventions. Where this is done at the strategic level, it can be described as the 'strategic intervention mix'. This refers to the mix of five key public sector tools that governments and organizations in all liberal democratic societies can use to deliver a better life experience for citizens (see Figure 5.7). This tool box has been called the 'deCIDES' strategic intervention mix framework (French et al., 2010). Each domain of this model in isolation has the potential to influence behaviour, and each has its associated strengths and weaknesses. However, the evidence is increasingly showing that orchestrating a coordinated response drawing from approaches across all of the five domains has the greatest potential not only to influence behaviour but also, importantly, to help sustain this influence

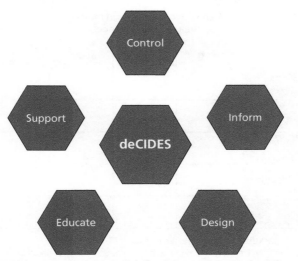

Figure 5.7 The deCIDES intervention mix model: five primary domains for influencing behaviour:
Design: create environments, products, services systems, technologies, and procedures that support individual and community health.
Control: use rules, legislation, monitoring, data, screening, enforcement, incentives, and disincentives to promote health.
Inform: inform, communicate, advise, raise awareness, remind, and encourage with facts, evidence, data, and information.
Educate: engage, empower, foster critical reasoning and health literacy, develop skills, and inspire.
Support: provide supportive products, services, and systems focused on prevention, care, treatment, and cure.

over time. Using isolated approaches can sometimes achieve short-term behavioural change, but the greatest challenges we face require us not simply to focus on changing behaviour but on maintaining and sustaining it.

A good example of such an approach is the national tobacco control campaign in England. 'Go Smokefree' uses a sustained approach and a wide range of interventions to reduce smoking (http://www.gosmokefree.co.uk). These include cessation services run alongside a national ban on smoking in public, combined with educational programmes and tax disincentives on the purchase of tobacco products.

If these five types of intervention are combined with the four forms of intervention—nudge, shove, smack, and hug—outlined in chapter three, a rich mix of potential interventions can be identified (see Figure 5.8). Any combination of these 20 possible ways to influence health behaviour can be tested against the criteria set out in Figure 5.6.

Each of these 20 ways to influence behaviour can also be focused on individual, group, organizational, environmental, and/or policy determinants. This represents a broad potential mix of interventions. One of the key principles to remember is to approach the selection of the interventions mix with an open mind. The situation, the nature of the health threat, the characteristics of the target audience, and the wider social and environmental influences on the problem should be key determining factors for selecting intervention types and forms alongside the selection filters set out in Figure 5.6.

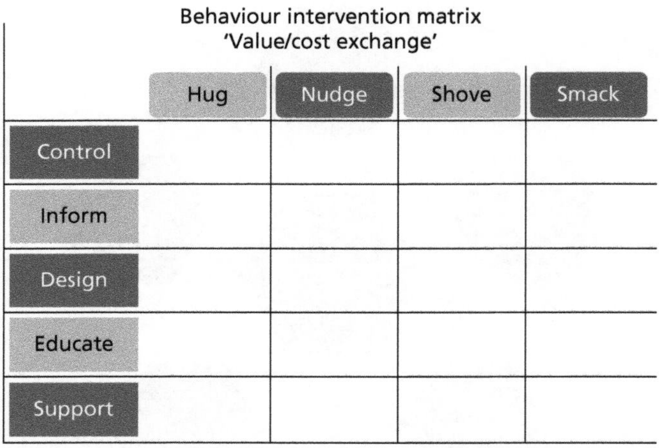

Figure 5.8 The social marketing intervention matrix.
Reproduced with permission from French J. Why nudging is not enough. *Journal of Social Marketing*. Volume 1, Issue 2, pp. 154–162, Copyright © 2011 Emerald Group Publishing Limited.

The need for vertical and horizontal integrated programmes

In addition to sustained social marketing programmes, there is also a need for vertical and horizontal integration of specific interventions. Social marketing programmes, like many other public sector, private sector, and NGO sector interventions, tend to have a bigger impact when national, regional, and local action is coordinated. Coordinated action across different sectors such as government, private, and NGO sectors can also improve the impact. Operational delivery responsibilities undertaken by different sectors or organizations can be clustered and related back to specific strategic areas of action to ensure that a consistent approach is maintained. In order for such a coordinated approach to work, there is always a need to develop clear systems for ensuring that all organizations know their own and the other organizations' responsibilities. Strong internal communication strategies, together with clear performance management and feedback systems, can help to ensure that social marketing strategies are effectively delivered. Chapter ten reviews how effective delivery coalitions can be developed and sustained.

Conclusion

In this chapter we have explored how the social marketing concepts set out in chapters two and three can be used strategically to ensure that understanding about target audience behaviour and preferences directly informs the identification and selection of appropriate health policy, strategy, and operational delivery. It should also be remembered that social marketing principles can be applied to influence the decisions and actions of politicians and service planners as well as citizens. Social marketing has the potential to be a key tool for convincing decision-makers and individuals who are in a position to influence overall health determinants and risk conditions to make significant changes to policy.

Much of the social marketing literature and most examples of practice currently lie in the operational field, where social marketing programmes or campaigns are developed to address specific topic areas and audiences. In contrast, a strategic social marketing approach is increasingly being developed to take a broader viewpoint. Strategic social marketing looks at ways in which a stronger citizen understanding and insight approach, aligned with more strategic audience segmentation work and whole-system planning, can inform policy development and strategic planning. A key challenge for social marketing, then, is to focus upstream—for example, to influence fiscal, food, and transport policy that can in turn have an impact on factors that affect people's health behaviour. A further challenge for social marketers is ensuring that the benefits of adopting a social marketing approach are fully understood. This is not, in many respects, about selling empirical evidence of the effectiveness of social marketing. It is about constructing a narrative that helps policy-makers and planners understand the rationale for social marketing and the value of its application across policy formulation, strategy development, and implementation. The first duty and task for many social marketers is to market social marketing to policy-makers and planners. Examples of how this has been done at a national policy level can be found in Lee and Kotler (2011) and French and Blair-Stevens (2006).

There are a number of tasks that social marketers need to consider when seeking to influence policy-makers and planners. These include asking and answering the following two questions.

- What are the policy-makers' and planners' needs?
- What will convince them that applying a social marketing approach will enhance the impact of their programme?

Having ascertained the answers to these questions, a number of other tactics can help to develop policy support for social marketing and embed it in the policy and planning process, including the following.

- Build a compelling story about the power of social marketing and promote it.
- Build a network of champions and advocates and support them with examples and evidence.
- Provide champions and advocates with opportunities to experience first-hand the power of applying a social marketing approach.
- Be constructively critical of current practice if it can be shown to be ineffective.
- Walk the corridors of power and influence, and take part in face-to-face selling of a strong customer-focused social marketing-informed approach.
- Celebrate and promote success.

There is, in effect, an 'exchange' (see chapter two) for policy-makers when considering the application of a social marketing approach. The costs for policy-makers are focused on the need to invest time in research and gathering users' views. The increased time and cost is a result of developing and synthesizing a more comprehensive array of different forms of evidence and influence on the policy-making process. This can also result in a delay in being able to deliver high-profile visible action, often in the form of a social advertising programme, if it is not supported by the evidence gathered. However, politicians get a more defendable programme of action, based on sound evidence and support from the intended audience. An end programme of action is more likely to be effective thanks to its explicit measurable objectives that can be used to inform the development of future interventions. Finally, politicians and planners get a programme of action that is not only fit for purpose but also one that can be tested for its utility because it has clear aims and objectives, and known input costs and outcome measures.

Self-review questions

1. What is the added value of social marketing to organizational strategy?
2. What are the key components of strategic planning?
3. What are the main differences between operational and strategic social marketing?

References

Bowman, C. (1990). *The essence of strategic management*. London: Prentice Hall.

CDC (2016). The community guide: what works to promote health? [website]. Atlanta, GA: Centers for Disease Control and Prevention http://www.thecommunityguide.org/worksite/supportingmaterials/IES-AHRFAlone.html

ECOM (2016). Effective Communication in Outbreak Management Programme: development of an evidence-based tool for Europe. Research project under the 7th Framework Programme of the EU (FP7-HEALTH-2011) [website]. Rotterdam: Erasmus MC.

French, J. (2011a). Business as unusual: the contribution of social marketing to government policy making and strategy development. In: G. Hastings, K. Angus, C. Bryant (eds). *The Sage handbook of social marketing*. London: Sage.

French, J. (2011b). Why nudging is not enough. *Journal of Social Marketing* 1(2): 154–162.

French, J., Apfel, F. (2014). *Social marketing guide for public health programme managers and practitioners*. Stockholm: European Centre for Disease Prevention and Control http://ecdc.europa.eu/en/publications/Publications/social-marketing-guide-public-health.pdf

French, J., Blair-Stevens, C. (2006). From snake oil salesmen to trusted policy advisors: the development of a strategic approach to the application of social marketing in England. *Social Marketing Quarterly* 12(3): 29–40.

French, J., Blair-Stevens, C., Merritt, R., McVey, D. (eds). (2010). *Social marketing and public health: theory and practice*, 1st edition. Oxford: Oxford University Press.

French, J., Gordon, R. (2015). *Strategic social marketing*. London: Sage.

Gordon, R. (2013). Unlocking the potential of upstream social marketing. *European Journal of Marketing* 47(9): 1525–1547.

Hornik, R. (ed). (2002). *Public health communication: evidence for behaviour change*. Mahwah, NJ: Lawrence Erlbaum Associates.

Kotler, P., Armstrong, G. (2008). *Principles of marketing*, 5th edition. Upper Saddle River, NJ: Prentice Hall International Editions.

Lannon, J. (2008). *How public service advertising works*. London: World Advertising Research Centre.

Lee, N., Kotler, P. (2011). *Social marketing: influencing behaviours for good*. New York: Sage.

Levitt, T. (1960). Marketing myopia. *Harvard Business Review 38* (July–August): 29–47.

Thompson, A., Strickland, A. (1987). *Strategic management: concepts and cases*. Des Moines, IA: Business Publications Inc.

Wensley, R. (2005). The basics of marketing strategy. In: M.J. Baker (ed). *The marketing book*, 5th edition. Oxford: Elsevier.

Chapter 6

Behaviour and how to influence it

Jeff French

Human behaviour is influenced by multiple factors that interact in dynamic ways.

Jeff French

Learning points

This chapter:

- explores why influencing behaviour is now a key facet of many social programmes and how new understanding about is being applied;

- introduces a tool box of potential intervention 'types' and 'forms' to influence behaviour that can be incorporated into a socially informed public health intervention mix;

- introduces readers to frequently quoted theories and models of behavioural influence and their public health operational assumptions and consequences;

- explains how an open analysis approach can help in the selection of appropriate theory and a mix of interventions to influence health behaviour.

Introduction to influencing behaviour

Human behaviour influences and is influenced by many factors, including the environment, individual personality and will power, physiology, genetics, culture, evolution, and technology. Behaviour is also influenced by social norms, upbringing, habits, economics, culture, communities, customs, and religion. Influencing behaviour sits at the heart of most public health programmes, be it influencing individuals to protect themselves and others from disease, influencing professionals to act in specific ways—for example, the take-up of evidence-based guidelines in medicine or nursing—or influencing policy-makers and politicians to adopt public health evidence.

Evidence- and theory-informed interventions aimed at influencing health behaviour are gaining the attention of policy-makers and professionals globally (Darnton, 2008; Jackson, 2005). This interest is supported by the growing body of evidence and accumulating experience in fields as diverse as increasing immunization uptake, malarial prevention, obesity, smoking, unwanted pregnancy, pandemic management, alcohol and drug misuse, breast feeding, and road safety.

One of the big challenges facing those responsible for developing and delivering programmes designed to influence health behaviour is to understand and make a reasoned selection and use of the many theories that have been articulated to inform programme design and delivery. The broad scope of theory and models, which is continuously expanding, can in fact be perceived as a barrier to its use. The literature in the field is 'enormous' (Jackson, 2005) and 'bordering on the unmanageable' (Maio et al., 2007). Time-pressured policy-makers and public health professionals may well be reluctant to engage fully with behavioural analysis and theory, even though they are aware of the insights they can bring (Michie et al., 2011). This reluctance indicates that one of the roles social marketing can play is to assist public health professionals to navigate their way through this seemingly complex field and distil practical insights for the theory of behavioural influence that can be used to select and shape public health interventions (French and Gordon, 2015).

The utility of behavioural theory

Traditionally, many behavioural theories and models have been developed within the discipline of psychology. Many of the models emphasize the importance of social pressures, knowledge, and beliefs in influencing behaviour. These, however, are now frequently criticized for being overly focused on individual rational choice and not taking account of wider economic, social, or environmental issues or non-rational choice, all of which can have a big impact on behaviour (Gordon, 2013). This realization is leading to a situation in which public health practitioners need to be familiar with a range of theory that can help them analyse problems and develop appropriate interventions. It is now the case that rather than using one theory, a combination of theories can be used to help design and deliver interventions (Green and Tones, 2010).

In a recent systematic review to examine the evidence for the effectiveness of interventions that use theories and models of behaviour change in the design and delivery of the prevention and control of communicable disease, commissioned by the European Centre for Disease Prevention and Control (Angus et al., 2013), 61 studies passed the critical screening methodology, 21 of which were designated as being of high quality. Of the high-quality studies, nine were successful in meeting their behavioural targets and six were not. The researchers then looked at the characteristics of the successful and unsuccessful programmes. What emerged was that studies that use theory to inform the design and evaluation of interventions, and that go beyond the use of just individual theories to encapsulate broader interpersonal and community theory, appeared to be more successful.

So while the evidence is not categorical, it is reasonable to conclude that the use of theory in the analysis of behavioural challenges and to inform planning interventions is likely to make a positive contribution to more effective and efficient programme delivery (Roe et al., 1997; Halpern et al., 2003). Using theory can also result in better planning and targeting, and the setting out of more explicit aims and objectives.

Behavioural theory and public health programme development

The focus for many public health programmes has been to seek to change behaviour using external drivers such as information provision, financial incentives and disincentives, and regulation. Such approaches will often be important tools, but the effectiveness of policy interventions is also dependent on understanding and reflecting what is known about the decision-making and what prompts people into action. Many influencing factors lie outside the rational domain, which most often seeks to apply strategies that emphasize awareness-raising and the use of restrictions, penalties, or rewards, all of which require rational considered engagement. However, recent developments in economic and behavioural theory are providing new insights about how many decisions are made in non-rational ways and how this new understanding can be used to build more effective and efficient social programmes. A cross-disciplinary field called 'behavioural economics' has emerged, which accepts that people are sometimes irrational, but believes that this irrationality can be understood and predicted and therefore used in the design of social programmes. Behavioural economics has been defined as 'the combination of psychology and economics that investigates what happens in markets in which some agents display human limitations and complications' (Thaler, 2000).

In 2000, Stanovich and West proposed a description of two distinct systems of cognition that influence decision-making based on emerging experimental studies. 'System 1' is more intuitive, reactive, quick, and holistic. When using system 1 thinking, we rely on a number of heuristics, situational prompts, readily associated ideas, and vivid memories to arrive at fast and confident decisions. System 1 thinking is particularly helpful in routine situations when time is short and immediate action is necessary. However, while system 1 is functioning, another powerful system is also at work, unless people specifically shut it down by, for example, drinking a lot of alcohol. 'System 2' is the more reflective thinking system that people used for making judgements when they find themselves in unfamiliar or complex situations and also have more time to weigh the options, costs, and benefits of a particular choice or course of action. It allows us to process abstract concepts, to deliberate, to plan ahead, to consider options carefully, and to review and revise our work in the light of relevant guidelines, standards, or rules of procedure. For most of the time, according to Stanovich and West (2000), we prefer to operate in system 1 mode.

This model has been expanded by Kahneman (2011) in his popular book *Thinking, fast and slow*, in which he rehearses how these two systems operate, how they influence each other and how they can be influenced. Kahneman gives many examples, backed by research studies that illustrate how factors such as cognitive ease, social norms, anchoring, availability, emotion, the impact of recent events, and framing all impact on decision-making.

A great deal of other work has been undertaken by behavioural psychologists, brain scientists, and biologists in recent years that has expanded our understanding about what influences non-rational or rapid decision-making. Major works in this area are those by Goldstein et al. (2007), Cialdini (2007), Ariely (2009), and Brafman and Brafman (2009). Two useful summary reviews of key strategies and tactics that can be derived from behavioural economic thinking are available from the New Economics Foundation (New Economics Foundation, 2005; Box 6.1) and the UK Government MINDSPACE review (Cabinet Office, 2010; Box 6.2).

The fact that those who are seeking to describe key principles of behavioural economics come up with slightly different sets of key principles illustrates the diverse nature of behavioural economics and its unfolding interpretation.

Nudging

In the 1980s Richard Thaler, an economist, began importing this new thinking into economics. This work was later captured in his popular book with Cass Sunstein, *Nudge* (2008). Nudges are a key mechanism for an approach to social transformation called 'liberal paternalism'. Libertarian paternalism, as advocated by Sunstein and Thaler (2003), seeks a middle ground between a state-dominated coercive paternalistic approach to creating social change and a more liberal approach that emphasizes free choice and the power of the market as the key driver. Thaler and Sunstein argue that nudges are a practice representation of this middle ground. They build

Box 6.1 New Economics Foundation summary of behavioural economics principles

1. Other people's behaviour matters

Behaviour of individuals is strongly influenced by other people's behaviours, from friends and family to community groups and classmates.

2. Habits are important

When we do something out of habit, we don't use much cognitive effort. Behaviour moves from being internally guided through attitudes and intentions to being controlled by environmental cues through habit.

3. People are motivated to 'do the right thing'

Individuals routinely forego narrowly conceived self-interest for the sake of altruistic motives.

4. People's self-expectations influence how they behave

People want their behaviours and attitudes to match. People are motivated to seek consistency between their beliefs, values, and perceptions.

5. People are loss-averse

People will go out of their way to avoid loss but will not go out of their way to gain.

6. People are bad at computation when making decisions

People put undue weight on recent events and too little on far-off ones; they cannot calculate probabilities well and worry too much about unlikely events; and they are strongly influenced by how the problem/information is presented to them.

7. People need to feel involved and effective to make change

If people feel helpless and out of control they are often incapable of doing anything to change their situation. Control of a situation can bring motivation.

Reproduced with permission from New Economics Foundation. *Behavioural economics: seven principles for policy makers*, London: New Economics Foundation, http://www.neweconomics.org/publications/entry/behavioural-economics, accessed 01 April. 2016. Copyright © 2005 NEF.

on Stanovich and West's (2000) work to identify what they call 'mindless choosing', which has a big impact on how decisions are made when we are not applying system 2 thinking—i.e. rational considered thinking. Thaler and Sunstein describe a set of concepts that can help those with the responsibility for developing choice situations to set up choices and prompts to behaviour that use mindless choosing. The hallmark of this kind of 'paternalism' is a focus not on tackling the determinants of social or health problems or on punishing 'bad' behaviour by interventions such as nagging people about what they should do. Rather, the focus is on incentivizing positive

Box 6.2 The nine MINDSPACE influences on behaviour

Messenger: we are heavily influenced by who communicates information.

Incentives: our responses to incentives are shaped by predictable mental shortcuts such as strongly avoiding losses.

Norms: we are strongly influenced by what others do.

Defaults: we go with the flow of pre-set options.

Salience: our attention is drawn to what is novel and seems relevant to us.

Priming: our acts are often influenced by subconscious cues.

Affect: our emotional associations can powerfully shape our actions.

Commitments: we seek to be consistent with our public promises, and reciprocate acts.

Ego: we act in ways that make us feel better about ourselves.

Adapted from Dolan P, Hallsworth M, Halpern D, Kind D, and Vlaev I. *MINDSPACE: Influencing behaviour through public policy—full report*. London: Cabinet Office and Institute for Government, Copyright © 2010 Crown Copyright.

choices by constructing choices that require little or no effort to result in a positive personal and social benefit. Thaler and Sunstein describe 'choice architecture' as the process of designing such systems and services. Choice architecture results in good social and personal choices. A classic example is that of establishing an organ donor scheme that automatically enrols every citizen unless they take action to opt out. In such schemes, typically over 95% of citizens remain in the scheme. In opt-in schemes that require action on the part of citizens to seek out and apply to be part of them, typically less than 30% of citizens sign up (Welsh Government, 2008).

Nudges can be characterized as:

- positive—i.e. they give positive rewards or only minor penalties;
- voluntary;
- avoidable;
- passive/easy—i.e. they require little effort and work on mindless choosing;
- low cost, to both the person targeted and to the government or organization utilizing them (and consequently they are highly cost-effective).

Weaknesses of a nudging-dominated approach to influencing health behaviour

From an ideological perspective nudging can also be criticized for adopting a neo-liberal, paternalistic approach rather than an approach that seeks to maximize personal decision-making and community empowerment (French, 2011). This kind of nudge paternalism is top down. Nudges are designed by 'choice architects' not by the people themselves; they are directive and they are controlling. In this sense, the application of a nudge-based approach to public health policy runs counter to a more citizen-focused public health response to issues such as pandemic events, smoking, etc.

A further problem is that liberal paternalism is not focused on tackling the determinants of issues such as obesity or drug misuse. It is clear that nudging people will seldom be enough to result in population-level improvements because in many situations evidence and experience make it clear that there is a need for other forms of intervention that address the economic, environmental, and social causes of disease. This conclusion was reached by the House of Lords review into behaviour change in public policy, which reported in 2011. The report, which reviewed how concepts such as behavioural economics were being used in government and the evidence for their effectiveness, came to the conclusion that it is important to consider the whole range of possible interventions when policy interventions are designed. The report stated:

> We place particular emphasis on this conclusion because the evidence we received indicated that the Government's preference for non-regulatory interventions has encouraged officials to exclude consideration of regulatory measures when thinking about behaviour change. Though there is a lack of applied research on changing behaviour at a population level, there is other available evidence that the Government need to use to better effect.
>
> (House of Lords Science and Technology Select Committee, 2011)

In general, the report found that to date there were few strong examples where behavioural economics had delivered substantial measurable improvements in interventions, and that more effort should be put into gathering such evidence.

The need to develop and apply comprehensive behavioural strategies

Positive rewards and mindless choosing will not work in all situations: critical reflection and judgement are also often needed when making many complex decisions to change (Grist, 2010). The crux of the matter is how to discern—based on theory, citizen insight, and evidence—what forms of social programme interventions will work in which situation, with specific target audiences. This is the essence of the social marketing process's contribution to public health planning and delivery. In some cases we may need to critically engage people in understanding a problem and helping to solve it. In some circumstances we may need to apply disincentives to dissuade bad behaviour such as smoking in the workplace. There are then a number of different 'forms' of intervention that can be used to influence health behaviour. The value/cost exchange matrix (French, 2011) set out in Figure 6.1 is a way to represent four common forms of

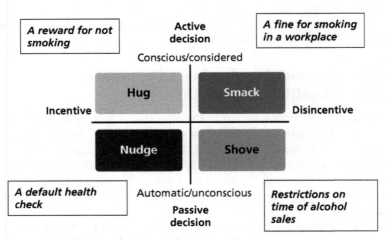

Figure 6.1 The social marketing value/cost exchange matrix.
Reproduced with permission from French J. Why nudging is not enough. Journal of Social Marketing, Volume 1, Issue 2, pp. 154– 162. Copyright © 2011 © Emerald Group Publishing Limited.

intervention that cover both active and passive decision-making and both positive and negative incentives and penalties that can be used in public health programmes. The matrix can be used as a conceptual tool for analysing what forms of intervention have, are, or could be used across a programme designed to influence behaviour.

Individual-level behavioural theories

The majority of models and theories of what influences behaviour and how it can be influenced are focused on individual decision-making and behavioural responses. The following brief selection of models cites some of the most commonly used and quoted models and theories used in public health practice.

Classical conditioning

This model (Pavlov, 1927; Skinner, 1953), based on empirical experimentation with both animals and humans, emphasizes the impact on learning of associations between stimuli and the subsequent behaviour. Classical conditioning occurs when an 'unconditioned stimulus', such as food, becomes associated with another stimulus, such as a bell. The establishment of such associations can be applied in many ways to set up either positive or negative associations and so influence behaviour. Classical conditioning theory can be applied in many fields associated with complex human behaviour as well as simple animal response situations. Even highly complex human behaviours can often be explained through long chains of such associations.

Classical conditioning has relevance for public health when rewards, incentives, punishments, and disincentives are being considered. Incentives and rewards include the use of conditional cash payments to promote behaviour such as taking children to school or taking up immunization. As with all public health tactics, incentives and penalties need to be developed based on an understanding of what the intended target audience considers to be appropriate, proportionate, and fair.

Motivation theory/Hierarchy of Needs

Motivation, according to Maslow (1954) and Herzberg (1966), is essentially a desire to behave or act in a particular way (Figure 6.2). There are a number of theories of motivation predominantly from the psychology field, some looking at general human motivation and others at more specific dimensions of human motivation. Maslow's Hierarchy of Needs is a prominent general theory developed by psychologist Abraham Maslow (1954) to describe and understand the pattern that human motivations generally move through. His theory proposed five layers of motivational needs from the most basic human needs for air, food, and water through to the most advanced needs for esteem and self-actualization. Maslow theorized that the most basic levels of human needs must be met before a person is motivated to desire secondary or higher-level needs.

Understanding people's motivations is a key component of gaining insight and trying to influence behaviour. Understanding levels of human motivation and the interactions between different motivations can help practitioners know how to appeal at various levels to people to change their behaviour (Lee and Kotler, 2011). However, social marketers have also recognized that it is less effective and ethically questionable to focus only on individual motivations; the motivations of communities and society around individuals should also be considered (Andreasen, 2002). Furthermore, Wymer (2011) has guarded against the majority of social marketing programmes being focused on individual motivation. This is because such a focus would draw attention away

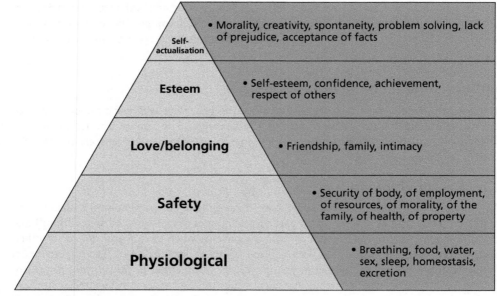

Figure 6.2 Maslow's Hierarchy of Needs.
Source: data from French J. (2011). Why nudging is not enough, Journal of Social Marketing 1(2): 154–16.

from more fundamental drivers of social problems. Therefore, motivation theory is of relevance but needs to be considered alongside other theories of wider societal and economic influence.

Cognitive Consistency and Dissonance Theory

Cognitive Consistency and Dissonance Theory (Festinger, 1957) proposes that people are motivated to seek consistency between their beliefs, values, and perceptions. The theory postulates that where there is a clash between people's actions and values or attitudes, people often resolve the discrepancy by changing their values or attitudes rather than their behaviour. For example, if someone agrees to take on a boring task for a very limited reward, there is a 'dissonance' between their behaviour (doing the task) and their reasoning (they would only do a boring task if there's a decent reward). One way out of this dissonance is to stop doing the task—i.e. change their behaviour; another is to change their attitude—i.e. convince themselves that the task is actually quite interesting.

Cognitive dissonance can be used in public health interventions through a process of highlighting clashes of behaviour and attitudes—for example, by highlighting differences between a favourable attitude to hand washing and actual poor practice as a way of triggering people to think about instigating a change in their behaviour. The theory proposes that by highlighting implicit cognitive dissonance people can become more aware and more mindful, and in so doing take more rational and considered control over their behaviour.

'Heuristics' and the consumer information-processing model

Tversky and Kahneman (1974) documented in detail how humans use mental shortcuts or 'heuristics' to make sense of their world, how they make decisions, and the impact this has on behaviour. Under normal circumstances heuristics do not present a problem, but in certain situations the use of these mental shortcuts can make people systematically prone to misjudgement and biases. Central assumptions are that individuals are limited in how much information they can process; in order to increase the usability of information, they combine bits of information into 'chunks', and employ decision rules to make choices faster and in a less stressful way (Bettman, 1979). Major heuristics include ones relating to availability, emotional stimulation, scarcity, fear of loss, peak experience, recency, and discounting over time. All of these potential biases can have large effects on decision-making and behaviour.

Many examples of heuristics such as fear of loss—e.g. loss of physical functioning or mental capacity—are powerful influences on people's behaviour. We know that the prospect of loss is often a more powerful motivator in decision situations than that of gain. Knowing this means that using fear of loss is often a better way to frame health messages than emphasizing the gains that people may get in terms of protection from the adoption of a recommended behaviour. For example, emphasizing the loss of happy times with children can be a more powerful motivator to stop smoking than appeals that emphasize a longer and healthier old age. Public health practitioners need to understand as part of their research efforts the heuristics that target audiences are using to make sense of the world and the particular behavioural responses that they are seeking to influence. This work is part of the insight development process that underpins social marketing practice.

Stages of change or Transtheoretical Model

The Transtheoretical Model (Prochaska and DiClemente, 1983) is perhaps one of the best known and most quoted models used in many public health behavioural interventions (Figure 6.3). It proposes five stages of people's readiness to change or attempts to change behaviour. The stages of change model treats behaviour change as a process that can be characterized by discrete ordered stages, but the stages are not necessarily passed through sequentially. People can enter and exit at any point and often 'recycle' through stages of change. One of the key limitations of the model is that it does not explain what the triggers to the different stages are; nevertheless, insights from other psychology models and from behavioural economics and social marketing may help to address this gap.

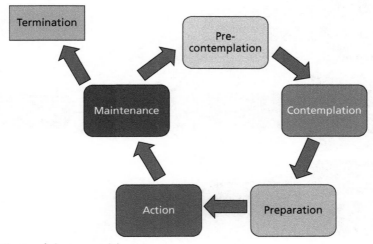

Figure 6.3 Stages of change model.

This model has informed many public health programmes which focus on gradually building people's willingness to take on large-scale behaviour changes such as stopping smoking or taking more exercise. The model identifies different elements/stages to behaviour change and attempts to disentangle these complex stages. This model can enable practitioners to develop both helpful segmentations of audiences and targeted interventions for people at different stages of change.

Theory of Reasoned Action/Theory of Planned Behaviour

The Theory of Planned Behaviour and its precursor the Theory of Reasoned Action (Ajzen, 1985; Fishbein and Ajzen, 1975) examine the relationship between behaviour and psychological issues including beliefs, attitudes, and intentions. The theory holds that 'behavioural intention' is the key determinant of behaviour and that an individual's attitude towards performing behaviour is one of the biggest influences on behavioural intention. Subjective norms are key to this influence—these are beliefs about what others think about the behaviour under consideration. In highlighting the importance of subjective norms the theory provides a conceptual link to interpersonal and community theories of behaviour change. The model was originally based on the assumption that humans are rational and that decisions and behaviours are under their control and develop from a set of reasoned decisions. However, in the 1990s Ajzen and Driver (1991) added an element that acknowledged the importance of factors beyond the individual's control, which impact on ability to change behaviour. This became known as the Theory of Planned Behaviour, which has been used by many public health programmes.

The Theory of Planned Behaviour adds 'perceived behavioural control': this is the amount of control an individual perceives they have over a behaviour and explains why behaviour or behavioural intention is influenced by factors beyond an individual's perceived control. The theory also highlights why knowledge alone does not necessarily lead to a change in a person's behaviour (see Figure 6.4).

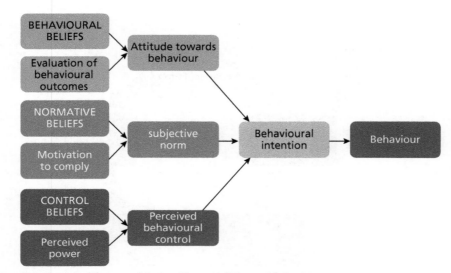

Figure 6.4 Theory of Reasoned Action/Theory of Planned Behaviour.

The Theory of Reasoned Action/Planned Behaviour can be used as a diagnostic tool when looking at health challenges. Each of the model's elements can be investigated to develop an understanding of factors that are influencing behaviour. The model can also be used to identify potential intervention points. For example, if people perceive that they have little control over malaria, one potential intervention approach might be to provide them with ways to exert more control, such as the provision of bed nets to use in their homes.

Protection Motivation Theory

Protection Motivation Theory (Rogers, 1975) considers that behaviour change may be achieved by appealing to an individual's fears. It identifies three components of fear arousal: the magnitude of harm, the probability of the event's occurrence, and the efficacy of the proposed protective response. Protection Motivation Theory suggests that these components combine to determine the intensity of the protection motivation, resulting in activity to protect oneself. This theory explicitly uses the costs and benefits of existing and recommended behaviour to predict the likelihood of behaviour change (Gebhardt and Maes, 2001). The theory assumes that the motivation to protect oneself from danger is a function of beliefs that the threat is severe, that the individual is vulnerable, that the individual can perform the coping or protective response, and that the coping response is effective at reducing or eliminating risk.

This theory has influenced many public health programmes that deal with risks associated with infections and chronic disease (see Figure 6.5). The implication of the theory is that people need to recognize risk and their vulnerability to it, and believe in the efficacy of the recommended action to reduce risk. This model can be used to guide research into an assessment of people's perception of risk and also their understanding and attitudes towards suggested actions that they can take to reduce their risk. The model can also be used to identify potential intervention opportunities related to each of the four factors that influence behavioural intention. For example, if people do not believe that eating less sugar will reduce their chances of obesity, novel ways of convincing them that this is in fact the case may be needed before they will be willing to change behaviour.

Interpersonal theories

Interpersonal models and theories focus on wider social interactions and the environment and how these affect behaviour. These models assume that people are strongly influenced by the opinions, views, beliefs, and values of people that they interact with—especially close relations and significant people in their lives.

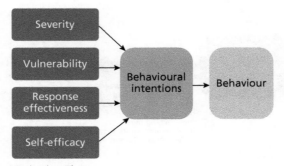

Figure 6.5 Protection Motivation Theory.

Social Cognitive Theory

Social Cognitive Theory (SCT) (Bandura, 1977; 1986) emphasizes the importance of enhancing a person's behavioural capability, self-confidence, skill, and competency when trying to influence behaviour. In SCT human behaviour is explained in terms of how personal factors, environmental influences, and behaviour continually interact (see Figure 6.6). SCT postulates that behaviour can be influenced by increasing knowledge and skills but also recognizes that behaviour is directly shaped by individuals' competencies and their beliefs in their own capabilities. Bandura argues that behaviour is a result of the constant interplay of personal factors (cognitive, affective/emotional, and biological events), environmental (external) factors, and how people interpret the results of their behaviour. SCT is based on the view that humans are instilled with certain capabilities, including:

- the capacity to symbolize (which enables us to extract meaning from the environment around us and solve problems);
- forethought (a capability to plan courses of action, anticipate, and set goals);
- vicarious learning (the ability to observe and learn from others);
- self-regulation (the potential for self-directed change);
- self-reflection (enabling us to make sense of our experiences and self-evaluation).

SCT also holds that each of us has different levels of these capabilities. Key to SCT is the concept of 'self-efficacy': this determines how we feel and think about ourselves and ultimately how we behave. Belief in self-efficacy can determine the amount of effort and perseverance people put into a task and how much resilience they display in adverse or challenging situations. Importantly, what we believe we are capable of may actually differ from what we can actually do.

The model implies that people's self-beliefs are more likely to influence what they do than their actual skills and competencies. Self-efficacy beliefs are influenced by four main sources:

- mastery experiences—personal experience of our own successes and failures;
- vicarious experiences—observing the success and failure of others;
- social persuasion—the direct influence of those around us;

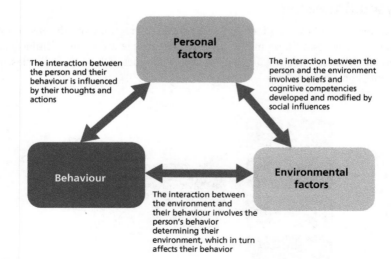

The interaction between the person and their behaviour is influenced by their thoughts and actions

Personal factors

The interaction between the person and the environment involves beliefs and cognitive competencies developed and modified by social influences

Behaviour

Environmental factors

The interaction between the environment and their behaviour involves the person's behavior determining their environment, which in turn affects their behavior

Figure 6.6 SCT.

◆ somatic and emotional states—i.e. stress, anxiety, and positive and negative moods, which can affect people's judgements of their personal efficacy, as can the physical condition or state of their body, such as how tired a person is or how hungry.

This theory can be used to help research the factors that exert an influence on decision-making and behaviour, and the interplay of the impact of these factors. SCT indicates that there are at least three potential ways to seek to influence behaviours. These are interventions aimed at influencing self-perception and understanding, actions that seek to influence environmental triggers, and prompts to behaviour and behaviours themselves. An example of influencing behaviour itself and this subsequently having an impact on personal perception and environmental factors would be the imposition of a ban on smoking in the workplace. Such an intervention directly targets the behaviour: this enforced behaviour change might lead to personal reconsideration of the need and desire to smoke. It might also lead to an impact on environmental factors such as the availability of cigarettes for sale at work, which in turn influences behaviour and personal desire to smoke.

Theory of Interpersonal Behaviour

The Theory of Interpersonal Behaviour (TIB), developed by Triandis (1977), takes account of individuals' less rational decision-making and the impact of habit on influencing behaviour (Figure 6.7). Habit is defined as a separate and key causal factor in the model, alongside attitudes, norms, roles, self-concept, beliefs, and attitudes to likely outcomes. TIB has been shown to be a good or better predictor of behaviour in situations where there is a significant habitual component. Embodied in the model is the premise that behaviour can follow two different paths: a deliberative path (via intentions) and an automatic path (via habits). This dual path theory is similar to system 1 and system 2 thinking, as defined by Stanovich and West (2000). Habits are bound up in this thinking, the two paths or processes run in parallel, one moderating the influence of the other.

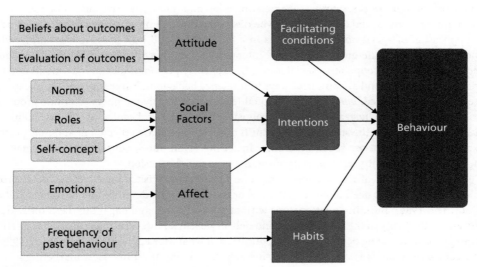

Figure 6.7 Theory of Interpersonal Behaviour.
Source: data from Triandis H. *Interpersonal behaviour*. Monterey, CA: Brooks/Cole. Copyright © 1977 Brooks/Cole.

The implication of the TIB model is that much of our behaviour and much of our decision-making is simply automatic or habitual. Therefore, appeals based on rational choice may have little influence on behaviour if the behaviour in question is following the habitual path. One of the best predictors of people's future behaviour is how they have behaved in the past. When developing intervention strategies the impact of any habitual responses needs to be fully considered. Helping people to first recognize and then change a habitual response can be a powerful way to bring about a change in behaviour. For example, if people who are trying to lose weight can be helped to first recognize the times of day and under what circumstances they are more likely to eat high-calorie foods through the keeping of a diary, they can then begin to put in place alternative strategies to prevent such habitual responses. A practical example would be the removal of a jar of cookies from the area in a kitchen where tea or coffee is made.

Community/group theories

Developments in the understanding of behaviour have also focused on the importance of behaviour in a community context; there is clearly a great deal of overlap between these theories and those that relate to interpersonal influence. These theories and models explore how social systems function and change and their impact on individuals and influencers. They also try to explain how behaviour change can be encouraged in groups and organizations. Such models have utility in informing and understanding approaches to influencing communities, the mobilization of intersectoral cooperation, and interorganizational change, as well as having a key impact on health communications and attempts to influence individuals' behaviour.

Social Capital Theory

The Social Capital Theory developed by Coleman (1988) and Putnam (1995) holds that social capital exists and can be measured in a community and that it is made up of the quantity and quality of social networks, interpersonal relationships, and the cooperative quality of a society's social interactions. Social capital can also be discerned through observation of the consistency of application of social norms and values in a community and how these norms informally and formally shape the quantity of social interactions. The core insight of this theory is that social networks and cooperative social norms have positive personal value to individuals and to wider communities and are powerful ways to influence behaviour. Three types of social capital are often distinguished: *bonding* social capital (e.g. among family members or ethnic groups), *bridging* social capital (e.g. across ethnic groups), and *linking* social capital (e.g. across political classes). Variations in the strength or weakness of social capital are reflected in and may partly explain variations in key social outcomes, including crime rates, educational performance, mortality and morbidity, economic performance, and social cohesion.

A key implication of this theory is that one of the prerequisites for effective social programmes may be the need to build, enhance, or incentivize the development of social capital (Bourdieu, 1986). Building relationships with target audiences and engaging them individually and collectively in the development and delivery of social interventions can be a powerful strategy for influencing behaviour. The application of what McKenzie-Mohr and Smith (1999) call community bases is an example of this approach being used in social marketing. This approach focuses on developing community capacity that can then be used to address other social challenges.

Diffusion of Innovations Theory

Diffusion of Innovations Theory (Rogers and Everett, 1995) addresses how new ideas, products, and social practices spread within a society or from one society to another. An innovation can be a product, service, idea, belief, attitude, or behaviour. An innovation presents a clear choice for an individual to continue with an existing activity, product, or belief or to embrace a superior one. Diffusion is facilitated through five key concepts: relative advantage, compatibility, complexity, observability, and trialling. Relative advantage is the extent to which an innovation is better than what it replaces. The concept of compatibility describes how well an innovation fits with the values, habits, experience, and needs of the intended audience. The concept of complexity acknowledges that people are more likely to make a behaviour change if the suggested innovation is easy to implement. Observability indicates how likely the innovation will be to produce tangible results and also how socially visible is it to other people. Trialability refers to the concept of 'try before you buy': innovations are more likely to succeed if individuals can try them before committing totally to them.

Populations can be classified by their approach to new innovations into five groups.

1. Innovators: this relatively small group will be the first to adopt the new innovations. They place a great deal of value on being the first to get the benefits of the new innovation and being seen to be innovators by other groups. They strongly influence the next group, the early adopters.
2. Early adopters: this is the second fastest category of individuals to adopt an innovation. These individuals have the highest degree of opinion leadership among the other adopter categories. Early adopters are typically younger in age, have a higher social status, have more financial lucidity, have advanced education, and are more socially forward than late adopters.
3. Early majority adopters: individuals in this category adopt an innovation after a varying degree of time. The time of adoption is significantly longer than the innovators and early adopters. Early majority adopters tend to have above average social status, have contact with early adopters, and show some opinion leadership.
4. Late majority adopters: individuals in this category will adopt an innovation after the average member of the society. Late majority adopters are typically sceptical about an innovation, have below average social status, and often have fewer financial resources. They are in contact with others in late majority and early majority, but have very little opinion leadership.
5. Laggards: individuals in this category are the last to adopt an innovation. These individuals typically have an aversion to change and change-agents and tend to be older. Laggards typically tend to be focused on 'traditional solutions' and have low social status and fewer financial resources. They are in contact with family and close friends but have very little to no opinion leadership with other categories.

In general, individuals who first adopt an innovation require a shorter adoption period than late adopters (see Figure 6.8). Within the rate of adoption there is a point at which an innovation reaches critical mass or tipping point (Gladwell, 2004). This is a point in time within the adoption curve that enough individuals have adopted an innovation in order that its continued adoption is self-sustaining.

Relevance for social marketing

These strategies all have relevance for implementing behavioural influence programmes. The recognition that there are normally different groups in society with regard to the

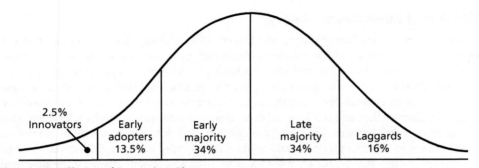

Figure 6.8 Diffusion of Innovations Theory.

adoption of a new idea or behaviour enables the development of targeted strategies aimed at each group. An example of such a segmented strategy might focus on having a social innovation such as eating less meat endorsed and adopted by a highly respected individuals or groups within a social network. This can help to create demand and desire for the innovation by early adopters and subsequently by the early majority group. The model also implies the need for very different mix of interventions when seeking to influence late majority and laggard groups. These groups might need special support programmes and/or more coercive interventions such as fines or prohibitions of certain behaviours such as smoking.

Systems Theory

Systems thinking (Checkland, 1981; Senge, 1990; Flood and Jackson, 1991; Argyris and Schon, 1996) is a set of theories developed as an approach to complex problem solving. Systems thinking is focused on understanding the total system of influences and how its components interact in a holistic way, rather than disassembling factors through a process of analysing individual elements. In this way, systems thinking is the exact opposite of much public health analysis that seeks to disassemble complex problems into discrete components that can be studied. Senge (1990) makes the distinction between 'detail complexity', which traditional analysis can deal with by disassembly, and 'dynamic complexity', which involves systemic interactions over time and generates emergent properties. Behaviour in systems thinking develops through continuous positive and negative feedback loops or interactions, rather than through simple cause and effect relationships. Systems thinking challenges the traditional approaches to behaviour change, which use theory to identify what works so that it can be replicated elsewhere. In contrast, systems thinking proposes an approach of reflective practice and continuous inquiry, not the implementing of set approaches or theories.

Systems thinking methods are particularly good for approaching messy problems, where diverse stakeholders are involved and causes and effects are multiple. Collective diagnosis of problems and collective development of solutions are key elements of systems thinking and organizational change models. Social marketing is a form of systems thinking: it rejects the notion that there is a single theory that can explain or solve most social challenges. Social marketing rather seeks to use a range of theories allied with a systematic and reflective process to develop bespoke strategies to influence specifically identified behaviours.

Needs, Opportunities, and Abilities Model

The Needs, Opportunities, and Abilities Model of consumer behaviour (Gatersleben and Vlek, 1998) is a good example of an ecological model that explicitly incorporates macro-economic and environmental influences with personal response factors (see Figure 6.9). It consists of an intention-based model of individual behaviour 'nested' within a model that shows the influence of macro-level factors. At the individual level, intentions are formed through both 'motivation' (which is driven by needs and opportunities) and 'behavioural control' or agency (which is driven by opportunities and abilities). At the macro level, needs, opportunities, and abilities are influenced by the five environmental factors: technology, economy, demography, institutions, and culture. The model incorporates a two-way relationship feedback loop between environmental factors and consumer behaviour.

The Needs, Opportunities, and Abilities Model provides a valuable demonstration of how macro-level factors can influence individual and group behaviour; it shows that focusing only on personal factors may not bring about sustained and large-scale population-level change. The model also shows how consumer or citizen behaviour influences societal factors, as well as being influenced by these factors. This interaction is missing from many other theories. One of the key implications of the model is the need to develop a strategy that includes a variety of intervention types and forms that work at multiple levels to influence behaviour. The model also makes it clear that there is a need to focus action on influencing people's expressed and felt needs, providing easy-to-access opportunities and incentives to behave in socially responsible and rewarding ways. Finally, it illustrates the need to ensure that people have the knowledge, skills, resources, and ability to adopt recommended behaviours.

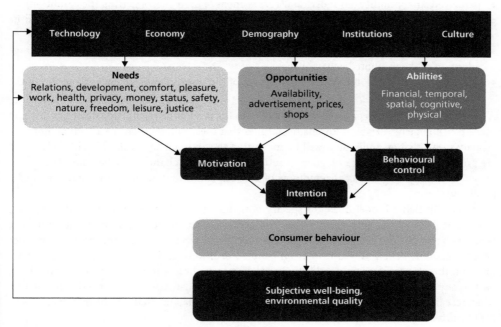

Figure 6.9 Needs, Opportunities, and Abilities Model.

Health-focused models

A number of health-focused models and theories of behavioural influence have been developed. These are a mix of individual, interpersonal, and wider systems types of model, reflecting many of the concepts identified in the brief reviews set out above.

Ecological Model

There is a growing consensus in many fields that social behavioural interventions should be based on what has been described as the 'Ecological Model' (Smedley and Syme, 2000). This approach views human behaviour as a form of complex ecology with multiple influences (National Institutes of Health, 2005). Health behaviour in this conception is influenced by a dynamic interaction between biology, psychological factors, and environmental influences. The relationship and influence of these factors is not static over time and can change depending on the life-course stage of individuals.

Health Belief Model

The Health Belief Model (Rosenstock, 1966) depicted in Figure 6.10 was one of the first social cognition models focused on health decision-making and behaviour. The model was further developed by Janz and Becker (1984) and colleagues in the 1970s and 1980s. Subsequent amendments to the model were made to accommodate evolving evidence generated within the health community about the role that knowledge and perceptions play in personal responsibility. The model suggests that belief in a personal health threat, together with a belief in the effectiveness of the proposed behaviour, will predict the likelihood of a behaviour. The four key constructs of the model are:

- perceived susceptibility (an individual's assessment of their risk of getting the condition);
- perceived severity (an individual's assessment of the seriousness of the condition, and its potential consequences);
- perceived barriers (an individual's assessment of the influences that facilitate or discourage adoption of the promoted behaviour);
- perceived benefits (an individual's assessment of the positive consequences of adopting the behaviour).

A number of mediating factors have been added to the model—these include demographic and socio-psychological variables. Rosenstock argues that these variables on their own do not necessarily mean that an individual will be motivated to carry out the desired health behaviour. He points to the importance of 'cues to action' to prompt a change in behaviour. These cues are either 'bodily' (e.g. physical symptoms of a health condition) or environmental (e.g. media publicity) events.

The Health Belief Model does not specify how different beliefs interact and influence each other, nor does it take into account environmental or economic factors that may influence health behaviours. The Health Belief Model also does not overtly consider the influence of other people's actions, beliefs, and attitudes on people's decisions. It does, however, indicate that a focus on threat, perceived vulnerability, and the efficacy of recommended actions should form part of any approach to influencing behaviour. The model can also be a useful diagnostic tool when research is being undertaken to understand potential factors that may be influencing people's health beliefs and behaviour.

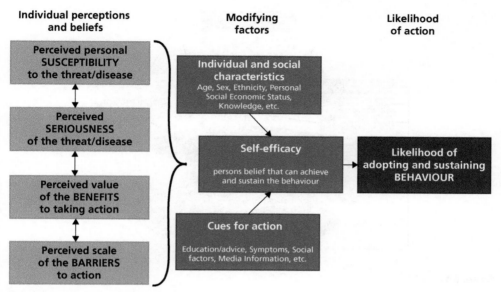

Figure 6.10 The Health Belief Model.

Health Action Model

The Health Action Model (HAM) (Tones et al., 1990; Tones and Tilford, 1994) conceptually incorporates the Health Belief Model and Fishbein and Ajzen's (1975) Theory of Reasoned Action (see Figure 6.11). HAM takes account of beliefs, normative influences, and motivating factors, including attitudes, along with other strong motivating forces such as hunger, pain, pleasure, and sex, in order to understand behaviour. Identity and self-esteem are key factors introduced by this model as important mediating factors. Self-esteem encompasses appearance, intelligence, and physical skills, as well as an individual's perception of how other people view them and the ability to make choices which are different from those of the group. In this model, behaviour change depends on:

1. a high level of self-esteem;
2. skills and strategies to resist peer group pressure;
3. an assessment of the pros and cons of change;
4. motivation to conform.

HAM is based on the idea that people with a high level of self-esteem and a positive self-concept are likely to feel confident about themselves; as a result, they will have the ability to carry through a resolve to change their behaviour. Conversely, people with a low level of self-esteem are likely to believe that they have limited control over their fate and will be less likely to respond to a health promotion message, no matter how convinced they are by it at an intellectual level. The model also emphasizes the need for facilitating factors, such as a supportive environment or the possession of personal skills, to support the translation of behavioural intention into action. HAM illustrates that people's health behaviour is dependent on both personal factors such as self-esteem and norms within communities and the wider macro-level social and economic conditions that affect their lives. Many of the factors that have an impact on people's health

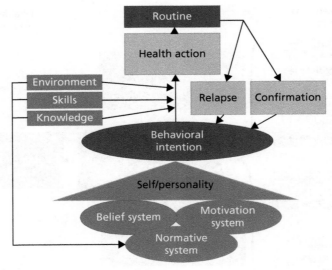

Figure 6.11 HAM.

behaviour can be at least partly and in some circumstances completely beyond their control. An implication of HAM is that public health programmes may need to focus on building up through community health education programmes self-esteem, health literacy, and health skills, as well as addressing wider influencing factors from the environment.

Developing an integrated theoretical framework to assist planning and delivery

A large number of behavioural theories and models can be used to inform the design and evaluation of effective and social behavioural influencing strategies. There is clearly a strong case for the application of theory in the development of interventions to change behaviour (MRC, 2007). However, many of the theories that can be used may be competing or partly overlapping, and as Noar and Zimmerman (2005) make clear, the use of many models to increase understanding is a useful approach. Nevertheless, selecting the most appropriate theories and models or elements of them will require the input of expertise from the relevant disciplines (Michie et al., 2005; Albarracin et al., 2005). The review, consideration, and selection of an appropriate theoretical foundation for any behavioural intervention is then a matter of some importance for at least three reasons. As Michie et al. (2008) argue:

1) Interventions are likely to be more effective if they target causal determinants of behaviour and behaviour change; this requires understanding these causal determinants, i.e. theoretical mechanisms of change.

2) Theory can be tested and developed by evaluations of interventions only if those interventions and evaluations are theoretically informed.

3) Theory-based interventions facilitate an understanding of what works and thus are a basis for developing better theory across different contexts, populations, and behaviours.

One of the first attempts made by practitioners to provide a unifying framework of various behaviour change influences was by the US National Institute of Mental Health, which convened

Table 6.1 Common key behavioural concepts

Element	Summary
Intention	To make a successful behaviour change an individual must form a strong positive intention or make a commitment to performing the behaviour. Therefore, some measure of intention should be included in the evaluation programme.
Environmental constraints	Barriers in an individual's environment may make behaviour change difficult, so a measure of perceived and/or actual barriers should be a key part of any evaluation programme.
Skills	An individual will need to possess the necessary skills to carry out the behaviour, so a measure of perceived skill level, combined with usage and awareness of any support and education tools, is an important element in any evaluation programme.
Attitudes	A positive attitude towards the behaviour change, particularly a belief that the advantage of making the change will outweigh the disadvantages, is an important step on the way to behaviour change. Evaluating attitudes and monitoring changes are therefore important measures.
Social norms	The influences of an individual's immediate support group as well as wider social influences in promoting the behaviour change are important indicators for evaluation. Measuring the perceived attitudes of friends, family, and 'society' could act as a proxy indicator here.
Self-image	The behaviour change needs to be consistent with an individual's self-image, so a way of capturing self-image and matching this with perception of the behaviour change will be useful.
Emotion	An individual's reaction to performing the behaviour change needs to be more positive than negative, so perceived emotion before performing the change and actual emotion once trialling it are good indicators of likelihood to continue with the behaviour change.
Self-efficacy	An individual's capabilities to perform the behaviour change in a range of circumstances and their belief in this are important in many of the models, so a measurement of perceived and actual capability is often key in evaluation.

a theorist's workshop to work through the key factors influencing behaviour and behaviour change (Fishbein et al., 1992). Drawing on this, Table 6.1 sets out the key concepts which reoccur in the models and theories reviewed.

This summary list seeks to concentrate the mind on the key elements that need to be considered when developing an intervention. The question of how these key elements can and should be applied was addressed in a review commissioned by the UK Government (Darnton, 2008) to clarify the use of models of behaviour change for research analysts. This aimed to improve advice to policy-makers seeking to influence behaviour related to social programmes and to evaluate such programmes. The report was designed to provide an overview of relevant models and theories and guidance on their uses and limits. It also makes it clear that there is no algorithm that can be applied to select models or theories: ultimately, a theory-based approach needs to be flexible to take account of different behavioural contexts and audience groups. This should also incorporate learning from practice, having identified what works in comparable interventions. The review sets out nine principles in a logical sequence (Box 6.3), but makes clear that they should not be regarded as discrete steps, with one being accomplished before moving on to the next.

Box 6.3 Government social research behaviour change knowledge review

1. Identify the audience groups and the target behaviour. If faced with a complex behaviour, break it down into its component behaviours and/or adopt a systems thinking approach.

2. Identify relevant behavioural models (use both individual- and societal-level models). Draw up a shortlist of influencing factors.

3. Select the key influencing factors used to design objectives in a draft strategy for the intervention.

4. Identify effective intervention techniques which have worked in the past on the influencing factors selected.

5. Engage the target audience for the intervention in order to understand the target behaviour and the factors influencing it from their perspective.

6. Develop a prototype intervention based on the learning from working with the actors. Cross-check this against appropriate policy frameworks and assessment tools. Pilot the intervention and monitor continuously.

8. Evaluate impacts and processes.

9. Feedback learning from the evaluation.

Adapted from Darnton A. *Government social research behaviour change knowledge review reference report: an overview of behaviour change models and their uses.* Centre for Sustainable Development, University of Westminster, Copyright © 2008 Crown Copyright.

Open analysis approach to selecting models and theories

In this final section of the chapter a suggested set of steps is set out for using existing and developing bespoke theories and models to inform your behavioural programme. The following four domains of influence on behaviour should first be considered:

1. bio-physical
2. psychological
3. social
4. environmental and economic.

The first step in the process of selecting a theory is to acknowledge the influence of these four domains and begin a review of potential influences on behaviour from these four perspectives. Using this frame of reference, potential models and theories can be sought that inform understanding about the impact of each of these four domains on behaviour.

The second task relates to the need to recognize that it is impossible for single practitioners to have detailed understanding of multiple theories or have the time or understanding to conduct exhaustive reviews of theory prior to any strategy or action being delivered. One way to reduce the effort required and to increase the theoretical frame of reference is the tactic of bringing together multidisciplinary teams from different backgrounds to select and develop the theoretical foundation of the intervention strategy. This approach will increase the range of theoretical models that will be applied in any given situation.

As discussed above, if theory is to be used to inform practice it is necessary to start by trying to get a clear understanding of what behaviour is occurring, and what different people know, think, and feel about it, before going on to pull down a theory to consider what might help inform or develop insight into why people are adopting a behaviour. In this way, a focus on the behaviour drives the selection and development of a theoretical perspective rather than practitioners using a process that starts with a theory and seeks to fit observed phenomena into it.

The final stages of selecting or developing theoretical understanding should involve the development of 'working propositions' of how to achieve and/or maintain the desired behaviour. These propositions will be based on existing theory and/or bespoke models developed from existing theory and informed by the observed influences on the behaviour under consideration. Interventions can then be developed based on these propositions and tested in pilots.

Conclusion

This chapter has explored the challenges for public health practitioners when seeking to influence behaviour to promote or maintain health. The complex web of influences on behaviour and the seemingly equal complexity associated with developing effective and efficient interventions have also been explored. The current tendency in many countries to rely on simplistic information transmission and legal and fiscal sanctions to influence health behaviour can reduce the impact of social programmes. This chapter has demonstrated that behavioural economics and the concepts that underpin it have important implications for the development of social interventions. This new understanding makes clear the need for strategies that go beyond just the transmission of factually accurate logical information as the main way to influence behaviour. The challenge now for social planners is to develop intervention programmes based on our understanding of both passive and active decision-making and wider systems influences on health behaviour.

The selective review of behavioural change theories and models in this chapter also illustrates that there is a great deal of understanding about the many factors at individual, group, and society levels that affect health decision-making and behaviour. It is clear that there is a need to place behavioural influence, which is the ultimate objective of a social marketing-based approach, at the heart of public health planning and delivery. The chapter has argued that when planning programme strategy, theories and models have practical utility and a central role in assisting with the selection design and evaluation of the effective programmes. We know that public health interventions that are based on theory are more effective. We also know that interventions that are systematically planned are more effective. Finally, we know that interventions that draw on knowledge about effective interventions and apply best practice are more effective. Interventions that do all of these things are not guaranteed to be effective and efficient but are much more likely to be so.

When constructing health behavioural interventions the use of several theories and models appears to assist with identifying the key elements which are of most use in explaining behaviour or predicting what will influence it. This understanding can be used as the foundation around which interventions can be designed. This is the approach that Darnton (2008) recommends. There will be occasions, however, when existing behavioural theory is not available or appropriate. In these circumstances it will be necessary to construct bespoke models and new theories to inform and guide the development of programmes. This chapter has demonstrated that theories and models are key tools that are vital in planning effective programmes. When planning interventions, practitioners and policy-makers should always start by seeking out theories and models that can help refine thinking about how to influence the specific behaviour they wish to have an impact on.

Self-review questions

1. How can the use of behavioural theories and models strengthen the development of social marketing planning and intervention delivery?

2. List the reasons public health practitioners need to understand and apply a broad range of behavioural interventions to tackle social challenges.

3. What are some of the key factors that influence health behaviour and decision-making at an individual level, an interpersonal level, and a wider social and environmental level?

References

Ajzen, I. (1985). From intentions to actions: a theory of planned behaviour. In: J. Kuhl, J. Beckman (eds). *Action-control: from cognition to behaviour.* Heidelberg: Springer (11–39).

Ajzen, I., Driver, B. L. (1991). Prediction of leisure participation from behavioural, normative, and control beliefs – an application of the theory of planned behaviour. *Leisure Sciences* 13(3):185–204.

Albarracin, D., Gillette, J., Earl, A., Durantini, M., Moon-Ho, H. (2005). A test of major assumptions about behaviour change: a comprehensive look at the effects of passive and active HIV-prevention interventions since the beginning of the epidemic. *Psychological Bulletin* 131(6):856–897.

Andreasen, A.R. (2002). Marketing social marketing in the social change marketplace. *Journal of Public Policy and Marketing* 21(1): 3–13.

Angus, K., Cairns, G., Purves, R., Bryce, S., MacDonald, L., Gordon, R. (2013). *Systematic literature review to examine the evidence for the effectiveness of interventions that use theories and models of behaviour change: towards the prevention and control of communicable diseases.* Stockholm: European Centre for Disease Prevention and Control.

Argyris, C., Schon, D. (1996). *Organizational learning II.* Reading, MA: Addison-Wesley.

Ariely, D. (2009). *Predictably irrational: the hidden forces that shape our decisions.* London: Harper Collins.

Bandura, A. (1977). Self-efficacy: toward a unifying theory of behavioral change. *Psychological Review* 84: 191–215.

Bandura, A. (1986). *Social foundations of thought and action: a social cognitive theory.* Englewood Cliffs, NJ: Prentice Hall.

Bettman, J. (1979). *An information processing theory of consumer choice.* Reading, MA: Addison-Wesley.

Bourdieu, P. (1986). The forms of capital. In: S. Baron, J. Field, T. Schuller (eds) (2000). *Social capital— critical perspectives.* Oxford: Oxford University Press.

Brafman, O., Brafman, R. (2009). *Sway: the irresistible pull of irrational behaviour.* London: Virgin.

Cabinet Office (2010). *MINDSPACE: influencing behaviour through public policy.* London: Cabinet Office.

Checkland, P. (1981). *Systems thinking, systems practice.* New York: John Wiley.

Cialdini, R. (2007). *Influence: the psychology of persuasion.* London: Collins.

Coleman, J. (1988). Social capital in the creation of human capital. *American Journal of Sociology* 94 (Supplement): S95–S120.

Darnton, A. (2008). *Government social research behaviour change knowledge review reference report: an overview of behaviour change models and their uses.* London: Centre for Sustainable Development, University of Westminster.

Dolan, P., Hallsworth, M., Halpern, D., Kind, D., Vlaev, I. (2010). *MINDSPACE: influencing behaviour through public policy. Full report.* London: Cabinet Office and Institute for Government.

Festinger, L. (1957). *A theory of cognitive dissonance.* Stanford, CA: Stanford University Press.

Fishbein, M., Ajzen, I. (1975). *Belief, attitude, intention and behaviour: an introduction to theory and research.* Reading, MA: Addison-Wesley.

Fishbein, M., Bandura, A., Triandis, H. (1992). *Factors influencing behaviour and behaviour change: final report—theorists workshop.* Bethesda, MD: National Institute of Mental Health.

Flood, R.L., Jackson, M.C. (1991). *Critical systems thinking: directed readings.* New York: Wiley.

French, J. (2011). Why nudging is not enough. *Journal of Social Marketing* 1(2): 154–162.

French, J., Gordon, R. (2015). *Strategic social marketing.* London: Sage.

Gatersleben, B., Vlek, C. (1998). Household consumption: quality of life and environmental impacts. In: K.J. Noorman, A.J.M. Schoot-Uiterkamp (eds). *Green households? domestic consumers, environment and sustainability.* London: Earthscan (141–183).

Gebhardt, W., Maes, S. (2001). Integrating social-psychological frameworks for health behaviour research. *American Journal of Health Behavior* 25:528–536.

Gladwell, M.(2004). *The tipping point.* New York: Back Bay Books.

Goldstein, N., Martin, S., Cialdini, R. (2007). *Yes! Fifty secrets from the science of persuasion.* London: Profile Books.

Gordon, R. (2013). Unlocking the potential of upstream social marketing. *European Journal of Marketing* 47(9): 1525–1547.

Green, J., Tones, K. (2010). *Health promotion: planning and strategies,* 2nd edition. London: Sage.

Grist, M. (2010). *Steer: mastering our behaviour through instinct, environment and reason.* London: RSA http://www.thersa.org/__data/assets/pdf_file/0017/313208/RSA-Social-Brain_WEB-2.pdf

Halpern, D., Bates, C., Beales, G. (2003). *Personal responsibility and behaviour change.* London: Prime Minister's Strategy Unit, Cabinet Office.

Herzberg, F. (1966). *Work and the nature of man.* Cleveland, OH: World Publishing.

House of Lords Science and Technology Select Committee (2011). *Behaviour change.* London: The Stationery Office http://www.publications.parliament.uk/pa/ld201012/ldselect/ldsctech/179/179.pdf

Jackson, T. (2005). *Motivating sustainable consumption: a review of evidence on consumer behaviour and behavioural change—a framework for pro-environmental behaviours.* London: Development Research Network and Defra.

Janz, N., Becker, M. (1984). The health belief model: a decade later. *Health Education & Behaviour* 11(1): 1–47.

Kahneman, D. (2011). *Thinking, fast and slow.* Oxford: Oxford University Press.

Lee, N., Kotler, P. (2011). *Social marketing: influencing behaviors for good.* New York: Sage.

Maio, G., Verplanken, B., Manstead, A., Stroebe, W., Abraham, C., Sheeran P., Conner, M. (2007). Social psychological factors in lifestyle change and their relevance to policy. *Journal of Social Issues and Policy Review* 1(1): 99–137.

Maslow, A. (1954). *Motivation and personality.* New York: Harper.

McKenzie-Mohr, D., Smith, W. (1999). *Fostering sustainable behaviour: an introduction to community-based social marketing.* Gabriola Island: New Society Publishers.

Michie, S., Johnston, M., Abraham, C., Lawton, R., Parker, D., Walker, A.(2005). Making psychological theory useful for implementing evidence based practice: a consensus approach. *Quality and Safety in Healthcare* 14: 26–33.

Michie, S., Johnston, M., Francis, J., Hardeman, W., Eccles, M. (2008). From theory to intervention: mapping theoretically derived behavioural determinants to behaviour change techniques. *Applied Psychology: an international review* 57(4): 660–680 doi: 10.1111/j.1464-0597.2008.00341.x.

Michie, S., Stralen, M., West, R. (2011). The behaviour change wheel: a new method for characterising and designing behaviour change interventions. *Implementation Science* 6:42. doi: 10.1186/1748-5908-6-42.

MRC (2007). *Developing and evaluating complex interventions: new guidance.* London: Medical Research Council http://www.mrc.ac.uk/complexinterventionsguidance

National Institutes of Health (2005). *Theory at a glance: a guide for health promotion practice,* 2nd edition. Washington, DC: US Department of Health and Human Services http://www.sbccimplementationkits.org/demandrmnch/wp-content/uploads/2014/02/Theory-at-a-Glance-A-Guide-For-Health-Promotion-Practice.pdf

New Economics Foundation (2005). *Behavioural economics: seven principles for policy makers.* London: New Economics Foundation.

Noar, S., Zimmerman, R. (2005). Health behaviour theory and cumulative knowledge regarding health behaviours: are we moving in the right direction? *Health Education Research* 20(3):275–290.

Pavlov, I.P. (1927). *Conditioned reflexes.* London: Oxford University Press.

Prochaska, J., DiClemente, C. (1983). Stages and processes of self-change of smoking: toward an integrative model of change. *Journal of Consulting and Clinical Psychology* 51: 390–395.

Putnam, R. (1995). Bowling alone: America's declining social capital. *Journal of Democracy* 6(1): 65–78.

Roe, L., Hunt, P., Bradshaw, H., Rayner, M. (1997). *Health promotion interventions to promote healthy eating in the general population: a review.* London: Health Education Authority.

Rogers, M., Everett, T. (1995). *Diffusion of innovations,* 4th edition. New York: The Free Press.

Rogers, R. (1975). A protection motivation theory of fear appeals and attitude change. *Journal of Psychology* 91:93–114.

Rosenstock, I.M. (1966). Why people use health services. *Milbank Memorial Fund Quarterly* 44(3): 94–112.

Senge, P. (1990). *The fifth discipline.* London: Random House.

Skinner, B. (1953). *Science and human behaviour.* New York: Macmillan.

Smedley, B.D., Syme, S.L. (eds). (2000). *Promoting health: strategies from social and behavioral research.* Washington, DC: National Academies Press.

Stanovich, K., West, R. (2000). Individual differences in reasoning: implications for the rationality debate? *Behavioural and Brain Sciences* 23: 645–726.

Sunstein, C., Thaler, R. (2003). Libertarian paternalism is not an oxymoron. *The University of Chicago Law Review* 70(4): Article 1.

Thaler, R. (2000). Behavioural economics. In: N.J. Smelser, P.B. Baltes (eds). *International encyclopaedia of the social and behavioural sciences.* Oxford: Elsevier.

Thaler, R., Sunstein, C. (2008). *Nudge: improving decisions about health, wealth and happiness.* New Haven, CT: Yale University Press.

Tones, K., Tilford, S., Robinson, Y. (1990). Health education: effectiveness and efficiency. London: Chapman & Hall.

Tones, K., Tilford, S. (1994). *Health education: effectiveness, efficiency and equity,* 2nd edition. London: Chapman and Hall.

Triandis, H. (1977). *Interpersonal behaviour.* Monterey, CA: Brooks/Cole.

Tversky, A., Kahneman, D. (1974). Judgment under uncertainty: heuristics and biases. *Science* 185:1124–1131.

Welsh Government (2008). *Opt-out systems of organ donation: international evidence review.* Cardiff: Welsh Government Social Research.

Wymer, W. (2011). Developing more effective social marketing strategies. *Journal of Social Marketing* 1(1): 17–31.

Chapter 7

Generating insight and building segmentation models in social marketing

Dominic McVey and Adam Crosier

A point of view can be a dangerous luxury when substituted for insight and understanding.
Marshall McLuhan, *The Gutenberg Galaxy.*
Reproduced with permission from University of Toronto Press,
Copyright © 1962 University of Toronto Press.

Learning points

This chapter:

- introduces the concepts of 'insight' and 'segmentation';
- gives an overview of how to build segmentations;
- provides an understanding of the importance of segmentation to social marketing initiatives;
- uses case studies to describe the construction and value of segmentations.

Introduction to generating insight and building segmentation models

One of the most important elements of the social marketing process is developing the in-depth understanding of the customer or citizen which forms the foundation for the choice of target groups and the construction of the intervention. The importance of insight in the development and design of interventions has continued to grow since a review of service transformation across the UK Government in 2006 concluded that 'we need to exploit customer insight as a strategic asset' (Varney, 2006: 88). Prioritizing this key benchmark of the social marketing process will deliver significant returns on investment.

Defining 'insight'

A useful working definition of 'customer insight' in the context of social marketing is provided by the Government Communications Network's 'Engage' programme, which classes it as:

> a deep 'truth' about the customer based on their behaviour, experiences, beliefs, needs or desires, that is relevant to the task or issue and 'rings bells' with target people.

> (GCN, 2009)

Insight is also defined by the way it is collected and used, and by two attributes in particular:

1. it draws on multiple sources of information, using these to build up complete pictures of customer needs and behaviours; and
2. it is essentially a business process, aimed at creating something which has value to the organization.

Generating insight

How do we generate consumer insight? There is usually no single source of insight generation but a combination of sources cross-referenced and triangulated to support recommendations. Practitioners should not rely only on research published in academic peer-reviewed journals but look across disciplines and source data generated from a plurality of methods. Examples include:

- the views of frontline staff, experts, and other stakeholders;
- data mining of customer databases and 'Big data'—e.g. Tesco Clubcard data;
- social media analysis—Facebook, Twitter, Instagram, Snapchat;
- customer/patient journey mapping;
- customer immersion techniques and ethnography (the scientific description of peoples and cultures);
- public consultations;
- usability testing and website analysis;
- qualitative research with the target group—focus groups, in-depth interviews, paired depths, deliberative workshops, etc.;
- formal and informal contact with representative bodies;
- the views of agents or intermediaries;
- written correspondence;
- media coverage;
- sales data;
- service evaluations;
- media analysis of press and broadcast coverage to understand the social, political, and cultural context;
- process evaluations;
- the process evaluations that accompany randomized controlled trials, controlled trials, and matched case controls;
- reviews of interventions' effectiveness;
- neuroscience—measuring consumer reaction using electroencephalogram (EEG) and magnetic resonance imaging (MRI);
- geodemographic databases;
- segmentation.

Before we take a look in detail at one aspect of insight generation—i.e. segmentation—we should remind ourselves of a basic difference between the commercial and social marketing use of such strategies.

Social marketing, inequality, and understanding disadvantaged groups

Social marketing tackles big social concerns such as health and crime, and requires an understanding not only of the mainstream audiences targeted by the commercial sector but also of the disadvantaged and marginalized groups in society. To create interventions that work with these groups requires greater understanding of their social circumstances and their ability to change within challenging environments. Interventions also need to build empathy and develop trust to sustain a continuing customer relationship with people who are not normally valued by commercial marketers as potential clients. Moreover, interventions targeted without adequate understanding of the groups they are meant to serve can result in a widening of the health inequalities between the rich and poor in society.

For example, despite the evidence of effectiveness of polices and interventions aimed at reducing smoking prevalence, there is little available evidence that these polices reduce inequalities. A review of systematic reviews undertaken by the Health Development Agency (HDA, 2004) showed little evidence of effectiveness of interventions to reduce inequalities.

While health promotion and social marketing in all its forms may contribute to the decline in overall prevalence of risky behaviour, there is evidence that some interventions may indeed be contributing to widening the gap in health inequalities. Smokers who live in more deprived neighbourhoods with higher levels of smoking prevalence are less able to respond and change their behaviour in response to health promotion interventions (Acheson, 1998). This does not mean to say that vulnerable groups do not exhibit resilience and change their behaviour—many of them do—but proportionately there is less change among these groups compared to the better-off smokers and this can result in a widening of the gap in health inequalities.

In 2010 Capewell and Graham cited evidence that cardiovascular disease prevention strategies for screening and treating high-risk individuals (which are contingent on action by individual patients and health care providers) may represent a relatively ineffective approach that typically widens social inequalities. The alternative approach of population-wide cardiovascular disease prevention—for example, legislating for smoke-free public spaces, appropriate food labelling, or halving daily dietary salt intake—are generally effective and cost-saving; there is also increasing evidence that they can reduce health inequalities. The authors conclude that the two approaches are complementary and support the dual strategy approach advocated by Rose (1992).

The dual approach is, in effect, a social marketing approach—i.e. individual behaviour change interventions used in conjunction with fiscal, legislative, and environment interventions. The social marketing approach, while theoretically sound, can fail because of a lack of insight into the lives of vulnerable and disadvantaged groups, coupled with a limited understanding of the substantial influence of the wider social determinants operating on the individual to limit their ability to live healthy lives. This has resulted in inappropriately targeted interventions which take little account of social deprivation. Interventions based solely on individual choice are unlikely to overcome the structural factors promoting inequalities in health. Campaigns targeting only an individual's behaviour, while working with the better-off groups, will generally have less effect on those that need them most.

Properly applied social marketing and health promotion techniques based on a deep understanding of people's lives, circumstances, and aspirations can help ensure that interventions are appropriately targeted. This, coupled with a mix of approaches—behavioural, fiscal, legislative, and environmental—can mitigate the possibility of widening the gap in health inequalities and may even narrow it.

With the widening gap in health inequalities, any strategy or intervention aimed at improving population health will merit rigorous assessment—at developmental and evaluation stages—of its potential impact on inequalities.

Quantitative and qualitative insight

As stated earlier, there is usually no single source of insight generation but a combination of quantitative and qualitative cross-referenced data. What is clear is that we cannot understand the complexity of people's lives by simply asking them questions. If we are to gain understanding of a person's world—their knowledge, attitudes, and beliefs, along with the social context in which they live and work—we need to see life from their perspective. The case study in Box 7.3 later in this chapter illustrates this point.

There are many useful statistical techniques available to explore large quantitative datasets, such as cluster analysis and multilevel modelling, all of which will reveal insights into people's lives. If, however, we are to uncover insights into how people's thoughts, feelings, objectives, and coping strategies influence their behaviours, we also need more open, qualitative techniques employing in-depth interviews, observation, and ethnography. The character Atticus Finch in Harper Lee's *To kill a mockingbird* (1960) puts it very well:

> You never really understand a person until you consider things from his point of view, until you climb into his skin and walk around in it.

Social marketers should always be aware that issues which have most traction with target groups may not be the obvious drivers of the behaviour change under consideration. The social marketer needs to look into people's lived experience: their more immediate situational needs in addition to the more upstream psychosocial determinants of the behaviour. For example, looking at the prevalence of smoking among single mothers living in more deprived communities in the UK, this has tended to be higher than the average for others in the same communities. Survey research reveals that they are aware of the risks, they want to give up, and many have tried to give up but failed. Using a variety of research methods, including ethnographic methods, researchers in the 1990s studied the lives of single mothers, revealing that smoking had a much more important meaning for this group. Social isolation, financial worries, and the challenges of raising children alone meant that smoking was one of the few pleasures left to them and provided a few minutes' break from life's stresses. Smoking was more than just a habit or addiction: it was a stress coping mechanism and a 'reward'. Smoking was more a 'friend' than an 'enemy' (Graham, 1993). If interventions were to be effective they needed to take account of this social and psychological context. This work was published in the 1990s, but many interventions aimed at disadvantaged single mothers still do not take account of these insights.

Segmentation

Building segmentations can generate new insights into the drivers and barriers to change and help target the right groups with the most persuasive approaches. Furthermore, segmentations are very valuable for condensing a complex array of data into a manageable, actionable form. Segmentation can be a powerful tool in understanding consumer groups and focusing resources where they are most needed. It is, therefore, a valuable addition to the insight toolbox. Generally, in the public health field, we cannot offer people a one-on-one service, so we need to segment audiences into homogeneous groups and tailor the proposition, as far as possible, to the groups' needs.

One of the challenges in social marketing is that consumers are constantly developing and adapting to life around them. Segmentation needs to do the same—it needs to be comprehensive and dynamic to take account of these changes and to spot shifts and trends in the lifestyles of customers.

Segmentation is a process of looking at the audience or 'market' and seeking to identify distinct manageable subgroups (segments) that have similar needs, attitudes, or behaviours. We all regularly segment people into groups. We talk about adults who are working and adults who are unemployed, single mothers who smoke and those who don't, and we subdivide these further by social class, ethnicity, level of income, use of public services, neighbourhood type, etc.

Traditionally, segmentation has focused on the use of demographics (age, sex, social class), geodemographics (type of neighbourhood), and epidemiological data. However, adding in attitudinal and psychographic data to provide a rounder picture of the segments is a good starting point for developing more sophisticated segmentation and hence more tailored interventions. Psychographic variables describe the individual in terms of their overall approach to life, including personality traits, values, beliefs, and preferences and are very useful for developing message propositions.

There are a wide range of segmentation techniques: sociodemographic, geodemographic, behavioural, epidemiological, psychographic, attitudinal, service utilization, and social network analysis, to name a few. They all, however, draw on a pool of common factors, as Table 7.1 shows. Most segmentations within public health use quantitative (measurable) data (for example, surveys, epidemiological data, or hospital episode data). There are, however, some good examples of qualitative segmentations (based on people's views, needs, and behaviours), which have drawn on in-depth interviews and focus groups to produce typologies of particular groups (see Box 7.2 later in this chapter). Although they cannot provide accurate estimates of the size of each segment, they do provide a rich description of the various groups and types emerging from the qualitative analysis and are very useful for developing propositions and defining the social marketing 'exchange'. Qualitative segments can be sized later using quantitative survey research.

Segmentation principles

When segmenting populations, the aim should be to define a small number of groups so that:

◆ all members of a particular group are as similar to each other as possible; and
◆ they are as different from the other groups as possible.

It is important for social marketers to know what differentiates one group from another, and equally important to know the similarities between people in a particular group. These allow us to create clusters of people and target our interventions at priority groups.

Key attributes of a good segmentation described by McVey and Walsh (2010) are the following.

◆ The segmentation should build on current knowledge.
◆ It should get us a step closer to knowing our audience.
◆ It should provide a common language for understanding people's motivations and behaviours.
◆ Utility/applicability: the segments should exist in the real world rather than simply being statistical constructs; the segment descriptions should make sense to the people who have to apply them; and the segmentation should add value and greater sophistication when developing and targeting interventions.
◆ Replicability: practitioners should be able to identify or recreate the segments in their own research.

Table 7.1 Factors common to segmentation approaches

Behaviour/current status	Demographics	Geographic	Activities and lifestyle	Attitudinal/ psychographic
◆ Dependency/ addiction issues ◆ How engrained is the behaviour—how long has it been sustained? ◆ Frequency of behaviour—e.g. regular, occasional, hardly ever, experimenting stage ◆ Occasion—e.g. social smoker, smoke after meal, never smoke at work ◆ Stage of change: e.g. contemplating change or have tried to change and relapsed ◆ Health status ◆ Are they in serious debt? ◆ Have they just experienced a major life event? ◆ Use of services—how often? What for? ◆ Habits ◆ Sales data: what people buy—healthy food, alcohol, cigarettes, condoms, etc.	◆ Age/life stage ◆ Gender ◆ Family size ◆ Income ◆ Social class/ occupation ◆ Education ◆ Religion ◆ Ethnicity	◆ Urban/rural ◆ Geodemographic ◆ Proximity to services ◆ Area deprivation Indexes ◆ Social capital indexes	◆ How do they spend their money? ◆ Where do they socialize and ◆ what do they do? ◆ What do they read, watch, and listen to, and what engages them most?	◆ Needs, desires, aspirations ◆ Beliefs and values ◆ Personality type ◆ Self-esteem, self-efficacy, locus of control ◆ Key influences in their life— parent, peers, partner, religion, and the media, role models ◆ Attitudes towards the issues in question, the service, the product, the organization, the government, health professionals— e.g. contemplating or tried and relapsed ◆ attitudes towards services (NHS, local councils, etc), customer satisfaction

- Stability: the segment definitions should be fairly stable, although the size of the segments may change over time as people migrate in and out of them.
- The segmentation should create a focus for our time and resources.
- It should not be too complicated: some of the most powerful segmentations are the simplest. As a rule of thumb, a manageable number will be in the range of three to eight segments.
- The segmentation should not be the final word but should allow room for new insight.

The type of segmentation adopted will depend on what you are trying to achieve. Regardless of the approach adopted, the resulting segmentation should be clear and actionable and help your team visualize the people you are trying to reach. A good strategic segmentation of all your customers, mapping their behaviours, service use, and attitudes, can provide a clearer understanding of the priority groups and be a valuable asset to your organization in planning programmes.

Segmentation starts with the consumers and how they should be served, rather than focusing on the product on offer. Messages, products, or services should be designed or redesigned around the priority segments. If done well, this will produce more satisfied consumers/patients and a more efficient delivery of your intervention.

Segmentations do not last forever and they need updating as media, services, and responses to interventions change. A well-constructed segmentation, however, which visualizes customers with clarity and insight, will result in buy-in from within your organization and its delivery partners, and can drive activity for years.

The stages in constructing segmentation

Stage 1. Identify potential target audiences

The first stage is to look at the behaviour or health problem that needs to be addressed and to collate existing data on the incidence or severity of the problem, the prevalence of risk factors, and estimates of the size of the groups affected (McVey and Crosier, 2013).

For example, looking at the issue of the uptake of pandemic influenza vaccination, the scientific evidence indicates that the impact of pandemic influenza will have varying affects on certain demographic groups:

- older groups;
- people who are chronically ill;
- pregnant women;
- children (targeting parents of children);
- marginalized groups (homeless, travellers, refugees, substance misusers).

There may be common drivers and barriers to vaccination uptake across all these groups and a composite of the measures may form the dominant dimensions/axes of the segmentation for the whole population. Alternatively, it may be more advantageous to segment within each population subgroup. These are decisions to make with research and programme specialists to ensure that the segmentation has utility to the people delivering the intervention.

Stage 2. What do we already know about these groups?

For many established health problems there will be existing data, reports, and reviews on the range of variables which will help build a detailed picture of the drivers and barriers to behaviour change. Some of these variables will be useful to include in a segmentation analysis, such as:

- knowledge and attitudes;
- perception of personal risk/personal susceptibility;
- general perceptions/beliefs/trust in authorities;
- locus of control/self-esteem;
- demographics and social deprivation;
- preferred information channels;
- use of services.

Before commissioning any new research, practitioners should review what is already known. There may be existing segmentations which fulfill the objectives of the research or others which can be readily adapted.

Stage 3. What data is available to build the segmentation model?

There may be sufficient data from existing sources: reviews, surveys, quantitative studies, and qualitative studies, which include measures on the key drivers/barriers to change within each of the key audiences.

Using existing data Based on the available review data, which includes knowledge, attitudes, and beliefs of priority groups, it may be possible to create a broad set of categories (or segments) of people who are more or less likely to respond to behaviour change messages. In the absence of any other data this will provide useful information about where resources should be targeted. If, however, quantitative data is available from contemporary evaluations or surveys, applying a more systematic analysis approach will improve the accuracy of the segment definitions, the estimated size of each segment, and hence the effectiveness of the targeting of planned interventions.

There may be existing raw data sources on the knowledge, attitudes, beliefs, and practices that are relevant to the behaviour in question. These data can be re-analysed to generate distinct segments. There are many approaches to analysing data to generate segments and it is important to have a plan of analysis which will meet the objectives for the segmentation. For example, if you wish to identify distinct segments within a subset of a population—e.g. older people—one approach would be to select this group from the dataset and define segments within this group. Take, for example, the issue of the low uptake of pandemic influenza vaccinations. Looking at a particularly vulnerable demographic group—older people—there are always at least two segments within the older population: those who are resistant to vaccinations because they do not feel at risk or are unable to attend vaccination clinics and those who do get vaccinated. Alternatively, you may decide to look at the whole adult population and identify a set of key characteristics of those who are not vaccinated, which in turn will define the particular segments across all demographic groups.

The more information you have on respondents' knowledge, attitudes, beliefs, and practices, the more detailed segment definitions you will be able to construct. It should be noted, however, that using too many variables to define your segments can overcomplicate the definitions and result in the segments having little use for those designing interventions and campaigns. Use only those variables which clearly have a strong influence on behavioural intentions or actual behaviour. For example, looking again at the uptake of pandemic influenza vaccinations, a sense of personal susceptibility, a belief in the severity of the disease, fear of side effects, trust in government information, or access to vaccines and antivirals all have a significant influence on vaccination uptake and should be prioritized for inclusion in any segmentation model.

Generating new data If there is insufficient data available from existing sources, new data should be collected which includes the relevant variables to quantify the measures at stage 2. These data will then form the primary source to develop the segmentation.

Stage 4. Decide what analysis is feasible with the data available

Ideally, if there is access to a dataset which contains some or all of the variables of interest it will be possible to conduct a number of different analyses to build a segmentation model—e.g. bi-variate analysis, factor analysis, cluster analysis, hierarchical cluster analysis, etc. Sometimes all that may be required is a straightforward bi-variate analysis within each group. Returning to the example of the uptake of influenza vaccination within the older population, if x% are non-compliant with vaccination measures and the main reason for this non-compliance is that they do not trust the government information, then that may be enough to identify a key segment for targeting.

If the data available is qualitative in nature, it may still be possible to identify key attitudinal segments which are resistant to behaviour change when it comes to vaccination or adopting non-pharmacological interventions. The qualitative analysis may describe several overall attitudinal/behavioural groups which can be quantified later with surveys.

Stage 5. Question the viability and utility of the segments

At the analysis stage a range of different segmentation solutions should be generated and the best solution chosen based on a number of criteria.

- Has the analysis resulted in a manageable number of segments? Three to eight segments is a good rule of thumb, as any more than this will result in a model which may be too complicated to be useful.
- Are the segments clearly defined and do they make intuitive sense to the social marketers who will have to use them in their work?
- Are there clearly defined channels of communication or interventions which can reach these segments?
- Are the segments distinct enough from each other to be useful to practitioners?
- Are the segments large enough to justify specific targeting and investment?
- Are some of the segments so intransigent that the likelihood of behaviour change does not justify investment in specific targeting?

Make use of robust objective analysis, and the common-sense judgements of your team to assess the segmentation against these criteria.

Stage 6. Reproducing the segments on subsequent surveys

If the segmentation is to be adopted by an organization and used to develop strategy and targeting at a local as well as national level, it is important that local practitioners can apply the segmentation to their own populations. After the extensive analysis to build the model it may become clear that only a small subset of variables are useful and should be included in the segmentation model. These key demographic/deprivation indices/ knowledge/attitudinal and behavioural variables can be included on a small questionnaire module to survey the local population and allocate respondents to each of the segments. See the case study in Box 7.1 in the next section for an example of this.

Three case studies

The case studies in Boxes 7.1–7.3 illustrate various approaches to developing insight and building segmentations. Some are examples of single-issue interventions with a local focus, and others include national segmentations which look at several health issues with common attitudinal, behavioural, and social determinants. Each case study features its own insight or segmentation challenges.

Conclusion

Developing an in-depth understanding of your audience using research and segmentation underpins effective social marketing. Many programmes jump too quickly into the design and implementation stage, without taking enough time to study the target group at the programme scoping stage. Social marketing, social advertising and health promotion are littered with examples of interventions which display little understanding of the beliefs and aspirations of their target audiences and why they behave as they do, often within socially and materially deprived communities.

Talking to people and 'walking in their space' for a while develops an appreciation of the challenges they face every day. Having this insight and knowledge will help with understanding

Box 7.1 Case study: using quantitative data to create a segmentation—the 'healthy life stage' segmentation

Working with the Department of Health (DH) for England, Word of Mouth Research Ltd and GfK Research Ltd developed a life stage segmentation which built on existing research and knowledge within DH and academia to create a segmentation of the nation's health—i.e. to define groups with varying degrees of motivation. The work focused on the drivers of behaviour across six key areas: smoking, obesity, alcohol, substance misuse, sexual health, and mental health (Williams et al., 2011).

Methodology

If we were starting from scratch to produce a health-related segmentation of the general population, we would look at an existing general population survey which included:

- health measurement across the six areas (for example, using knowledge, attitudes, beliefs, and behaviour studies);
- an assessment of risk, self-esteem, and locus of control;
- indicators of motivation to change;
- environmental or structural measurements—deprivation indicators and social norms;
- people's use of services and their views about services;
- lifestyle indicators: social life, family life, aspirations, what people read, what they watch;
- their views about professionals and government; and
- demography: sex, age, class, ethnicity, etc.

Using this data we would conduct a factor analysis and a cluster analysis. These are statistical techniques commonly used to analyse survey data into a number of segments. Unfortunately, no such dataset exists. Government surveys and campaigns tend to concentrate on single issues. Occasionally, some smoking surveys ask about alcohol use or a sexual health survey asks about alcohol use prior to sexual activity. The Health Survey for England covers many of the behavioural indicators of interest but includes very few attitude questions. Very few health surveys include attitude questions and fewer still ask about self-esteem, locus of control, or perceived social norms. Campaign tracking studies usually have more detailed attitude statements, but again they tend to focus on single issues. There are valid reasons for this deficit. Apart from the difficulty of getting buy-in from several government departments with different responsibilities and funding streams, there are considerable methodological challenges in condensing all the issues into an interview of between 45 and 60 minutes.

In the absence of this cross-issue survey with motivational and environmental indicators, the healthy life stage hypothesis was created from extensive desk research and stakeholder interviews with the DH and others with expertise in behaviour change.

Segmentation

Three overarching dimensions were identified as having the greatest significance when identifying population segments most likely to adopt 'at risk' behaviours in relation to health. These are:

- the circumstances/environments in which people live—the 'environment' dimension;

- ◆ their attitudes and beliefs towards health and health issues and the sense of control they have over their health—the 'motivation' axis;
- ◆ age/life stage—the 'life stage' axis.

Constructing the motivation dimension

Some of the constructs relevant to the motivation dimension, such as self-esteem and locus of control, have a considerable body of literature behind them exploring the relationship between these variables and health behaviours. Other constructs such as health fatalism, having a short-term view of life, and the role of external and internal aspirations have been less well researched but had featured regularly in the qualitative research conducted when developing interventions for DH. The only psychological constructs included were those which had been robustly shown to have an impact on health behaviour, and for which reliable measurement indicators were readily available.

The scales selected were anticipated regret, aspirations, attitude to risk, attitudes to healthy living, behavioural intentions, fatalism, health as a value, health consciousness, health locus of control, self-efficacy, self-esteem, self-positivity bias, self-regulation, social desirability bias, and perceived parental autonomy support. A number of stages of piloting were conducted to explore options for reducing the list of statements to a manageable number in a statistically robust way.

Constructing the environment dimension

Following a rapid review of the literature, the established and easily accessed indices of multiple deprivation (DCLG, 2007) were chosen as the axis for the social and environmental dimension of the segmentation.

Methods

Following stratification, a random sample of 4,928 adults aged 16–74 years living in England were interviewed face-to-face on all these measures using a 60-minute questionnaire.

Generating the segmentation: a two-staged approach

When segmenting a population, the aim should be to define a small number of groups so that all members of a particular group are as similar to each other as possible and are as different as possible from the other groups. A cluster analysis generates segments and diagnostics which assess these attributes.

The segmentation was built in two stages: first the population was segmented by health motivation, and each motivation segment was divided by the environment dimension represented by indices of multiple deprivation. Next, the distribution of the final segmentation solution within each of the defined life stages was calculated to produce the final overall segmentation solution.

The segment descriptions

The segments were named based on an analysis of their responses to the attitude statements on the questionnaire. While providing a simple label for communicating the findings, segment names tend to be very reductive and can lead to a skewed representation of the data. A better description of people in each segment is given by constructing a brief pen portrait based on respondents' attitudes (Table 7.2).

Table 7.2 The segment descriptions

Segment	Size, age, proportion in routine and manual occupation	Description of segment
Unconfident fatalists	Population size: 18% of 16–74 year olds = 6.8 million adults in England Average age = 46.8 years (average age of whole sample = 42.7 years) Proportion in routine and manual occupations = 43% (average for the whole sample = 35%)	Overall, they feel fairly negative about things, and don't feel good about themselves. A significant proportion feel depressed. They feel that a healthy lifestyle would not be easy or under their control. Generally, they don't feel in control of their health anyway. They are quite fatalistic about health and think that they are more likely than other people of the same age to become ill. Their current lifestyles aren't very healthy, and their health isn't currently as good as it could be. They know that their health is bad and that they should do something about it, but feel too demotivated to act.
Live for todays	Population size: 25% = 9.5 million adults Average age = 42.4 years Proportion in routine and manual occupations = 42% (average for the whole sample = 35%)	They definitely like to 'live for today' and take a short-term view of life. They believe that whatever they do is unlikely to have an impact on their health. They tend to believe in fate, both where their health is concerned and for other things in life. They value their health but believe that leading a healthy lifestyle doesn't sound like much fun, and think it would be difficult. They don't think they are any more likely than anyone else to become ill in the future. They tend to live in more deprived areas. They don't feel that good about themselves, but they feel more positive about life than the 'unconfident fatalists'. They are the segment who are most likely to be resistant to change and don't acknowledge that their behaviour needs to change, unlike the 'unconfident fatalists'.
Hedonistic immortals	Population size: 19% = 7.2 million adults Average age = 36.1 years Proportion in routine and manual occupations = 25%; (average for the whole sample = 35%)	These are people who want to get the most from life and they don't mind taking risks, as they believe that this is part of leading a full life. They feel good about themselves and are not particularly motivated by material wealth or possessions, or how they look. They know that their health is important to avoid becoming ill in the future, but feel quite positive about their health at the moment and don't think they'll be becoming ill any time soon. Maybe because of that they don't really value their health right now. They are not fatalistic about their health and don't have a problem with leading a healthy lifestyle, believing that it would be fairly easy and enjoyable to do so. They say they intend to lead a healthy lifestyle; however, they feel that anything that is enjoyable, such as smoking and drinking, cannot be all bad.

Segment	Size, age, proportion in routine and manual occupation	Description of segment
Balanced compensators	Population size: 17% = 6.5 million adults Average age = 41.2 years Proportion in routine and manual occupations = 35% (average for the whole sample = 35%)	They are positive and like to look good and feel good about themselves. They get some pleasure from taking risks. However, they don't take risks with health. Health is very important to them, and something they feel in control of. A healthy lifestyle is generally easy and enjoyable. They are not fatalists when it comes to health and understand that their actions have an impact on their health both now and in the future. They believe they are much less likely to become ill than their peers. If they do take some health risks, they will use compensatory mechanisms to make up for this, such as going for a run in the morning having eaten a big meal or drunk too much the night before.
Health-conscious realists	Population size: 21% = 8.0 million adults Average age = 46.7 years Proportion in routine and manual occupations = 27% (average for the whole sample = 35%)	These are motivated people who feel in control of their lives and their health. They generally feel good about themselves, but have more internally focused aspirations to better themselves, learn more, and have good relationships, rather than just aspiring to looking good and acquiring wealth. They tend not to take risks and take a longer-term view of life, and that applies to their health too. Their health is very important to them, and they feel that a healthy lifestyle is both easy to achieve and enjoyable. They also take a realistic view of their health: of all the segments, they are the least fatalistic about their health, and don't think they are any more or less likely than other people to become ill. Unlike the 'balanced compensators', they don't use compensatory mechanisms. This may be because they are so health-conscious that there's no need for them to balance out health behaviours.

Each of the five segments exists in deprived and affluent areas to a greater or lesser degree. The five segments can be broadly mapped onto the hypothetical segmentation matrix showing the segment distribution by motivation and deprivation (Figure 7.1).

However, this is not the final segmentation. Life stage is an important driver for many behaviours. For example, moving from school to college or school to work, having children, getting divorced, looking after relatives, and the whole landscape of retirement can create positive and negative health opportunities for people, and this has to be factored into the segmentation (Table 7.3).

Pulling the three dimensions (environment, motivation, and life stage) together creates a richer segmentation without adding more complexity. Within each life stage all of the five motivation segments exist to a greater or lesser degree. It should be acknowledged that working with three dimensions rather than two is relatively unusual in segmentation, but it is

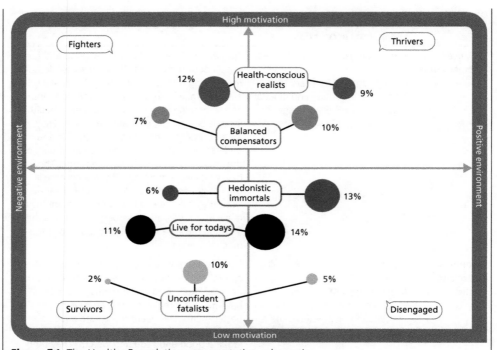

Figure 7.1 The Healthy Foundations segmentation schematic.
Reproduced with permission from Williams B, McVey D, Davies L, and MacGregor E. *The Healthy Foundations lifestages segmentation research: report No. 1: creating the segmentation using a quantitative survey of the general population of England.* London: Department of Health, Copyright © 2011 Crown Copyright, http://www.nsmcentre.org.uk/sites/default/files/301846_HFLS%20Report%20No1_ACC.pdf, accessed 09 Aug. 2016.

Table 7.3 Life stages

Life stage	Age range
Childhood	0–11 years
Discovery teens	mainly 12–15 years put could go up to 18 years
Freedom years	mainly 16–24 but could go up to 40 years
Young settlers (no dependents)	mainly 25–39 years
Young jugglers (with dependents)	mainly 25–39 years
Older settlers (no dependents)	mainly 40–59 years but could go up to 65 years
Older jugglers (with dependents)	mainly 40–59 years but could go up to 65 years
Alone again	mainly 45–59 years but could be as young as 20 or as old as 75 years
Active retirement	mainly 60–74 years but could go up to 80 years
Ageing retirement	mainly 75 years plus but could be as young as 60 years

clear from research that the ambition of the task (looking across the entire population on a range of health issues) required this extra level of sophistication if the work was to be useful for public health practitioners.

The allocation algorithm—'the profiler'

The original questionnaire for this study was just over an hour long. Using only 19 questions from the study and a simple spreadsheet algorithm, it was possible to allocate respondents to one of the five motivation segments to an accuracy of 88%. Using only six questions, it is possible to allocate respondents to one of the five motivation segments to an accuracy of 67%. Either of these small questionnaires could be added to existing national and local health and lifestyle questionnaires to identify the segment grouping for each respondent.

What does the segmentation tell us?

What is partially captured in this simple and intuitive segmentation schematic is the interaction between *structure* and *personal agency*. To a fair degree, the two axes of the segmentation reflect these variables and, therefore, capture a key feature neglected in many segmentations: the influence of social deprivation and social inequalities on personal motivations to change and vice versa.

The primary aims of this segmentation were to locate the greatest need in the population, to identify what can reasonably be achieved by typical intervention approaches, and to articulate which interlocking deprivation and motivation factors should be taken into account when designing new approaches. Further qualitative work was conducted with representatives from each segment to further understand the drivers and barriers to change and to assess the types of intervention approach most likely to work with each group (Smith et al., 2011).

Among the many uses of this strategic segmentation was the exploration of cross-issue interventions, combining health messages with delivering a more holistic customer-centred approach. For example, rather than simply targeting people's smoking behaviour or drinking behaviour separately via different interventions or services, it may be valuable to explore the common drivers for both behaviours within each segment and address them concurrently.

References

DCLG (2007). Indices of deprivation 2007 [website]. London: Department of Communities and Local Government http://webarchive.nationalarchives.gov.uk/20100410180038/http://communities.gov.uk/communities/neighbourhoodrenewal/deprivation/deprivation07/, accessed October 2015.

Smith, A., Heslington, L., La Placa, V., McVey, D., MacGregor, E. (2011). *The Healthy Foundations lifestage segmentation research report No. 2: the qualitative analysis of the motivation segments.* London: Department of Health http://www.thensmc.com/resource/healthy-foundations-lifestages-model-report-2, accessed 9 August 2016.

Williams, B., McVey, D., Davies, L., MacGregor E. (2011). *The Healthy Foundations lifestages segmentation research report No. 1: creating the segmentation using a quantitative survey of the general population of England.* London: Department of Health http://www.nsmcentre.org.uk/sites/default/files/301846_HFLS%20Report%20No1_ACC.pdf, accessed 1 October 2015.

Box 7.2 Case study: using qualitative data to create a segmentation—the 'Medicines management behaviour change' project

The problem

The estimated annual cost of wasted medicines to the NHS is more than £300 million or £1 wasted for every £25 spent.

The project

This project used a social marketing approach to examine the use of medicines by patients and health care professionals across the north-east of England and to suggest ways to improve adherence to medicine taking, improve health outcomes, and reduce wastage in target groups (patients and health care professionals).

There already existed a number of research studies examining intentional and unintentional barriers to medicine adherence. It is estimated that up to 50% of non-adherence is intentional. Broadly, this relates to social and psychological factors such as lack of knowledge of the benefits of adherence; previous experience or anticipation of unpleasant side effects; previous experience of medicine taking as painful or stigmatizing; beliefs that medicines are ineffective or that there is an alternative; low self-efficacy; lack of high-quality, professional support; lack of familial support; fear of running out of medicines; belief that refusing medicines may 'offend' general practitioners (GPs) or be interpreted as recovery, which may affect benefit payments or relationships; and financial barriers. There is also extensive evidence that mental illness is a significant risk factor here.

Unintentional non-adherence tended to relate to systems, processes, and environmental factors generally beyond the control of the patient; complex treatment regimes; capability and capacity; forgetfulness; misinterpretation; access to medicine-taking support—where patients are housebound or in 'assisted living' housing; change of medicines and/or appearance of medicines; unduly long prescription durations; inconsistent or conflicting advice or prescribing; repeat treatment prescribing and dispensing; lack of medicine use support in home settings; and life and routine-breaking events.

These issues were explored in more depth via qualitative research to create patient/customer journeys and a segmentation identifying the key target groups and the appropriate interventions to reach them. The findings are based on more than 1,000 pages of transcripts from 29 in-depth interviews with health care professionals; 21 patient interviews; 13 interviews about repeat prescribing and medicine use reviews conducted with pharmacists or GPs); eight interviews with housebound patients recently discharged from hospital; two focus groups with patients; and 13 self-completed pharmacy surveys.

Results

There were many complex and valuable insights from this research which needed summarizing into an easily understandable form. These included attitudinal, behavioural, and demographic variables, as well as data on patient journeys and health system factors which encourage or hinder medicine adherence. These were broken down into manageable units of analysis and then recombined into more easily understood and hence actionable findings (Crosier and McVey, 2012).

Adherence spectrum

Based on the available data a 'spectrum of adherence' was created, which described the various reasons for a patient's adherence or non-adherence (Figure 7.2).

Patient journeys

A number of patient journeys were constructed from the qualitative data which described a patient journey from receiving a repeat prescription to having a medicine use review with a pharmacist or GP, and then the journey from home to hospital and back again, and the effect on medicine adherence during these stages.

The range of interventions

There already existed a number of possible interventions for improving medicine adherence and reducing waste; these were combined with a few additional interventions suggested by the research which could be deployed at particular points on the patient journey:

◆ developing a medicine value campaign and a practitioner toolkit—raising awareness about medicine waste and setting norms in the Clinical Commissioning Group;

◆ promoting the Green Bag scheme to minimize waste;

◆ replacing managed repeats with repeat dispensing;

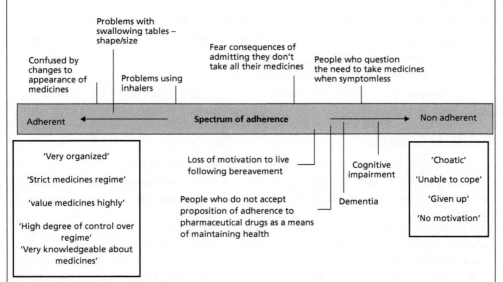

Figure 7.2 The spectrum of adherence.
Reproduced by kind permission of Adam Crosier and Dominic McVey, Copyright © 2012 Adam Crosier and Dominic McVey.

- providing more domiciliary medicine use reviews/home visits to support medicine taking for the housebound;
- inviting selected patients to attend their medication review and referring to a community pharmacy for a targeted medicine use review if the need for support is identified;
- improving communication between professional groups: GPs, hospitals, community pharmacists, community nurses, and between professional groups and the patient.

Segmentation

Based on the insights gained from the study, a segmentation of the patient group was proposed. The purpose of this segmentation was to:

- identify the behavioural and attitudinal traits that may be more or less modifiable in relation to non-adherence;
- focus attention on key groups within the overall 'over 60, long-term condition' patient group, where actions may be best targeted.

Both health professionals' and patients' interviews identified attitudes and behaviours that were used to construct the segmentation. This reflects learning about the 'spectrum of adherence', key situational, and life stage factors, as well as motivational factors including attitudes and norms.

Naming segments should provide an identifiable shorthand for a set of characteristics which can be communicated easily across professional groups.

Three segments were identified. Naming them after UK television cooks caught the attention of the professional audience and the names became the shorthand descriptors when discussing each group:

- *GORDON* (**G**enerally **O**lder **R**egularly **D**ischarged cha**O**tic and **N**on-adherent)
  - patients frequently re-admitted to hospital—older, more ill, and frequently non-adherent and chaotic;
- *HUGH* (**H**ousebound; **U**nlikely to **G**et GP's **H**elp)
  - patients who are effectively 'hidden' from services—likely to be housebound, living alone, lacking family support, on repeat prescription but not having their health needs monitored, and visible to health services only when a crisis occurs;
- *DELIA* (**D**oing **E**verything for **L**iving; **I**n general **A**dherent)
  - younger, in better health, not housebound, with family support.

Overlaying the segment definitions onto the various patient journeys provided a useful analysis of the key journey points for each segment and the most appropriate interventions to apply.

As this was a qualitative segmentation, it was not possible to size groups but this could be done using service and survey data. What can be said with a fair degree of confidence is that these attitudinal and behavioural segments exist and operate within these patient journeys and that specific segments are more likely to respond to the targeted interventions suggested for each of them (Figure 7.3).

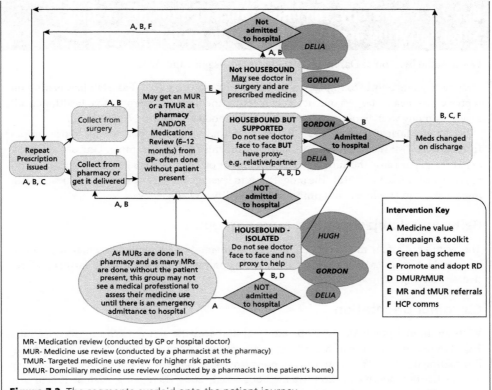

Figure 7.3 The segments overlaid onto the patient journey.
Reproduced by kind permission of Adam Crosier and Dominic McVey, Copyright © 2012 Adam Crosier and Dominic McVey.

This research deconstructed an opaque problem with many complex dimensions into several clearly defined facets (the adherence spectrum, patient journeys, segments and intervention options) and then combined them onto a more easily digestible and hence actionable form.

Reference

Crosier, A., McVey, D. (2012). *Presentation to the North East of England Medicines Management Behaviour Change Project*. Hampton: Word of Mouth Research www.womresearch.org.uk, accessed August 2016.

Box 7.3 Case study: the importance of audience insight—Suraj, ensuring access to the poor in rural Pakistan

Contributed by: Komal Daredia, Qaiser Jamshad Asghar, and Asma Balal

Despite ongoing efforts to improve access to family planning (FP), Pakistan lags behind on reproductive health targets, particularly meeting the need for reproductive health and FP services among women of reproductive age (Mahmood and Dur-e-Nayab, 2000).

In 2008, Marie Stopes Society Pakistan, a leading global partner of Marie Stopes International (MSI), launched its Suraj social franchise (SF) programme. One of the largest networks in Pakistan, the Suraj SF network consists of 550 providers in peri-urban and rural areas (Saeed and Khan, 2010). The model aims to leverage the private sector to achieve health impact and equity while maintaining service quality and efficiency.

Behavioural objectives and target group

The overall goal of the model is to increase uptake of modern FP methods by married women of reproductive age (MWRA), especially focusing on young MWRA in their early reproductive years living in rural Pakistan.

Customer orientation

With an annual population growth rate that outpaces the slowly declining fertility rate, Pakistan may become the fifth most populous country in the world by 2050 (NIPS and ICF International, 2013). The contraceptive prevalence rate is low for a middle-income country and the use of modern contraceptive methods is only 26%. There is a persistent 20% unmet need for FP services (NIPS and ICF International, 2013).

MWRA in rural areas are less likely to use contraception (31%) than their urban counterparts (45%) (NIPS and ICF International, 2013). These women tend to be impoverished and have low literacy and poor access to accurate information about FP. Due to patriarchal cultural norms, they often lack access to household finances and have limited decision-making powers, and thus have low self-efficacy for seeking FP services (Saigol, 2011).

The social offering

The Suraj SF network offers rural, underserved, and poor communities a range of affordable and high-quality FP options for the healthy spacing of pregnancies, as well as counselling services. The majority of the Suraj network members are mid-level providers such as nurses or midwives. Suraj providers are trained in FP methods, basic business skills, and other network standards. Each Suraj franchise has one dedicated field health educator (FHE) to promote awareness and uptake of modern FP methods among MWRA and market Suraj in the catchment community. FHEs also distribute free FP service vouchers to MWRA who are identified as poor or who do not have personal access to household funds. In terms of competition analysis, most people in Pakistan seek services at private facilities due to perceptions of poor quality as well as lack of available drugs, equipment, or sufficiently trained staff at public facilities (Zaidi et al., 2013). Private sector service provision in rural areas is relatively low and tends to centre on product delivery over service delivery. The Suraj SF network's focus on service delivery through its unique quality assurance approach positions it differently from the other providers in the community.

Audience insight and segmentation

FHEs conduct *mohalla*: meetings with groups of MWRA within their neighbourhood. During these meetings, FHEs create awareness about available FP services among non-user MWRA, and they also follow up with current clients or those who showed an intention to adopt an FP method. The FHEs, like providers across the Suraj network, are mostly female, in order to increase the comfort of the interaction and gaining insights from women in the target population (Figure 7.4).

Baseline research indicated that prominent reasons for unmet need of FP are lack of access to services (such as an inability to pay or lack of transportation) and unfavourable attitudes towards FP methods (Azmat et al., 2012). Evidence from other studies indicates that decision-making for FP at the household level is strongly influenced by patriarchal norms, and that even with the right information and access to FP services, women are often unable to make the decision to adopt FP. These findings suggested a need to address community-level issues of inclusion, social capital, community capability, and empowerment.

The insight-informed intervention mix

The Suraj service offering is complemented by a behaviour change strategy called IRADA (improving reproductive health through awareness, decision and action) led by FHEs and community mobilizers. Popular opinion leaders facilitate social action projects to address the underlying societal factors that present barriers to access for women. Widespread branding of Suraj, provision of culturally congruent health education materials, a toll-free number for information and counselling services, street theatre, and films and songs enhance visibility

Figure 7.4 The Suraj Social Franchise programme: providing reproductive health and family planning support to peri-urban and rural communities in Pakistan.
Reproduced by kind permission of Marie Stopes Society Pakistan, Copyright © 2016 Marie Stopes Society Pakistan.

and lead to uptake of service provision. The Suraj SF network brings many individual private providers under an umbrella entity that is big enough to yield benefits of economies of scale—combined supply chains, training, supervision, branding, and communication—and yet nimble enough to respond to individual clients' needs. Suraj clinics are thus able to offer affordable and high-quality FP services.

Results and learning

Between November 2008 and February 2015, Suraj reached almost 1.5 million clients, 30% of whom accessed FP services using free service vouchers. Nearly half of these clients received intrauterine device services, indicating that the programme successfully addressed myths and misconceptions and increased access to this long-term method.

The Suraj SF network was recognized in 2014 as the highest-scoring network on MSI's internal quality audit, which is used across 17 MSI country programmes operating social franchise networks. It was also awarded the 2011 International Quality Award by the Global Health Group, University of California, San Francisco.

Suraj has also demonstrated that private providers are willing and able to offer high-quality FP services and are willing to invest in their own clinics to meet franchise network standards. In an uncertain funding environment, this result suggests that Suraj-trained providers will be able to sustain quality FP service provision to meet the needs of their communities.

References

Azmat, S.K., Mustafa, G., Hameed W., Ali, M., Ahmed, A., Bilgrami, M. (2012). Barriers and perceptions regarding different contraceptives and family planning practices. *Pakistan Journal of Public Health* **2**(1).

Mahmood, N., Durr-e-Nayab. (2000). An analysis of reproductive health issues in Pakistan. *The Pakistan Development Review* **39**(4): 675–693.

NIPS, ICF International (2013). *Pakistan demographic and health survey 2012–13.* Islamabad and Calverton, MD: National Institute of Population Studies and ICF International.

Saeed, R., Khan, F.K. (2010). *Case study: 'Suraj'—a private provider partnership.* Karachi: Marie Stopes Society.

Saigol, R. (2011). *Women's empowerment in Pakistan—a scoping study.* Islamabad: Aurat Publication and Information Services Foundation.

Zaidi, S., Rabbani, F., Riaz, A., Pradhan, N., Hatcher, P. (2013). *Improvement in access and equity for maternal and newborn health services: comparative advantages of contracted out versus non-contracted facilities.* Islamabad: Research and Advocacy Fund, British Council.

the audience 'exchange' and with building strong message propositions which will be relevant and salient to the target group. If applied appropriately, this will result in interventions with the best chance of success. At the very least it will help avoid the costly errors associated with poorly conceived programmes which neglected to take the time to listen and understand their audiences.

Self-review questions

1. How can the use of segmentation strengthen the development of public health social marketing planning?

2. List the reasons segmentation in public health is essential for the delivery of more effective and efficient behavioural interventions.

3. Describe the key stages in the development of a segmentation model to inform public health interventions aimed at influencing health behaviour.

References

Acheson, D. (1998). Independent inquiry into inequalities in health—report. London: Department of Health.

Capewell, S., Graham, H. (2010). Will cardiovascular disease prevention widen health inequalities? *PLoS Medicine* 7(8): e1000320 doi:10.1371/journal.pmed.1000320.

GCN (2009). Engage programme [website]. London: **Government Communications Network** https://www.comms.gov.uk/, accessed February 2009.

Graham, H. (1993). *When life's a drag: women, smoking and disadvantage.* London: The Stationery Office.

HDA (2004). *The effectiveness of public health campaigns: consumers and markets. Briefing No. 7, June 2004.* London: Health Development Agency.

Lee, H. (1960). *To kill a mockingbird.* Philadelphia: Lippincott: 30.

McVey, D., Crosier, A. (2013). *Guide to segmentation in relation to pandemic influenza E-Com@Eu Programme Work Programme 3. EU Seventh Framework programme.* Liphook: Strategic Social Marketing Ltd.

McVey, D., Walsh, L. (2010). Generating insight and building segmentations—moving beyond simple targeting. In: J. French, C. Blair-Stevens, D. McVey, R. Merritt (eds). *Social marketing and public health: theory and practice,* 1st edition. Oxford: Oxford University Press.

Rose, G. (1992). *The strategy of preventive medicine.* Oxford: Oxford University Press

Varney, D. (2006). *Service transformation: a better service for citizens and business, a better deal for taxpayers.* London: The Stationery Office.

Chapter 8

Commissioning social marketing

Jeff French

Nowadays people know the price of everything and the value of nothing.
Oscar Wilde, *The Picture of Dorian Gray*

Learning points

This chapter:

◆ provides guidance on how and when to commission all aspects of social marketing from scoping, testing, enacting and learning, and follow-up action;

◆ provides an understanding of the fundamental concepts of commissioning social marketing programmes, projects, interventions, research, and evaluation;

◆ covers the essential elements of developing tender documents, procuring suppliers, selecting potential suppliers, and managing the supplier–client relationship;

◆ gives guidance on how to manage suppliers and assess progress and value for money.

Introduction to why quality commissioning is key to successful social marketing

Pigott (2000: 156) defines commissioning as: 'the strategic activity of assessing needs, resources and current services, and developing a strategy to make best use of available resources'. Countries from all over the world spend huge amounts of money, time, and effort setting up, delivering, and attempting to evaluate programmes aimed at influencing behaviour. Many developed countries also spend a great deal of money on aid programmes in developing countries aimed at influencing health behaviour in relation to issues such as malaria prevention, HIV prevention and management, and basic sanitation programmes. Unfortunately, many of these programmes are poorly set up and consequently perform less well than they could have if the people commissioning the programmes had taken a more systematic approach to setting out more precisely what they were hoping to achieve, how learning would be captured, and how programme evaluation and reporting would be carried out.

Commissioning in the not-for-profit sector is a key means for securing best value and quality improvement in public services. The term 'best value' means both the best possible outcome and the best possible return on the investment. Best value is also concerned with the quality of service provision—this implies that in addition to effectiveness and efficiency measures, an agreed set of quality standards and metrics also need to be included within commissioning frameworks.

The commissioning of social marketing initiatives and other activity that puts people at the centre of service delivery is part of this wider set of responsibilities. Effective commissioning of such initiatives should lead to improved impact and outcome of social marketing programmes and enhance the quality, responsiveness, and efficiency of these interventions. Good commissioning also leads to improved understanding of service users' or target audiences' needs and helpful feedback about what worked, what did not, and why this was the case. This kind of feedback should result in a cycle of positive progressive improvement in programme design and delivery.

Commissioning is essentially transformational and not just transactional. It incorporates 'contracting' and 'procurement' as mechanisms for achieving higher commissioning objectives. Those who are leading the commissioning need to display visionary leadership and to operate with tact, assertiveness, and skill.

> *They draw legitimacy from being seen to be engaged with communities, with service providers and with partner agencies drawing complementary views into a credible and coherent plan to which all sign up—putting the 'mission' into commissioning.*
>
> *Increasingly commissioners will be locally perceived as investors; that is, they commission to achieve the greatest health gains, return on investment and reduction in inequalities at best value. The process is often referred to as 'commissioning for improved outcomes'.*

(NHS, 2007: 5)

Commissioning can take place between public sector organizations, where one branch of the service acts as an executive commissioning agency and the other acts as a delivery arm. However, in social marketing, commissioning often involves outsourcing or buying in specialist services from external private sector or third sector suppliers. 'Outsourcing' can be defined as the provision, generally by a third party, of defined services and activities, typically involving a transfer of assets, intellectual property, and/or staff. Organizations across the private, public, and third sectors are increasing the number of functions they outsource and are becoming the holders of a variety of outsourcing contracts. As outsourcing increases, and with it the interdependence between commissioners and suppliers, the nature of contractual arrangements is changing from being prescriptive and punitive (driven by bottom-line performance) to a situation that is more relational, and based on greater transparency, trust, and working towards a common goal over time (Box 8.1).

Decisions about what to commission should be informed by answers to questions such as the following.

◆ Can suppliers provide the service at lower cost?
◆ Are specialist suppliers needed for a defined time period?
◆ Do suppliers have skills that are not available internally?
◆ Are there opportunities to reduce risk by using suppliers?
◆ Is there is a need to reduce core organizational running costs or simplify internal systems?

Nussle and Orszag (2014) and colleagues argue that too often policy-makers rely on instinct, or special interests, when deciding how to invest taxpayers' money. Data from the US Government

Box 8.1 Case study: two examples of how poor commissioning supports ineffective and inefficient intervention continuation

Scared Straight (USA)

Scared Straight is a programme that started in New Jersey in the USA in the 1970s. The programme brings at-risk youths face-to-face with prison inmates, aiming to scare the young people into not committing crimes by talking to them about the brutality of life in prison. This project programme became more widely known from a 2013 reality TV show called *Beyond Scared Straight*, which takes viewers inside prisons for young people to explore their lives and their reactions to being in prison.

Evaluation has shown, however, that Scared Straight and similar programmes are effective—at *increasing* criminal behaviour. Research conducted by Petrosino et al. (2013) and researchers at the Campbell Collaboration showed that instead of turning young people away from criminality, the programmes actually made things worse. Of those who attended the programmes there seemed to be an increase of approximately 12% in the proportion who went on to commit a crime.

21st Century Community Learning Centers (USA)

The American government's after-school programme, 21st Century Community Learning Centers, has not demonstrated any positive effect on academic outcomes among elementary-school children. It has been shown, however, to significantly *increase* the number of school suspensions and incidents requiring other forms of discipline.

In the mid 2000s the government planned to halve the funding of this programme owing to its weak performance. However, following lobbying by many provider organizations and personalities such as Arnold Schwarzenegger, the government agreed to restore all funding. In 2015 the programme was granted more than $1 billion a year in federal funds.

References

Petrosino, A., Buehler, J., Turpin-Petrosino, C. (2013). Scared Straight and other juvenile awareness programs for preventing juvenile delinquency: a systematic review. *The Campbell Collaboration Library of Systematic Reviews* 9(5).

U.S. Department of Education (2016). Programs: 21st Century Community Learning Centers [website]. Washington, DC: U.S. Department of Education http://www2.ed.gov/programs/21stcclc/performance.html, accessed 2 September 2016.

Office of Management and Budget's Program Assessment Rating Tool (2015) shows that less than $1 out every $100 spent by the government is backed by even the most basic evidence that the money is being spent wisely. In their book *Moneyball for government*, Nussle and Orszag (2014) describe how Billy Beane, general manager of the Oakland Athletics baseball team, transformed baseball by using an approach he called 'moneyball'. He proceeded by ignoring scouts' opinions and preferences for players and instead used data to select and build championship-contending teams, despite a limited budget. *Moneyball for government* encourages governments at all levels to increase their use of evidence and data when investing limited taxpayer money. The three basic 'moneyball' principles are that governments at all levels should:

1. build evidence about the practices, policies, and programmes that will achieve the most effective and efficient results so that policy-makers can make better decisions;
2. invest limited taxpayer money in practices, policies, and programmes that use data, evidence, and evaluation to demonstrate they work;
3. direct funds away from practices, policies, and programmes that consistently fail to achieve measurable outcomes.

Governments that use the moneyball approach focus on outcomes and results, rather than on the provision of service, numbers of people served, or activity levels. Data and evidence is used to continuously improve quality and impact, while also reducing duplication and cutting pointless red tape. Governments that apply this approach also invest in scaling-up innovations that work and in enabling communities to collaborate and to use data and evidence to achieve significant community-wide improvements.

Think about strategy as well as about operational tactics

One of the key issues for commissioners is deciding whether they are going to apply a social marketing approach to their overall strategic development or just to specific behavioural challenges and interventions. The following set of questions is designed to help you think through which approach you wish to take. You will be adopting a 'strategic social marketing' approach if you answer yes to most of these questions.

◆ Do you want to help inform your organization's wider policy context and/or related strategic plans?
◆ Do you want to look at a number of behavioural challenges, rather than just focusing on a single behaviour?
◆ Do you want to identify and consider potential connections and synergies between different topics or issues and their related behaviours?
◆ Do you believe that there is an opportunity and value in looking at behaviour 'in the round' before selecting a specific topic or issue?

If you answer yes to the majority of the following questions, you will be adopting more of an 'operational social marketing' approach.

◆ Have you ruled out undertaking a strategic review of the causes of a behaviour, current activity, and possible interventions that you want to influence?
◆ Have decisions already been taken to tackle a specific topic or issue?
◆ Are you clear about what type of social marketing research development you will carry out?
◆ Are you clear about the type or form of intervention you want to commission?

Characteristics of commissioning excellence

A number of characteristics are shared by efficient commissioners of social marketing initiatives, regardless of whether they are taking a strategic or operational approach. These are shown in Box 8.2.

Writing a tender document

Having decided whether you are taking a more strategic or operational focus, the next step is to develop a tender document (a 'brief') that sets out what you wish to commission. The way that tenders need to be put together varies significantly between organizations, and the form and

Box 8.2 Characteristics of commissioning excellence

Excellent commissioners:

♦ collaborate with organizations that share the same strategic and operational goals, and share intelligence and collaboratively plan with partners and stakeholders;

♦ are guided by what works and foster communities that contribute to the design, delivery, and evaluation of social marketing interventions;

♦ specify behavioural outcomes that are clearly set out and communicated;

♦ set out explicit ethical processes that should be followed;

♦ use intelligence and information from target audiences alongside other forms of data and evidence to inform and shape the specifications for social marketing interventions that are to be commissioned;

♦ demonstrate clear evidence of rigorous monitoring of suppliers and holding suppliers to account for delivering programmes to agreed levels of quality, value, and impact.

Source: data from Dr Foster Intelligence. *Intelligent commissioning: intelligence*, Issue 2, September 2007. London: Dr Foster Ltd., Copyright © 2007 Dr Foster Ltd.

focus of the document will vary depending on what type of service you are commissioning and what stage of the initiative you are at. However, the first thing to do is to speak with whoever is in charge of approving and monitoring such documents if you work in an organization with a specialist commissioning or procurement function, to ensure that you are following the correct procedure and including all the elements your organization requires.

The time spent developing your brief is time well spent. It will save time and money later. Sometimes, however, less can be more: do not clutter the brief with unnecessary background information or statistics that are irrelevant. Some examples of what tender documents might focus on are contained in Figure 8.1.

Tender documents range in length and complexity, but there are common features that should appear. The following checklist has been developed from the guidance given in the CD-ROM 'CDCynegy Social Marketing Edition Three' (CDC, 2006). Before applying it, however, you should also make a judgement about the scale and focus of the work that you are intending to commission, as this will also help inform how comprehensive your tender needs to be.

General information

♦ **Overview of the tender and the issue(s) being addressed**: this is an explanation of why you are producing a tender and the issue(s) being addressed. As well as providing a description of the issue(s), you should set out relevant research data, evidence, and research.

♦ **A clear statement of aims and objectives**: what are your initiative's aims and objectives? Include a description of your organization's current and past work and research in the area.

♦ **Budget/funding level**: you may choose to give an indicative budget or not, depending on your organization's approach. There are advantages in indicating the scale of your available budget, as this helps applicants tailor their proposals. But some organizations prefer not to disclose the available budget in the belief that this will help promote cost competition and keep costs lower.

♦ **Project timescale**: this should include the contract period, start date, and end date.

♦ **Anticipated outputs**: this should specify the expected outputs (such as reports, presentations, and reviews) and dates for their delivery. It should also include the timetable for application and decisions.

Scoping tenders
- Desk-based evidence reviews
- Desk-based data reviews
- Desk-based policy reviews
- Stakeholder surveys and interviews
- Target audience knowledge, attitude, and behaviour surveys
- Target audience service experience surveys or observations
- Development of initial segmentations
- Development of propositions
- Competition analysis
- Review of exiting social marketing case studies on similar topics and/or target audiences
- SMART objectives

Development tenders
- Development of intervention methods and materials
- Pilot of services changes, products, and campaigns
- Development of segmentations and user understanding
- Development of insight and testing propositions
- Testing creative executions
- Coalition building
- Community engagement
- Development of evaluation plans and systems
- Risk analysis

Delivery tenders
- Service delivery contact
- Community engagement programme delivery
- Stakeholder engagement programme delivery
- Media campaign delivery
- Partnership building and coalition formation and management
- Policy lobbying
- Organizational change
- Programme management

Evaluation tenders
- Evaluation of intervention processes
- Evaluation of short-term intervention impact
- Evaluation of knowledge and attitude change
- Evaluation of behavioural change
- Evaluation of physiological change
- Evaluation of partnership and coalition
- Evaluation of specific program and/or campaign elements
- Cost–benefit analysis
- Return on investment analysis

Follow-up tenders
- Project publicity
- Project write-ups
- Conference presentations
- Publications
- Evaluation launches
- Political dissemination strategies

Figure 8.1 Commissioning tenders in social marketing.

Scope of work

This should include:

- a **detailed description of the work to be completed**:
    - specific activities to be undertaken;
    - products to be delivered or developed;
    - research or pre-testing activities to be carried out;
    - evaluation to be designed or carried out;
    - number of items, workshops, staff, or other quantities you expect to be delivered;
- **reports and/or updates you require** during the course of the work, and the means for delivering these;
- **follow-up and dissemination activity required;**
- **ethical considerations.**

If you are commissioning promotional work the promotion commissioning checklist set out in Box 8.3 can help you determine what mix and weight of interventions you need to commission.

Box 8.3 Promotion commissioning checklist

Programme summary

Aim to be achieved

Audiences: primary, secondary, and tertiary

Primary SMART objective

Secondary SMART objectives

Management approval granted for this activity: Yes No

Budgets
Total promotion budget
Channels and methods

TV

Radio

Cinema

Press space

Digital

Mobile/Tablet/Text, etc.

Gaming and in-game promotion

Website

Email

New digital channels

Digital display (e.g. banners, etc.)

Biddable media (e.g. search, Facebook, YouTube)

Virals

Direct marketing, including door drops

Video on demand (VOD)

Online video promotions

Paid-for social media advertising

Second screen promotions

Media sponsorship and support (paid for)

Blogging

Advertorials

Word of mouth

Billboards and other ambient

Product placement

Affiliate/paid-for search marketing/click to call

Print materials

Events

Sponsorships

Timing

When each of the activities will start and end:

Focus

Location for each promotional intervention:

Country/region/city/area (specify):

Supplier details

- **Eligibility criteria:** this sets out who may apply. You may have a requirement that the service is provided by a local supplier or one that has specific skills such as language skills, public relations, media buying and planning, direct marketing, merchandizing, new media, creative development, research or survey design, and delivery. You may require submissions only by agencies with certain experience (e.g. marketing, public relations, marketing research, specific ethnic group marketing, youth marketing and public education, grassroots organizing, crisis management, and special events).
- **Invoicing:** this includes requirements for invoicing arrangements, timing, and process.
- **Acceptability of joint applications or consortium bids:** you may accept a lead agency affiliated with other agencies with relevant experience (e.g. lead agencies without ethnic marketing experience may still be considered as long as they make it clear in their proposal which subcontractors they would partner with to create the plans for ethnic minorities).
- **Potential/perceived conflict of interest:** you should require a statement of disclosure of affiliation or contractual relationships, direct and indirect, with any agency that you feel is incompatible with your organization's values and/or the aims of the initiative you are funding. You should also ask for details of any other current or previous relationships with such organizations.
- **Supplier questionnaire:** this should include:
  - questions regarding agency mission and philosophy;
  - CVs of the staff who will be working on the project agency;
  - years in business;
  - relevant social marketing experience including past *pro bono* work;
  - financial track record (ask for last three years' audited accounts);
  - examples of past good work and contacts for references;
  - information about how the agency uses research in developing, executing, and evaluating campaigns.
- **Performance requirements:** set out the expected performance required and over what time frame. Also set out any penalty clauses, incentives, and contract break points that you wish to include.

- **Format for the proposal**: these may include ideas for how the work will be developed and delivered, including;
  - supplier name and address;
  - tax and company reference numbers;
  - lead contact information;
  - rationale for the project;
  - proposed approach;
  - mix of interventions and tasks;
  - timetable;
  - stakeholder and partnering arrangements;
  - research and evaluation elements;
  - outline of budget allocations;
  - approach to ongoing tracking and reporting; and
  - examples (include the standard format for cover sheet, budget, and action plan, e.g. as appendices).

Having a standardized approach to submission formats that can be set out as online application forms can help prevent glossy or lavish applications that may distract from a systematic assessment of the applications based on their content.

Process for preparing and submitting proposals

- **Application deadlines:** include letters of intent (confirming intent to submit a full proposal) and complete proposal package.
- **Key contact information at your organization**: include information on how to submit questions and how they will be responded to. It is good practice to make a public record of all questions submitted by potential suppliers and the answers given, so that these can be seen by all potential suppliers. It is also a good idea to include a question-and-answer sheet with the tender documentation, as this will help reduce the number of subsequent enquiries.
- **Instructions for how to submit an application:** this should include a date and time, the number of copies required, and whether fax or email versions are acceptable. You should also include instructions for oral presentations, including the time, date, location, and form of presentation or pitch interview.
- **Instructions for how to withdraw an application** should be included.
- **Reasons for disqualification:** these may include
  - incomplete or late submission;
  - failure to meet requirements;
  - submitting an application with false, inaccurate, or misleading statements; and
  - unwillingness or inability to comply fully with the proposed contract provisions.

Review, evaluation, and selection

You will need to set out the criteria for evaluation and, ideally, the respective weighting given to each criteria. You can use the guidance in this chapter concerning the assessment of suppliers and their proposals as a basis for agreeing what factors you are looking for.

Other inclusions and issues

As stated in the preceding sections, you will need to be clear on your organization's rules about how contracts should be signed and who can sign them. Other issues that should be built into tender documents include:

◆ reasons for termination of contract;
◆ the right to remove or replace subcontractors;
◆ the responsibility or liability for costs incurred by bidders prior to contract award;
◆ the confidentiality policy; and
◆ your organization's terms and conditions (e.g. intellectual property rights, payments, indemnity, liability, insurance, termination, and records maintenance).

Creating a positive pitch meeting environment

When conducting a meeting with possible suppliers so that they can pitch their proposals to you, it is important to remember that a pitch meeting should not be viewed as performance but rather as a dialogue. As a potential client, you need to create a positive experience in which the potential suppler and your organization can gain the best possible sense of what is on offer in terms of skills, experience, and ideas from both sides. When you are planning pitch meetings, consider the following questions.

◆ Do you need a facilitator for the meeting?
◆ Did you answer all of the agencies' questions prior to the pitch?
◆ Have you provided all the research reports and other background material that the supplier might need?
◆ Are you going to hold a single meeting or a set of meetings before you make decisions?
◆ Have suppliers had a reasonable amount of time to prepare?
◆ How will you react to challenges to the brief from the supplier?
◆ Do you have a set of explicit written criteria that all those people on the selection panel will use to evaluate each pitch?
◆ What system have you put in place to feed back to all those who pitched?
◆ Are you putting in place a system for suppliers to give you feedback on the process?

It is simply good practice to treat suppliers that have put effort and expense into pitching for work with respect and ensure that good relations are maintained. Even if a given supplier did not win the contract, you may want to work with them in the future.

Assessing social marketing supplier proposals

Organizational capacity

If you are supporting specialist commissioners to commission social marketing initiatives, or are commissioning on their behalf, you may be using approaches and tools that differ from those they usually use. They need your input and support to critically assess the suppliers that are pitching for work and the proposals they bring forward. You need to be aware, and to make colleagues aware, that there are many suppliers who do not have a deep understanding or track record in delivering successful social marketing programmes but who are skilled in pitching for work. Therefore, it is important that companies bidding for work are interviewed consistently and rigorously to ensure that what they plan to deliver is actually what you require and that you yourself are satisfied that they can deliver it. It is also important that you have systems and resources in place to ensure the ongoing management and monitoring of supplier organizations throughout the contract period, and not just at the start.

Assessing potential suppliers

There are several important issues to consider when assessing the competence and track record of potential social marketing suppliers (Government Communications Network, 2007).

◆ Establish that the potential supplier understands your aims and objectives—do they understand the strategy behind them and how the work you are commissioning will add value?

◆ Look for a track record of effectiveness as well as attractiveness. Were previous initiatives 'fit for purpose' rather than just looking good? Look for evidence of clear behavioural change measures.

◆ Consider supplier size, resources, and position in the market, including the strength of the proposed project team and organizational management team.

◆ Check that they demonstrate a professional understanding of social marketing principles and concepts.

◆ Establish whether they demonstrate an ability to use research techniques to segment, target, and design interventions that meet the needs of distinct target groups.

◆ Check for evidence of an ability to customize solutions. Is there evidence in the supplier's submission that they can understand your challenge, or are they just applying an approach they have used before?

◆ Consider whether they have provided evidence of genuine audience and stakeholder engagement, partnerships, and collaborative delivery.

◆ You will usually want to appoint an organization that has a track record of collaborative delivery and ability to manage local stakeholders and partners. Ask for references and evidence of such work.

◆ Check that the supplier demonstrates a good understanding of your sector and the issues you are concerned with.

◆ Ensure that the supplier is committed to delivering against your targets and clear about the consequences of failing to deliver.

Assessing social marketing proposals checklist

You can use the checklist set out in Table 8.1 to assess the strength of social marketing proposals.

Other recommendations for commissioning suppliers

Avoiding conflict of interest

It may be worth checking out other clients of your proposed supplier to ensure that there is no conflict of interest with your eventual intervention. This is particularly pertinent if agencies work for both commercial and public sector organizations.

Beware of 'add-ons'

In pitching for your commission, an organization may include a few promotional freebies, contests for kids, freephone calls, or helplines, for example. Although these ideas may appear to offer value for money, they may not actually help you archive the results you want; so question how such 'add-ons' will contribute to the overall initiative.

Table 8.1 Checklist for assessing social marketing proposals

Programmes displaying these characteristics are likely to be effective	Yes	No	Unsure
A systematic scoping and development phase has been built into the proposal.			
The proposal contains the need to gather and synthesize insight into the proposed target audience.			
The supplier aims to develop a clear 'exchange proposition' through which advantages of the proposed behavioural change will be spelled out in a way that the target group believes.			
Measurable behavioural goals have been or will be set, and there is a clear process for this.			
Interventions proposed are informed by relevant theoretical models.			
Interventions proposed are informed by a review of evidence about effectiveness.			
Data reviews have been used to inform the development of the proposed strategy.			
Systematic short-, medium-, and long-term planning are clearly set out.			
If appropriate, the plan includes action to establish multisector delivery coalitions to assist in development, delivery, and evaluation.			
The proposed budget allocation is realistic enough to develop, deliver, and evaluate the aims and objectives of the initiative.			
Competitor analysis has been or will be undertaken, and measures to address competitive factors feature in the proposal.			
The proposal sets out a multicomponent strategy that can be delivered in an integrated way.			
There are clear plans to involve the target group in intervention development, implementation, and evaluation.			
Mechanisms will be put in place to coordinate international, national, regional, and local action if appropriate.			
The proposed initiative is complementary to the current policy and delivery environment.			
The plan sets out how any relevant ethical issues will be addressed.			
A comprehensive evaluation strategy is proposed covering process, impact, and outcome evaluation.			

Ongoing management of the organization you commission

Once you have commissioned a supplier and have agreed objectives, it will be necessary to ensure that the supplier is monitored and managed in terms of their performance and that a strong two-way flow of information is maintained over the contract period.

Normally, some form of management group or programme board, consisting of key commissioners and representatives from the supplier agency, will agree to meet to keep the initiative under review, monitor progress, and agree to changes as the programme proceeds. Such a group should work to an agreed set of terms of reference that indicate to whom the group reports in the commissioning organization. The group should also be the forum for resolving issues and challenges that arise as the programme proceeds. The group or committee should meet at appropriate intervals and receive milestone reports from the agency.

It is important not to let the supplier lead the intervention down a route that is not based on hard evidence or goes against what you want. At all stages of an initiative, commissioners should be able to evaluate progress against the original brief to ensure that the initiative remains focused on the original aims and objectives.

Making the most of current evidence

It is widely recognized that investments in social marketing are hampered by a lack of clear and consistent measures of their impact, which leads to inadequate funding (Bennett, 2003; Jackson, 2005; Hay, 2006). However, there is also a growing evidence base that proves that social marketing not only works but is also cost-effective (Hornik, 2002; McDermott et al., 2006; Gordon et al., 2006; Stead et al., 2006; Lister, 2007); see also chapter five).

A key task for any social marketer is to assess the current evidence base. Rather than undertake a systematic review of the evidence, it is usually more practical to search the evidence reviews and 'reviews of reviews' that have been carried out by others and to draw on case study databases. One of the best sites dedicated to providing evidence-based meta-reviews of marketing and communication services is the CDC Community programme. This site publishes guidance and review documents that bring together current evidence about best practice: http://www.thecommunityguide.org/about/What-Works-Health-Communication-factsheet.pdf

Using information gathered from these and other sources will help you answer questions about the probable effectiveness of your eventual intervention. However, commissioners must be aware that only by undertaking a thorough development phase and field testing process with the intended target groups can a more accurate assessment of impact be arrived at.

Ensuring return on investment

One of the central issues facing any marketing agency or marketing managers in the non-governmental organization (NGO), for-profit or not-for-profit sectors is demonstrating that investment in marketing makes a direct impact on the bottom line of the organization they work for. The plain fact is that we are all competing for investment in our initiatives. It is right that senior management in any organization should ask the three key tough commissioning questions:

1. Will it work?
2. What return do I get for my investment?
3. Is it value for money?

Those seeking to attract investment into marketing initiatives to address social issues are going to have to get smarter about setting out clear answers to these questions and being held to account for delivery against any investment made.

In the private sector, the return on investment (ROI) is the annual financial benefit of an investment minus the cost of the investment. In the public sector, the ROI is the cost reduction or cost avoidance obtained after an improvement in processes or systems, minus the cost of the improvement. In recent times, the ROI has been enhanced by the notion of the 'triple bottom line' (Elkington, 1997). This equates to an expanded baseline for measuring organizational performance, adding social and environmental dimensions to the traditional financial 'bottom-line' results. Social marketers will need to set out the likely impact on the environment and the wider social impact of their intervention to build a picture of the total impact of the intervention.

Focusing purely on the financial aspects of ROI, Table 8.2 sets out the kind of ROI analysis that social marketers should include in their proposals for funding. These kinds of

Table 8.2 Example estimates of ROI on a proposal to extend social smoking cessation clinic opening times

Numbers of current attendances annually	1,000
Percentage increase projected by increasing opening time	10%
Number of new clients	100
Percentage of new clients expected to quit	25%
Number of additional quitters	25
Average cost saving per quitter	£3,000
Annual gross cost of savings (25 × £3,000)	£75,000
Annual costs of providing extended opening	£20,000
Net cost savings	£55,000
ROI (£20,000–75,000)	3.5 : 1 or 350%

assessments are also helpful as tools for tracking programme performance. They not only set out a clear economic case but also provide commissioners with hard numeric measures for assessing ROI.

Is it value for money?

Value-for-money audits are non-financial audits, usually built into summative evaluation strategies, to measure the effectiveness, economy, and efficiency of investing in marketing. They do not question the policy itself; they examine the focus on the efficiency and implementation as measured against the initiative's goals and overall scale of the project. Value-for-money audits should also be accompanied by a cost–benefit analysis, which is a technique to compare the various costs associated with an investment with the benefits that it proposes to produce.

Both tangible and intangible returns should be addressed and accounted for. Marketers should use cost–benefit analyses to assess the return they get in terms of behavioural change for each of the investments made in a programme. For example, what generated the most contacts from the public about advice to recycle: the website? the telephone advice line? the drop-in centre? and what was the cost of each of these contacts (the number of contacts against the cost of providing the service)? Clearly, how the ultimate benefit of a programme is defined will be specific to the intervention.

Two final points about funding and cost assessment

When investing in social marketing, there is a threshold point that must be reached in terms of population awareness and action before the ROI can be measured. In an environment in which there is increasing competition for attention and engagement, social marketing programmes are often not funded to a sufficient level so that they can 'cut through' to their intended groups. Low levels of investment are often compounded by stop–start approaches to investment. Consequently, and importantly, the amount to be invested to achieve measurable impact on behaviour in target groups is a key factor to be determined in the development stage of any social marketing programme (for more detailed guidance on the development stage, see chapter three).

A second key recommendation for commissioners is to set a time frame over which investment needs to be maintained to achieve the targets of the programme. If investors are not able to commit sufficient funds over the required period, they must be made aware that the impact of their more limited investment may be reduced further by a lack of perseverance. Impact over time is a key issue to be addressed when putting together a full business case for investing in social marketing.

A three-step process for social marketing commissioning and budget allocation

French and Mayo (2006) recommend that social marketing budgets are allocated in three steps, rather than allocating a fixed amount at the start of an initiative, to ensure that a rigorous marketing development process is adhered to.

First, allocate a budget to scope an issue (see chapter three), understand the issue to be tackled, understand the audiences and assets that exist or that could be brought into play, and define the obstacles to success. As chapter three sets out, the key output from this scoping phase is a 'scoping report', which outlines the initial insights that will be taken forward into the development stage and explains how these insights were generated.

On completion of the scoping stage, and based on the scoping report, commissioners should allocate a budget for the testing phase of the project or programme (see chapter three). During the development phase, suppliers should work up the proposals, undertake field testing, and refine (or, if necessary, redesign) the proposed interventions so that they meet the initiative's requirements and are acceptable to the target groups.

Following the testing phase, a full plan for enacting the project or programme can be developed. This should form the basis of funding allocations to scale up and fully implement the recommended interventions and evaluate their impact (see chapter four).

If commissioners apply this three-step approach to budget allocation and it is complemented by marketers in the public sector setting out evidence for their recommendations, estimates of projected savings, and a value-for-money analysis, the chances of well-executed social marketing interventions will increase. We will also start to build a robust, costed evidence base for social marketing that will inform future planning and delivery, which will itself lead to greater investment in social marketing. Building this virtuous circle of practice should be a primary concern for all marketers.

One final point is the need to avoid panic-buying of interventions. In circumstances where additional funds become available at short notice and they must be spent rapidly—for example, near the end of the financial year—try to avoid spending for its own sake. Rather, try to invest in developmental work or research and testing if you do not have a well-researched and evidence-based programme or one that needs upscaling ready to go.

Conclusion

Commissioning social marketing is a key activity for an ever-increasing number of public service workers. Commissioning is a straightforward process, but it does demand a systematic approach and the proactive management of prospective and successful suppliers. Commissioning social marketing can be a highly cost-effective way of drawing on the necessary specialist skills that may not be present within public or third sector organizations. Commissioning is, however, not without risk.

Commissioners need to dedicate sufficient time and resources to constructing a thorough and fair process and actively managing the chosen suppliers, while evaluating their delivery against the brief that they successfully competed for. There are many generic guides to commissioning, and further free online guidance documents can be found at the Strategic Social Marketing website: http://strategic-social-marketing.vpweb.co.uk/Free-Tool-Box.html.

Self-review questions

1. Why is effective commissioning important in social marketing?

2. What are some of the main elements of effective commissioning?

3. When developing a brief for a new social marketing project or programme what are some of the main elements of the tender document that you would expect to be included?

   Use the following briefing template to set out a programme of work that you wish to put out to tender. If possible, use it for a real project, but if this is not appropriate, select a project that you would like to commission. Set a budget for the work and then attempt to fill in as much of the form as you can. If you get stuck at any point, refer back to the advice in this chapter and others in the book that deal with specific issues.

   - Title of project/programme
   - Background, context, and rationale for the project/programme
   - Purpose (focus of the project, scoping, development, implementation, evaluation, follow-up, or a full end-to-end programme):
     - aim(s)
     - objective(s)
     - target audience(s)
   - Requirements (brief description of project/programme)
   - Time frame (programme start and end date)
   - Organizational, technical, and/or scientific requirements or standards such as compliance with national guidelines
   - Intended audiences:
     - primary
     - secondary
     - tertiary
     - intermediate
   - Explicit skills and experience that the agency must have
   - Key partnerships and stakeholders that will need to be engaged
   - Ethical issues and requirements (involvement of ethics committee in research activity)
   - Incentive, bonus, and/or penalty schemes
   - Declaration of any conflict of interests
   - Branding requirements
   - Sign-off procedures
   - Reporting arrangements and milestones
   - Evaluation required
   - Financial arrangements, payment, and invoicing
   - Specific contractual and legal clauses, including intellectual property rights
   - References and examples of similar or relevant work

References

Bennett, J. (2003). Investment in population health in five OECD countries. Paris: Organisation for Economic Co-operation and Development.

CDC (2006). CDCynergy Social Marketing Edition Three [CD-ROM]. Atlanta, GA: Centers for Disease Control and Prevention.

Dr Foster Intelligence (2007). *Intelligent commissioning: intelligence*, Issue 2, London: Dr Foster Intelligence.

Elkington, J. (1997). Cannibals with forks. The triple bottom line of the 21st century business. Bloomington, MN: Capstone.

French, J., Mayo, E. (2006). It's our health! London: National Consumer Council.

Gordon, R., McDermott, L., Stead, M., Angus, K., Hastings, G. (2006). A review of the effectiveness of social marketing physical activity interventions. Stirling: Institute for Social Marketing.

Government Communications Network (2007). Engage. London: Cabinet Office http://www.comms.gov.uk/engage, accessed March 2009.

Hay, D.I. (2006). Economic arguments for action on the social determinants of health. Ottawa: Public Health Agency of Canada.

Hornik, R.C. (ed). (2002). Public health communication: evidence for behaviour change. Mahwah, NJ: Lawrence Erlbaum Associates.

Jackson, T. (2005). Motivating sustainable consumption: a review of evidence on consumer behaviour and behavioural change. Surrey: Network Centre for Environmental Strategy, University of Surrey.

Lister, G. (2007). Prevention is better than cure: cost-effectiveness of interventions aimed at promoting health and reducing preventable illness. London: National Social Marketing Centre.

McDermott, L., Stead, S., Gordon, R., Angus, K., Hastings, G. (2006). *A review of the effectiveness of social marketing nutrition interventions.* Stirling: Institute for Social Marketing.

NHS (2007). *World class commissioning: competencies.* London: NHS Commissioning Team Directorate.

Nussle, J., Orszag, P. (eds). (2014). *Moneyball for government.* Washington, DC: Disruption Books.

Office of Management and Budget (2015). Program Assessment Rating Tool Explained [website]. Washington, DC: Office of Management and Budget http://web.archive.org/web/20080616222524/http://www.whitehouse.gov/omb/part/, accessed 17 July 2015.

Pigott, C.S. (2000). *Business planning for healthcare management.* Buckingham: Open University Press.

Stead, M., McDermott, L., Gordon, R., Angus, K., Hastings, G. (2006). *A review of the effectiveness of social marketing alcohol, tobacco and substance misuse interventions.* Stirling: Institute for Social Marketing.

Chapter 9

Social marketing on a small budget

Jeff French

Less is more.

(Robert Browning, *'Andrea del Sarto (called
"The Faultless Painter")'*, 1855)

Learning points

This chapter:

- provides an understanding of how social marketing principles can be applied to the development of even small-scale behavioural projects;
- explains how social marketing principles can be applied without the need for a large budget for research, development, or implementation or evaluation;
- explains how to get help in your own area from social and professional networks, and how to tap into international support networks.

Introduction to social marketing on a small budget

The title of this chapter implies that it is possible to conduct social marketing with a small or no budget. While 'no resources' is a fairly clear statement, the word 'small' needs clarification. For the purposes of this chapter, it is assumed that we are talking about a situation in which a practitioner or concerned individual has only their own time or, in the case of an employed worker, no more than 10% or less of their employed time to allocate to a social marketing project.

This chapter could be considered as a form of applying *'Jugaad'* thinking and principles. *Jugaad* is a Hindi word that describes a simple fix or solution to a problem or challenge (Radjou et al., 2012). It is used to signify creativity to make existing things work or to create new things with few or no resources. *Jugaad* is also increasingly being accepted as a management technique (Radjou et al., 2010) and is recognized all over the world as an acceptable form of frugal development. *Jugaad* thinking is about applying simple principles and creative thinking to solving immediate problems. While it is true that social marketing programmes often require investment in market research and analysis, as well as time to plan and test possible interventions, the key added value of social marketing comes from adopting the social marketing mind-set set out in chapter two of this book.

For large-scale, regional or national social marketing programmes it is wise to invest in building up an accurate picture of subsegments of the population through market research and analysis of the behavioural challenges to be tackled. It is also wise to take time to develop and test interventions and to employ specialist agencies and consultants to help develop, deliver, and evaluate interventions. However, many of these elements of social marketing can still be applied without access to the kinds of funding or human resources needed for large-scale programmes.

Social marketing on a small budget

The essential 'must have' in any social marketing programme or project is the application of the social marketing mind-set. This is a way of thinking that embodies:

- the key concept, principles, and techniques of social marketing;
- the systemic analysis of problems and the application of a systematic set of processes to investigate, develop, implement, evaluate, and share what has been learned.

It is very important to be realistic about the scope of what can be achieved with few or no resources. This important consideration is also true for social marketers who have access to large budgets. Priorities always need to be agreed, and the limits of the focus of a particular programme need to be spelled out clearly. On a small budget, the need for clarity of purpose and the scope of what can reasonably be expected are even more important if we are not to set ourselves up for failure.

There are four things to constantly hold in your mind when you are developing social marketing interventions, especially when you have limited resources.

1. What explicitly are you trying to achieve in terms of behaviour?
2. Who precisely are you trying to help?
3. What interventions will these people value and collaborate with?
4. How will you measure and report on what happens?

As social marketers, our job is to create systems, environments, products, and services that people say help them to behave in socially beneficial ways. Social marketing programmes also need to be designed in such a way that target audiences value and can take advantage of them. If we are successful, we will not only see lots of people taking up the targeted behaviour but we should also see them promoting the behaviour to others, thus creating a multiplying effect related to our marketing interventions.

Scoping on a small budget

This section sets out how to apply the first stage of the STELa social marketing planning tool set out in chapter three on a small budget. For more details about STELa see the European Centre for Disease Prevention and Control's free planning guide (French and Apfel, 2014).

Making the most of all your assets

If you think like a social marketer, you will regularly start to spot opportunities for developing, delivering, and evaluating your programme. One of the best ways to start this process is 'asset mapping'. As chapter three explains, in the scoping stage you need to discover as much as you can about the audience, the behavioural issue that you are trying to address, and what is influencing it. This process should, however, focus not purely on the problem but also on the solution and the assets that you could use to tackle the issue.

Asset mapping is a process of identifying all the resources that exist in a community or area to deal with an issue such as obesity, crime, or poor education attainment. It is also a process guided by the view that issues are best tackled by community-led action and engagement. A good way to start is by drawing up a list of:

- local politicians;
- local community groups;
- civic organizations;
- religious and cultural groups;
- key community leaders;
- relevant companies;
- not-for-profit organizations;
- media assets such as local newspapers and digital social networks.

You can add to this list other key individuals or groups that may be interested in or that are already seeking to influence in a positive way the problem you want to tackle.

In the first instance, you should target those organizations and individuals that have a deep concern about the issue or have the resources or existing contacts with the target audiences you are seeking to influence. Setting up meetings and discussions with these groups should be an early priority in your programme: from these you can develop a broader picture of potential alliances that could help tackle the issue. Often these groups also have intelligence and data about the problem and the target audiences that can help you start to develop a potential set of interventions.

Research and analysis on a small budget

One of the big costs in large-scale social marketing programmes is that of gathering research data about the target audience. There are resources in most communities, however, that can help reduce the need for this expenditure.

Libraries

Local or regional public and academic institutions' libraries can be of tremendous help in researching what is known about the issues you are trying to tackle and the audience you are trying to reach. Librarians and, increasingly, information scientists are employed by libraries to assist students and researchers in finding the data they need. Get to know your local library and seek access to any academic institutions' libraries that are in your area. Get to know what services they offer and ask librarians for assistance.

Public sector information services

Many local public and civic institutions (including planning, health, economic, housing, police, education, fire and rescue, water, power, telecommunications, and media organizations) employ information scientists, researchers, statisticians and geographers, and epidemiologists. As part of your asset mapping, create a map or list of such services. Arrange to visit or contact the organizations or departments and discuss:

- the issue you are trying to tackle;
- your data needs;
- how they may be able to help you;
- if they have already undertaken research projects that may help you;
- if any data they have is freely accessible to you.

Local private sector companies

Local companies and corporations routinely collect customer, market research, sales, and service data. Obviously some of this data is highly confidential; however, companies are increasingly making such data available, suitably anonymized, especially in areas of public concern such as health and the environment. Sales data of items such as energy-efficient light bulbs, fruit, and vegetables, and service data such as the number of plastic bags given away are being shared for free with the public sector as part of companies' corporate social responsibility agenda. It is recommended that you discuss your issue with local companies and ask how they might be able to help you build a picture of the people and issues you are trying to tackle, using their data. Remember also to think about what is in it for the company and how you can reward them for cooperation. For example, setting up a photo call and a news feature with local media can be a good way of persuading and rewarding such cooperation. Clearly, you need to be aware that private sector organizations may have a biased way of presenting their data.

Local universities, colleges, and schools

Learning institutions are assets in terms of knowledge management and research. Many institutions have students and staff who are looking for research topics that will form part of their academic work and count towards qualifications. Many students are also looking for socially relevant research projects and work experience. These institutions often have highly skilled staff that can help with research design and analysis as well as desk-based searches of existing research. When approaching such institutions, it is worth stressing the contribution of your project to the local community and the benefits, to the institution, of being seen as partner. It is also important to understand the time cycles of such institutions. There will be certain times of the year when decisions are being made by students and staff who may be looking for research projects. Also bear in mind exam timetables and coursework-submission deadlines.

The third sector

International, national, and local non-governmental organizations (NGOs), foundations, charities, and other third sector organizations are a great source of research and intelligence data. Many have well-developed, searchable websites dealing with specific issues. Many also employ information specialists and researchers who are willing to help you for free. A call or email to these specialists is worthwhile, but make sure you are as clear as possible about what you are asking for, as this will help them help you. Obviously you need to be aware of any possible bias that the organization may have.

Specialist marketing agencies

As part of your asset mapping you should also locate and record details of any local marketing, market research, campaign, public relations, advertising, and creative agencies that work in your area. These companies may provide you with insight into the issue you are dealing with, examples of what works, or advice. Some companies have a policy of doing a certain amount of *pro bono* or unbilled work for causes and issues that they believe are important. When approaching specialist marketing or market research agencies, make it clear that you are not a fee-paying customer in the very first meeting. Share your problem with the agency, what you know and don't know, and who is already helping you, and then set out a specific request for support. It is much better to go with a specific request and then be prepared to alter this than go with a vague request for help.

Part of any deal for free support work needs to include a clear agreement about how and when the company will be credited for its support. It is an absolute must that you draw up a written and signed agreement of what the company will deliver, over what time frame, and to what success criteria. Even if no money is changing hands, such an agreement is important for both you and the company to ensure absolute clarity about the nature of the relationship and the support that is being pledged.

Marketing and market research using target audience meetings

A good way to gather views and develop a deeper understanding with regards to audience views about the issue want to influence is to invite members of the target audience you are trying to help to a meeting to discuss and explore the issue. The setting up, management, and reporting of these meetings will, however, need careful planning. Inviting in audiences for this kind of meeting can make those responsible for delivering existing services nervous, as they feel they may be exposed to criticism that is sometimes very vocal and even aggressive. When you are planning this kind of 'meet the audience' session, set out answers to the following eight questions to help you plan the event.

1. Have I set out clear aims and objectives for the meeting?
2. Have I got a representative sample of the audience I want to learn from?
3. Have I engaged and got the commitment of all relevant officials (who should also be present) and are they happy with the proposed focus of the meeting and the methods that will be used to engage the audience and report on what is discussed?
4. Have I made it easy and attractive for the audience to participate (have I considered issues of time, location, family support such as child care, physical access, and transport)?
5. Are the methods that will be used to engage the audience appropriate, and will they work?
6. How will I handle any conflict or dissent in the meeting?
7. How will the meeting be facilitated—do I, or whoever will facilitate the meeting, have the skills, personal qualities, and audience respect to succeed?
8. Do I have a way of capturing what comes out of the meeting in a way that is respectful, appropriate, and as accurate as possible?

You also need to remember to treat your target audiences and coalition partners with respect. This means treating information you have gathered as sensitive and confidential, and keeping people informed about what you are doing, what you are discovering, and what you plan to do about it.

Online evidence and networks

Evidence about what works from other social marketers and academics who have tried to tackle similar issues with similar groups is beginning to be systematically collected and reviewed. The following websites, list servers and associations can all help you scan what has been tried and link you with people who are working or who have worked on similar issues.

Associations and networks

The International Social Marketing Association: http://www.i-socialmarketing.org/
The European Social Marketing Association: http://www.europeansocialmarketing.org/
The Australian Association of Social Marketing: http://www.aasm.org.au/
The Asian Social Marketing Network: http://www.asiansmn.ning.com

The Social Marketing Listserv: http://socialmarketers.net/mailman/listinfo/socialmarketing_
socialmarketers.net

Guidance

French, J., Apfel, F. (2014). *Social marketing guide for public health programme managers and practitioners.* Stockholm: European Centre for Disease Prevention and Control http://ecdc.europa.eu/en/publications/Publications/social-marketing-guide-public-health.pdf

CDC (2007). *CDCynergy Lite: social marketing made simple.* Atlanta, GA: Centers for Disease Control and Prevention http://www.cdc.gov/healthcommunication/cdcynergylite.html

Testing and development on a small budget

Here, we set out how you can go about developing and testing possible interventions related to the behaviours that you want to influence. A more comprehensive description of this stage is set out in chapter three.

Using partnerships to deliver your marketing interventions

Perhaps the single most powerful way to enhance the amount of resources that you can bring together to tackle a social issues is to develop a coalition or partnership focused on solving an agreed social challenge. The decisions of who to convene and what the agenda ought to be are critical to the success of almost all social marketing efforts. Even those running major campaigns spend a lot of time and money on building partnerships. Do not underestimate the importance of this role. Avoid getting bogged down in a process of just building and maintaining good relationships. This can easily become an end in itself. Remember that the point of investing some of your limited time and resources in a relationship is to get a payback that outstrips the effort you have to put in. Box 9.1 provides a checklist for getting the most out of your partnerships.

A key partner both for promoting your programme and for market research are the media, whether local radio, newspapers, television, or the Internet. The media are normally viewed simply as marketing channels, but they are also a business sector, as well as a collections of individuals, and are a powerful force in shaping popular societal agendas. It is often worthwhile to invest time in recruiting key editors, writers, or broadcasters as key partners in your delivery coalition.

Box 9.1 Managing partnerships checklist

1. Anticipate partners' needs and be proactive in tackling them.
2. Always be 'positive' and adopt a 'can-do' attitude.
3. Be flexible to requests from partners.
4. Keep people informed, even if there is nothing to report.
5. Put effort into marketing your successes and celebrating together.
7. Acknowledge and praise partners at every opportunity.
8. Take partners to lunch or coffee to build personal relationships.

When building partnerships with the media, it is important to treat them like any other key audience or potential partner. Get to know how they operate and their needs, likes, and dislikes. Ask yourself these questions.

- Who are the media's key influencers?
- What issues are they interested in?
- What kinds of projects or causes have they taken up?
- What are they against?
- What do I want them to do?
- What do I want them to stop doing?

As with any other partner, building trust with local media organizations and individuals is important. Many people working in the media industry rightly view themselves as being an important part of the democratic system. They are used to being lobbied and told half-truths, so it's important to build up trust by being open and honest with them. One of the best ways to build up trust is to volunteer to provide media with content related to your issue that they can use. For example, media companies are increasingly staffed by very few people, and they are often hungry for copy and ideas to fill their programming schedules. Offer to write, at no cost, a regular feature of an agreed length and to an agreed style on your issues, or give some interviews for free to your local radio station, newspaper, bloggers, and/or TV station.

Generating funds for your programme

If you have little or no funding, a first task may be to secure a small budget to help you research, test, deliver, and evaluate your intervention. This budget might simply be agreement from your managers that you can use some of your time on this project. There are a number of ways to raise funds that can generate interest and engagement in your project at the same time. These methods include:

- asking possible donors to give direct funding or to provide goods and services that can be sold;
- asking donors and/or communities to give prizes that can be given or raffled off to promote the issues you are dealing with—for example, a voucher for a free haircut from a barber shop can be used as a prize for people who attend a session about exploring why a community does not come forward for immunization;
- staging community events to both raise awareness of the issue and generate donations—for example, a coffee morning to raise awareness and generate funds to tackle littering in an area.

Often, local business people are more willing to help if they believe that the issue that you are concerned with is something that they would want to be associated with, because either it will give them good publicity or it is something that may adversely affect their business if it is not tackled—for example, food hygiene and fire safety. So when planning your project, consider who might be sympathetic, who might have something to gain, and who might see the project as a way of enhancing their reputation or brand.

Kotler and Lee (2007) suggest that, when trying to persuade potential funders to support social marketing programmes, the same principles we apply to understanding and influencing any other type of audiences still apply. This means that there is a need to identify and prioritize possible funders and to segment them, using criteria appropriate to the issue and sector you are looking at. Next, there is the need to articulate clear and specific requests. Invest in understanding the potential funders and develop a strategy using all elements of the marketing mix to create the best possible chance of the funder deciding to support the programme. One key process

---

Box 9.2 Possible costs and benefits of partnerships

Possible costs

- Reputation and/or brand damage
- Time cost: the need for a full scoping and development before impact is observable
- Resource costs, management time, and programme budget

Possible benefits

- Reputation and/or brand enhancement
- Community engagement and corporate responsibility
- Market intelligence gained
- Demonstrable improvement in a cause they care about

---

is to set out the exchange that is on offer to potential funders. When working out the exchange, you should set out both the costs and benefits (see Box 9.2 for examples) in terms that the potential funder will be able to understand and relate to.

When meeting potential funders, prepare for the meeting by using the following checklist to structure what you want to cover in the meeting. Make the possible funders aware:

- that you understand the issues and have done your research;
- that the proposal meets their priorities as set out in any application criteria;
- of the envisaged outcome;
- of how you will measure progress;
- of key milestones;
- of how budgets will be applied, and what the likely cost of success per person will be;
- of who else is supporting the project and what other pledges of funding and support you have;
- of what you would like them to do;
- of what you would like them to fund.

Do not use moral arguments about why a potential funder should support you; use arguments that demonstrate that a real difference can be achieved. And be realistic: do not over-promise what you can deliver. Sue Adkins sets out a lot of helpful additional advice about how to work with corporate partners in her book *Cause-related marketing* (1999).

If you are approaching funders through a formal application, make sure that you fill in application forms in the way prescribed by the funder and that your request is compatible with the selection criteria set out in the guidance to applicants. If you are unsure about any aspect of a funding application procedure, it is always best to contact the organization and seek clarity before proceeding with the process, as you may waste a great deal of your—and the funder's—time if you submit applications inappropriately or in a form that does not meet the required specification or timetable.

Field testing interventions on a low budget

Before an intervention is fully implemented, it should be tested and refined based on the feedback received. While you may not have sufficient budget to undertake a full pilot and extensive field testing, it is possible to conduct mini-pilots and refine promotional material and/or service changes.

The following list of ideas for low-cost testing and refinement is not exhaustive but gives some practical ways that you can refine your intervention prior to full implementation.

- Ask a small number of your target group to read and comment on the written material you produce.
- Ask colleagues to review your plans, intended materials, and approach.
- Stage a role play in which you or a colleague act as a member of the target audience coming into contact with the new service, and note what happens.
- Audio record the reactions of a small number of people to the new service or material.
- Conduct a peer appraisal of the new service or approach, having tried the new system for a week.
- Keep a written record of users' reaction the new service or product.
- Ask colleagues to observe the audience reaction to the project and give you feedback

Testing or piloting should be a feature of your development process. It is usually a good trade-off in time and effort to undertake a test or pilot of any intervention before implementing it fully. On occasion, pilots will indicate that despite the development work and research you have undertaken, the interventions you have selected do not work as intended. Without piloting you run the risk of committing time and resources to interventions that may not work and might even make things worse.

Enacting your project with a small budget

It is important to remember that large budgets are no guarantee of success: much has been achieved through local interventions that have relied heavily on partnerships and a deep understanding of both the issue to be tackled and the triggers that bring it about. What we also know is that well-planned and well-managed interventions that have clear aims and objectives, regular management input, review, and evaluation tend to be much more effective and efficient.

Promoting and managing social marketing in your organization

As part of your day-to-day work, you may be required to review, participate in, or approve projects. These tasks are opportunities to influence the management culture of your organization and to get it to be more marketing orientated. When reviewing such proposals, you should consider the following three questions.

- Has an understanding of the target audience been used to influence the proposal, and if so, how?
- What is the specific behavioural objective?
- Is there a clearly articulated value proposition that the intended audience is likely to positively respond to?

You should try to get everyone in your organization to start thinking about the benefits of new services, products, or systems from a user's point of view. In addition, try to get people to set explicit behavioural objectives that can be measured. These should be challenging but realistic. Usually the weakest parts of most social interventions will concern the evidence for an intervention, the understanding of the audience, and the proposed impact of the proposed intervention. As chapter three explains, it is vital to ensure that clear, measurable objectives are set and that interventions are pre-tested as thoroughly as possible.

Making the most of every face-to-face opportunity

Every one-to-one meeting and face-to-face encounter you have, and every committee meeting and event you attend, is a free marketing opportunity. Face-to-face communication is the most powerful channel there is, so use these opportunities to the full to gather information, build partnerships, and spread your ideas.

To get the most out of these opportunities, you need to think about the people you are meeting (your customer or audience). Consider how you can convey your key ideas and requests in a way they will relate to. Think about and write down the key phrases or words that you will need to use. It is a good idea not to talk theory but to give real-life practical examples, quoting actual people and explaining how they are affected by the issue to bring it to life. In addition, do not forget that every face-to-face encounter is an opportunity for market research. Apply active listening skills and note what is being said. Make a record as soon after the meeting as you can: it is a good idea to carry a small notebook with you to capture these kinds of encounters. Another good tip is always to have a business card with you to give to people you meet. The card can even spell out the core objectives of your project as well as your contact details. Business card distribution and collection is a very cost-effective way to promote your project and record people who might be willing to help you deliver it.

Talks, workshops, and seminars

A great way to gather views from, inform, or influence target audiences is through talks, workshops, and seminars. Presentations are a very low-cost way of interacting with medium-sized groups of people, and they also allow for two-way interaction. If you think like a marketer when planning and organizing presentations, you will ensure that you give thought to the people coming to the meeting prior to giving your presentation.

- Who are they?
- What are their views likely to be?
- What troubles them?
- How can you help them?
- Why are they coming?
- What do they expect to get from the event?
- Are there different subgroups within the audience?

Next, think about what you want them to understand, know, and feel. You should also be clear about what you want to get from them. For example, do you want them to:

- commit to doing something;
- feel that something must be done about the problem you are tackling;
- help with a proposal or research project; or
- better understand an issue or a demonstration?

Remember never to make a presentation about data without relating the data to a story about a real person; this will help your target group to understand the issue and your intended solutions.

Every meeting with a partner, potential partner, or even somebody representing the competition is a marketing opportunity. Do remember also that marketing is not about selling your ideas and persuading the other person to change against their will, but rather it is about finding an idea or an action that meets your goals and the goals of your target audience. This means active listening and a willingness to modify *your* ideas in the light of what you hear and learn.

Creative input for free

For social marketers, creative thinking can be an important and effective process to bring your ideas about how to help people change. Always be on the lookout for innovative and inexpensive ways to promote your campaign or project. Look out for new combinations of marketing methods that are being used nationally and locally, and try to tap into free sources of creative thinking. Ideas can come from the commercial sector as well as the public sector. You can also get great creative ideas by asking local schools or college students to work on ideas as part of design, marketing, art, or social programmes they are studying. Local artists, designers, media workers, and marketing firms can also be persuaded to help for free. As suggested earlier, when developing your asset map make a list of all possible creative resources that may be of use to you in your local area.

Using newsletters and bulletins

With cheaper and increasing access to low-cost software, and the falling costs of setting up web-based social networks, surveys, blogs, and electronic newsletters, it need not be an expensive exercise to produce good-quality e-newsletters and other forms of content which can act as a vehicle to communicate general or targeted messages to your target groups.

Newsletters and other forms of contact with supporters such as surveys can also help you generate more supporters and funds for your intervention. If you are interested in carrying out free online surveys take a look at Survey Monkey, and low-cost websites can be developed by people with no programming expertise at sites such as Vistaprint.

You can also explore possibilities for fundraising by, for example, selling advertising space on your e-newsletter to people who want to raise their profile or communicate with the same audience as you. Businesses, NGOs, or third sector organizations may also consider sponsoring your newsletter or buying advertising space on your webpage. You should also consider setting up a Twitter account and linking with professionals interested in the issue via LinkedIn.

Swapping advertising space

If you publish a newsletter, blog, or podcast, other publishers may be prepared to give you free or low-cost space if you provide a reciprocal arrangement. If you have a small budget, you can try negotiating with local media (e.g. local newspapers) for discounted advertising space. If the timing or placing of your advertisement is not important, try negotiating a discount for placing an advertisement at the last minute, if the newspaper cannot sell the space at a commercial rate.

If you do work with partners and organizations, set up agreements to cross-promote interventions or share the cost of advertising and promotions. Remember that partners represent you and what you are trying to achieve. See also tips on making the most of people and partnerships, described above.

Making the most of your content

You can save a lot of time and money by making the content of your communications work as hard as possible for you. For example, you can use articles or news items you have written more than once, editing and/or updating them if necessary. Make a list of all possible outlets for content you produce, and contact each outlet on a rolling basis to see if they are prepared to carry it.

Prize draws, lotteries, and contests

Contests, lotteries, and prize draws are a great way to set up an 'exchange' (see chapters one and two) and to encourage people to participate in your social marketing intervention. For example, children's painting or poster-design competitions that focus on the issue you are tackling are a cheap way to engage large numbers of people and generate media attention. You can also set up competitions or lottery schemes through which people can win prizes if they participate. You can even give as a prize something you already own, manufacture, or produce and which others will find valuable (e.g. cakes, food, or new but unwanted gifts). The awarding of a prize can also create a good news stories for the local media, again increasing the number of people who will hear about your intervention. Bear in mind that it may be necessary to obtain legal advice before running a competition or a lottery.

Online marketing

As more and more people gain access to the Internet, it becomes an increasingly important marketing, social networking, and communication channel. It is simultaneously a global and a very local tool. Below, we list some ways your social marketing intervention can exploit the Internet with no budget other than that needed for web connection.

Email marketing

Over 40% of all emails are now classed as 'spam' (the online equivalent of junk mail), so email marketing is getting an increasingly bad press. However, a good email can still receive a high response rate and have real impact. The key things to focus on are:

- personalizing the email rather than making it a general one;
- targeting the recipient's interests and needs;
- keeping it short, interesting, and to the point;
- providing an easy way to respond and a call to do something to follow up for those who chose do so.

As with all forms of contact from people who show an interest in your intervention, you need to respond to email replies quickly and effectively. It is a good idea to send out emails in phases or batches if you are contacting a lot of people so you have time to deal with responses in a timely and personalized way.

Building your own website

If you have a subscription to an Internet provider, it is easy to set up a website. Many providers even give free software that helps you design your site. A website can be a great marketing tool for providing information about what you are doing, how to contact you, and to gather people's views.

Linking to other websites

Getting other websites to link to yours is not only free, it can also help with your search-engine rankings, as many search engines now factor 'link popularity' into the relevancy of their search results. Site linking is also a good way to build relationships with partner and stakeholder organizations.

Email signature file

Use automated signature files, which can be set up to appear at the bottom of every email you send out. These are like little poster cards, helping you promote your social marketing intervention and its key messages. The signatures can be changed and updated on a regular basis as you develop your intervention.

Discussion groups, forums, message boards, and news groups

An excellent way to increase awareness of your intervention is to take part in online discussion groups and message boards and to contribute to news and interest groups. You can even set up new social network groups to serve or communicate with the specific groups of people you are trying to help, and/or with partner organizations and individuals who support your project. For example, set up a LinkedIn group for all the nurses working on a project to reduce the overprescribing of antibiotics in a hospital to share information, experiences, and tips.

Press releases

The press release is a great low-cost way to get media attention. But you have to have some *real* news before you decide to use press releases: your story has to be newsworthy and told in a way that a journalist would find interesting and relevant. If it is not, there is little chance of it getting the desired result.

Make sure your press release is attention grabbing. Try to think creatively about an angle that will interest both the media outlet that will read it and your target group and the organizations they interact with. Also, try to come up with an interesting and attention-grabbing title. For example, dressing up in a funny costume or getting photographs taken with a local personality or politicians to publicize the issue you are focused on can be a good way to create a lot of attention. A good picture is worth a thousand words.

Other ways of promoting your intervention

- Print some postcards or write letters to your target group, highlighting your intervention. Include links to a follow-up website or telephone number.
- Set up a press conference, rally, picnic, or awareness 'launch meeting' for all the people who have said they will help you.
- Set up a public signing of a petition for action, and invite the press and photographers for a photo-shoot of the event. Make sure to think of some memorable images for them.
- The presentation of a petition to an important local person is a great way to get lots of media coverage for free.
- Print, or hand-make if necessary, business cards that promote your intervention.
- Place signs that publicize your intervention in your workplace, in your car, and at other outlets that will display them for free (e.g. hospitals, schools, libraries, and shops).
- Join professional face-to-face and online social groups to network with other people, and volunteer to speak at local group meetings and seminars.
- Talk with local colleges, schools, and universities, and offer workshops on the issue your social marketing intervention is seeking to address.
- Participate in community events (e.g. carnivals, parades, picnics, fairs, fun runs, and walks) to promote your interventions.
- Listen to radio phone-in talk-shows, and when the topic is relevant to your issue, call in and offer your opinion and advice.

Learning and evaluation on a small budget

Chapters three and four provide a lot of advice and information about how to evaluate a social marketing intervention (Step 4 of the STELa framework). It is possible to evaluate social marketing interventions on a low budget but, as with the rest of the advice in this chapter, it is even more important to be very clear and realistic about what can be done. The key tasks are:

- setting aims and objectives;
- identifying evaluation indicators;
- choosing research to gather evaluation data;
- disseminating evaluation results and follow-up action.

Setting aims and objectives

Although this section does not seek to repeat the information that chapter four provides on set-ting aims and objectives, it is important to reiterate that without clear and SMART objectives, evaluation of programmes becomes very problematic. If clear and precise objectives are set, the method of measuring them becomes much easier. Measurement does not have to be expensive or complicated. For example, you can track responses to a feature in a newspaper by asking all the people that contact you what prompted the contact and recording how many say it was the newspaper feature.

With a small budget, some evaluation methods (e.g. extensive longitudinal tracking studies involving lots of people) are not possible, unless sponsorship can be found. It is also not appro-priate to spend a disproportionate amount of your time or resources on evaluating small inter-ventions. A good rule of thumb is that evaluation should take up no more than 10% of your total resources, be that time or funding, and no more than 5% if the total project value is less than £100,000 or $200,000 (providing you are adhering to what professional and research institutes consider to be best practice).

Evaluation methods open to people working with a small budget include:

◆ short, multiple-choice questionnaires;
◆ changes in service or product uptake ;
◆ short open-ended questionnaires (of no more than ten questions);
◆ reviewing existing service utilization data;
◆ a small number (less than 15) of audience interviews;
◆ group discussions;
◆ producing a narrative case study based on personal reflections;
◆ capturing audience stories using a recording device;
◆ video, audio, or photographic recording of the project;
◆ document analysis—for example, how many times the issue was an agenda item on an important committee or how many times it was mentioned in the local newspaper;
◆ studies focused on observing behaviour of target groups.

You may need specialist help to set these approaches to evaluation up if you are not experi-enced, for example, in developing questionnaires or interpreting numerical or qualitative data (Box 9.3).

Follow-up on a small budget

As chapter four explains, the utility of an evaluation depends on what you do with the results. Evaluations should lead to answering questions such as the following.

◆ What element of our intervention had the biggest impact on behaviour?
◆ What were the most efficient things we did?
◆ What partnerships worked well and who else could we work with?
◆ What should change in the future delivery of the project?
◆ What improvements to our research methods do we need to make?
◆ What further information do we need?

Follow-up to evaluation is important because it is a way of maintaining a relationship and showing respect for funders, partners, supporters, and the target group(s) of the intervention. You should aim to provide some form of feedback to the target group and anyone who has

Box 9.3 Example: co-observation and supportive feedback

Two midwives wanted to evaluate their antenatal education programme. In addition to designing a short questionnaire with the help of a local university researcher (which they gave out to their classes at the end of the sessions), they also set up a process of co-observation and feedback. The co-observation consisted of each of the midwives observing and feeding back to the other on their sessions' educational plan, the conduct of the session, and the audience reaction against a pre-agreed set of criteria that included:

- clarity of aims and objectives;
- content, method, and evaluation of the session;
- the conduct of the session;
- verbal and non-verbal communication;
- level of interaction with the class; and
- how questions were dealt with.

The midwives used the observations and the results from the survey to review and modify their programme on an ongoing basis.

helped with the intervention, including funders, staff, and sponsors. Ideally, you should also give some form of feedback on your intervention to others running—or planning to run—similar projects, so that knowledge about what does and does not work can be disseminated. You can do this by publishing your results and learning in professional newsletters and journals and by giving presentations about your work and posting details of what you found on your website.

Do not delay the dissemination of your findings, as their importance and relevance can decrease over time. Set a deadline for getting results published or being put before relevant stakeholders.

It is important not to hide negative findings. Learning that something has not worked is very valuable and will help others not to make similar mistakes. If your intervention has not worked, the key point is not to beat yourself up about it but to understand why it did not work and then to set in train actions to improve impact and efficiency next time around.

Conclusion

It is very possible to deliver social marketing on a small budget. The key factor is to apply a systematic approach to understanding the behavioural challenge from a citizen perspective and build interventions around this insight. There are many free resources that can be used to help with this process. Practitioners also need to gather together all the assets that exist in their professional, social, and community networks to help to develop, deliver, and evaluate their interventions. Starting planning from a perspective of what is to be achieved rather than with an emphasis on using allocated resources can in fact be more effective than a budget-driven approach.

Self-review exercise: develop a micro-social marketing plan

Think of a real-life situation that you think could benefit from the application of social marketing principles but for which you have few or no resources other than your time. Set five headings that relate to the key planning documents needed for each stage of the STELa framework outlined in this chapter and chapter three. Consider what three to five actions you could take to develop:

- a scoping report;
- a testing plan;
- an enactment plan;
- an evaluation and follow-up plan.

Limit yourself to no more than five bullet points for each of these micro-plans.

References

Adkins, S. (1999). *Cause-related marketing: who cares wins.* Oxford: Butterworth Heinemann.

French, J., Apfel, F. (2014). *Social marketing guide for public health programme managers and practitioners.* Stockholm: European Centre for Disease Prevention and Control http://ecdc.europa.eu/en/publications/Publications/social-marketing-guide-public-health.pdf

Kotler, P., Lee, N. (2007). *Social marketing.* Thousand Oaks, CA: Sage.

Radjou, N., Prabhu, J., Ahuja, S. (2010). Jugaad: a new growth formula for corporate America. *Harvard Business Review Blog Network*, 25 January 2010.

Radjou, N., Prabhu, J., Ahuja, S. (2012). *Jugaad innovation: think frugal, be flexible, generate breakthrough growth.* San Francisco, CA: Jossey-Bass.

Chapter 10

Building social programme coalitions

Jeff French

Coming together is a beginning, staying together is progress, and working together is success.

Henry Ford

Learning points

This chapter:

- discusses the importance of establishing and managing partnerships as part of social marketing programmes and short-term interventions;

- sets out some of the differences between partnerships with the for-profit sector, the not-for-profit sector, communities, and non-governmental organizations (NGOs);

- explores some of the differences between partnership development and stakeholder management and explains how to manage both as part of a social marketing programme or project;

- discusses how to select appropriate partners, develop partnerships, and evaluate their contribution to solving behavioural challenges.

Introduction to building social programme coalitions

Building and sustaining a dynamic, productive, culturally rich, and healthy society presents real challenges that no single sector or organization can tackle alone. We know that in many circumstances interventions that are perceived to be led by the government or governmental agencies are seen as intrusive or a turn-off to some potential target audiences. The task when tackling many complex social challenges that have a large behavioural component, therefore, requires the contribution and coordination of all relevant resources held by communities and organizations across all sectors. For this reason many social marketing programmes start by building delivery coalitions among all those who can help.

If social marketing is to tackle issues such as health inequality successfully, one of the most important types of partnership it needs to develop is between the private and public sectors. Although there are many examples of social marketing initiatives that have relied on partnership between these sectors, many public sector staff are still reluctant to work with the private sector owing to ethical considerations or fears that the private sector will take advantage of public sector endorsement. In extreme cases, public sector workers believe that the private sector is the 'enemy' and that capitalism and consumerism sit at the root of many of society's problems. Conversely, the private sector can be nervous about working with the public sector because it sometimes perceives it to be slow, bureaucratic, and—in the case of some countries—corrupt and/or poorly managed.

As described by Crisp (2007), there are real challenges associated with developing health-focused partnerships to deliver social projects, improve health, prevent disease, and tackle inequality. As Crisp points out, the basic actions that need to be taken to empower people to choose positive health behaviours and prevent disease include:

◆ building a supportive social network and strong communities;
◆ ensuring that people are protected by laws that reflect fundamental human rights and responsibilities;
◆ providing appropriate information at the right time and place;
◆ ensuring that people have access to the resources they need;
◆ providing goods and services that meet people's needs;
◆ establishing markets that work for the benefit of both people who use and those who profit from them; and
◆ ensuring that the environment people live in is safe, healthy, and inspiring.

Clearly the public, voluntary, and private sectors all have key roles to play in delivering these activities. Nationally and locally, cross-sector partnership can increase the impact of most health programmes; conversely, a lack of such partnerships can limit the impact and reach of many health programmes.

There have always been partnerships focused on promoting health. The public sector in many countries relies on businesses to supply it with goods and services, and is clearly a significant customer for the private sector, enabling it to create wealth and employment opportunities, which in turn contributes to well-being and social development. The public sector also relies on the voluntary sector and the communities it serves to supply volunteers and to deliver support programmes that complement public sector initiatives. Governments, NGOs, and foundations all supply funding for research and support local community interventions. Communities themselves supply cultural, spiritual, educational, and support services, as well as economic goods and services that make for vibrant social environments, which are the very stuff of social capital (Putnam, 2000). See chapter thirteen for a review of how social franchising, which is often a partnership between governments, NGOs, and the private sector, is being used to promote the delivery of high-quality health interventions in many developing countries.

The 2004 Global Corporate Citizenship Initiative survey showed that over 90% of the chief executives surveyed believed that the world's development challenges cannot be met without partnership (World Economic Forum, 2005). The respondents felt that partnerships between business, government, and civil society would play a major role in addressing key developmental challenges.

However, official government or public sector agency guidance about working with the private sector, and sometimes the voluntary sector, is often framed defensively and seeks to minimize risk (NHS Management Executive, 1993; Department of Health, 2000; WHO, 2000; NHS Scotland, 2003; Audit Commission, 2005). While it is appropriate to minimize risks, there is also a need to harness the power, influence, and know-how of all potential partners if we are to make progress in tackling the huge health challenges that we face. There is a need to move away from passive forms of partnership that merely seek private sector or foundation funding for government- or NGO-driven initiatives towards more jointly developed and sustained initiatives. New cross-sector health partnerships need to be developed that encourage sharing of intelligence, expertise, and resources. One of the challenges in developing cross-sector programmes is to begin to build a dialogue between potential partners around areas of mutual concern.

Building partnerships with the private sector

An important opportunity for those leading health-focused social marketing interventions is the increasing enthusiasm of many sections of the private sector for supporting social marketing initiatives. While there have always been commercial drivers for effective partnerships, there are now additional compelling social drivers concerned with tackling some of the key challenges facing the world today, as discussed in chapter one. Developing a sustainable economy, a pleasant and productive environment, and a healthy population are all key goals of the public sector, but they also represent the best long-term strategy for the private sector in its mission to benefit shareholders in a socially responsible way. In short, the key challenges facing society today, including poverty, poor health, sustainable consumption, inequality, and climate change, require coordinated effort between the state and the private sector. A full discussion and guidance on how social marketing can be enhanced by working with companies as part of the corporate social responsibility agenda can be found in *Corporate social responsibility: doing the most good for your company and your cause* (Kotler and Lee, 2006). In addition, the Economist Intelligence Unit (2008) concluded that there are already many examples of successful private sector organizations supporting health and social programmes in partnership with both the governmental and the NGO sector. The success factors highlighted by the report include the following.

◆ To be successful, corporate citizenship must be driven from the top, but leaders of this initiative are needed at all levels of the firm.

◆ Significant companies find ways to channel the passion of their employees into corporate citizenship activities. Such activities help firms to recruit better-quality workers and retain them.

◆ To convince senior executives that corporate citizenship is effective, the financial benefit must be clear. Companies must set ambitious goals, along with ways of keeping track of progress towards them.

◆ Companies have discovered that financial advantages can accrue from forming partnerships with non-traditional stakeholders. These include local, state, and federal government, as well as activist groups and NGOs.

The Ministry of Foreign Affairs of Denmark has instigated a public–private partnership (PPP) programme to promote sustainable PPPs. It recognizes that private sector involvement is crucial to achieve the development goals of the international community (Ministry of Foreign Affairs of Denmark, 2006). PPPs continue to be promoted as a core part of policy by institutions such as the UN (2003) and UNAIDS (2007). The private sector is increasingly being seen as a route to reach and connect with different societies or specific communities, as stated by the former Secretary-General of the United Nations Ban Ki-Moon: 'It is clear that none of the Millennium Development Goals can be achieved without the active involvement and engagement of business. At the same time, there is increasing realization within business that it cannot survive or thrive if societies fail or if people feel that their security is threatened. Building healthy and inclusive societies, sustainable markets, combating corruption and safeguarding the environment is just as important for Business as it is for the United Nations and its member governments.' (Ban, 2008) (Box 10.1).

Box 10.1 Case study: School Food Trust Partnership with Walt Disney Motion Pictures International

In 2008 the School Food Trust—the organization charged by the UK government with trans-forming school food—partnered with Walt Disney Motion Pictures International on High School Musical 3 to encourage more children to eat healthy school food. By working with a brand phenomenon the Trust was able to engage with children at primary and secondary school levels, using a variety of communications channels. Through interactive competi-tions and carefully targeted public relations, the campaign attempted to influence children by offering them a chance to win a ticket to the premiere of the film if they ate a school meal. Over 70,000 children entered the 'Magic meal ticket' competition.

Working with an international, long-established film company brought with it superb benefits of strong brand allegiance and media engagement; however, the multilayered sign-off processes and contractual arrangements of the film's stars resulted in regular delays and changes to the overall project brief. Nevertheless, taken as a whole, the campaign was a sig-nificant success and the benefits far outweighed the difficulties encountered.

The private sector is increasingly keen to get involved in achieving public sector objectives. The reasons companies might want to partner the public sector include those related to their overall financial performance, such as:

- strengthening brand position, company reputation, and corporate image;
- increasing customer loyalty;
- attracting and motivating high-quality employees;
- differentiating themselves from competitors;
- increasing their appeal to investors;
- entering a new market;
- increasing sales;
- influencing public sector policy;
- promoting products or services.

In addition to these financial reasons, companies are also driven by objectives that relate to both social and environmental bottom lines. Such objectives include:

- being altruistic for its own sake—giving something back;
- meeting corporate social responsibility targets;
- meeting environmental and sustainability targets;
- responding to staff and board wishes to support community or health issues.

Ethical considerations

There are obviously many benefits to using PPPs in social marketing initiatives that include amplification of behavioural influence and campaign messaging, target audience reach, sus-tainability, and positive associations with trusted commercial brands. However, not-for-profit agencies and governments should proceed with due diligence when establishing and managing partnerships with the private sector. The European Commission's guidelines (2003) set out a range of recommendations to be considered before creating a PPP.

- There should be detailed analysis of the costs and benefits of private sector involvement ver-sus public sector alternatives.

◆ Both parties should appreciate the appropriateness of working together in a partnership—this could be through their organization type or the specific focus of the issue, such as nutrition.

◆ Detailed analysis of the full costs to all parties should be calculated before the partnership starts.

◆ There needs to be sufficient structure, management, and ability to implement an intervention effectively.

◆ The relationship should achieve the objectives of both parties.

◆ Finally, a PPP should only be used if it can be clearly demonstrated that it will add additional value to other approaches.

Another consideration before embarking on PPPs for social marketing is to ensure that the process is open to scrutiny (National Institute for Public Health and the Environment, 2006). This will help to ensure transparency in management and reporting and to prevent problems arising.

Building partnerships with communities

As well as working with the private sector to develop more sustained and social marketing pro-grammes that have greater reach, social marketers also need to consider how they work with communities to develop programmes that have relevance and utilize the existing assets within communities to tackle the health issue under consideration. The World Bank (2008) defines empowerment as: 'the expansion of assets and capabilities of poor people to participate in, nego-tiate with, influence, control, and hold accountable institutions that affect their lives'. According to Wallerstein (2006), societies where people play an active role in the social, economic, and cultural life will be healthier than those where people face insecurity, exclusion, and depriva-tion. Wallerstein has furthered our understanding of the nature of empowerment by describing how it is both an outcome of and an intermediate step towards a healthier life status. As such, it can be seen as both a goal and a mechanism for achieving better personal health and improving disparities in health experience and outcomes. Wallerstein recommends that effective empow-erment strategies that health promotion interventions use should include:

◆ increasing citizens' skills, control over resources, and access to information relevant to pub-lic health development;

◆ using small group efforts, which enhance critical consciousness on public health issues, to build supportive environments and a deeper sense of community;

◆ promoting community action through collective involvement in decision-making and participation in all phases of public health planning, implementation, and evaluation, use of lay helpers and leaders, advocacy and leadership training, and organizational capacity development;

◆ strengthening healthy public policy by organizational and interorganizational actions, trans-fer of power and decision-making authority to participants of interventions, and promotion of governmental and institutional accountability and transparency;

◆ being sensitive to the health care needs defined by community members themselves.

Other reviews have reported that health development initiatives based on participatory approaches are more likely to be successfully implemented (Bonnefoy et al., 2007). Some have also shown that community-based approaches which combine many different risk factors into one 'package' tend to be more effective (Ministry of Health Planning, 2003).

Community-based approaches can follow a similar path to empowerment. A review of ran-domized control trials (Gillies, 1998) found that the greater the representation of the local community in health promotion programme design and delivery, the greater the impact and the more sustainable it is. Activities that help to increase community engagement include:

◆ volunteer activities;
◆ peer programmes; and
◆ durable structures to facilitate planning and decision-making, such as the use of local committees and councils.

The case study from Madagascar set out in Box 10.2 illustrates the power of joint programmes between international organizations such as international agencies, in-country government agencies, NGOs, and the private sector.

Box 10.2 Case study: stimulating the creation of a private sector market for improved fever case management in Madagascar—the power of partnerships

Rova Ratsimandisa, Cristina Lussiana, Hana Bilak, Stephen Poyer, Nikki Charman, and Stephanie Dolan

Aims

In Madagascar the private sector distributes 80% of antimalarial drugs, primarily through drug stores, pharmacies, and retailers (ACTwatch 2015). While the availability of rapid diagnostic tests for malaria (mRDTs) has increased in the public sector, diagnostic services are practically nonexistent in the private sector, often leaving potentially life-threatening febrile illnesses being mistreated. This is the result of a lack of incentives for providers to stock mRDTs, low consumer demand, and the absence of regulatory environments mandating mRDT use.

The aim of the UNITAID Private Sector RDT project[1] is to create a private sector market for mRDTs by:

◆ increasing access to and demand for quality-assured mRDTs;
◆ improving private providers' fever case management skills; and
◆ increasing public–private engagement.

Behavioural objectives and target group

In 2010, the World Health Organization (WHO) recommended that all suspected malaria cases be diagnosed with either mRDTs or microscopy, before being treated with artemisinin-based combination therapy (ACT). Overuse of ACT is problematic because the correct treatment for other life-threatening illnesses is withheld and the risk of resistance to artemisinin is increased.

To stimulate a private sector market for mRDTs and promote rational treatment, the UNITAID project identified three target groups for intervention:

◆ consumers, to increase demand for mRDTs;
◆ private health providers, to improve their use of mRDTs;
◆ regulatory authorities in a position to modify policy.

Customer orientation and social offering

For consumers, the primary barrier to informed demand was lack of knowledge about the benefits of diagnosis and mRDTs.

There were two barriers to mRDT uptake among private providers.

◆ Technical specifications were restrictive and only one brand of quality-approved mRDT was eligible for use, leaving no room for healthy competition in the market.

◆ In the absence of any formal regulation about types of providers allowed to perform mRDTs, physicians considered it their prerogative and were resistant to private retailers performing such tests.

Target audience engagement and exchange

The UNITAID project targeted consumers through communication campaigns to improve their health-seeking behaviour by using a mix of communication materials, mass media, community-based outreach, and point-of-sales materials.

Private health providers were supported through training, formative assessments, and supervision visits to improve performance.

Regulatory authorities were invited to a series of meetings convened by the National Malaria Control Programme to discuss barriers and benefits to mRDT market development. Regulations governing the sale and use of mRDTs were developed in collaboration with the Programme and WHO, together with regulatory authorities, private sector representatives, and pharmacists' and physician's associations.

Competition analysis

At the start of the UNITAID project, lack of competition and competing interests in the mRDT market were identified as barriers to achieving its goals. Despite the national policy to test all fever cases prior to treatment with ACT, no legal framework authorized private providers to perform such tests. Physicians were reticent to let other providers carry out tests: they felt that doing so would drive consumers away from them.

Audience insight and segmentation

A total market approach was used to shape local markets to:

◆ increase access to and demand for mRDTs—for both providers and consumers;

◆ ensure service quality—tracking and improving private providers' quality in mRDT performance;

◆ create an enabling policy environment—working in partnership with the Ministry of Health.

Integrated intervention mix

Partners developed fever case management marketing plans to inform strategies for the 4Ps—product, place, price, and promotion. The UNITAID project also developed audience profiles to identify factors associated with providers' and clients' behaviour, tailored mRDT marketing plans based on those profiles, and identified appropriate market positioning.

Two campaigns were developed to increase demand for mRDTs.

◆ 'It's good for me': for consumers, mass awareness campaigns stressed the importance of being correctly diagnosed before being treated.

◆ 'It's good for business': for providers, mRDT use and adherence to WHO guidelines were positioned as methods to improve case management skills and increase credibility in the community.

The project ensured quality of service by training private providers and carrying out supportive supervision, thereby improving providers' case management skills and adherence to national guidelines—i.e. only giving an ACT when the patient had malaria. In addition, the project worked with the Ministry of Health to overcome the two policy barriers for increasing uptake of mRDTs: the product offer was broadened and a legal framework for mRDT use was created.

Co-creation through social markets

The UNITAID project is based on national and international partnerships. The national partnership consists of the public sector (Ministry of Health and National Malaria Control Programme) and the private sector (PSI, physicians' and pharmacists' associations, pharmaceutical wholesalers). The local WHO office acts as the link between both entities. The international partnership consists of PSI, WHO, the Foundation for Innovative Diagnostics, and the Johns Hopkins School of Public Health. Local support through the Ministry of Health was vital for policy-related issues, and the Ministry was engaged from the start of the project through the local WHO office. This engagement ensures sustainability of the market.

Systematic planning

The UNITAID project's total market approach examined the core supply/demand functions of the mRDT market, critical market support functions, and key policy/regulatory issues. It also targeted the main policy players, identified their capacities and incentives to build the market, and facilitated their increased role in tackling policy barriers.

Results and learning

Partnership activities in Madagascar have resulted in the following.

◆ 60 private providers were trained in the use of mRDTs, representing over 9,000 fever cases managed at 52 private facilities between April and December 2014. During that time, the testing rate increased from 69.2% to 92.7% (unpublished project monitoring data).

◆ Technical specifications for mRDTs were modified for procurement in the private sector, opening up the market to more than one supplier. All authorities and partners working on malaria control in the country endorsed the decision.

◆ In September 2014 the Ministry of Health enacted a legal framework, which allows all health providers in the public and private sectors to perform malaria diagnostic testing using mRDTs, providing they have been appropriately trained (Figure 10.1).

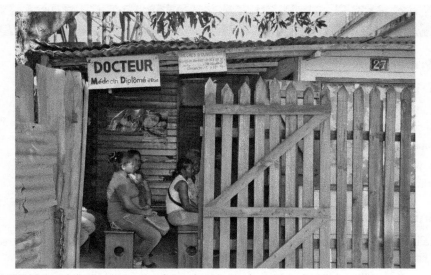

Figure 10.1 Rapid diagnostic testing for malaria in Madagascar.
Reproduced by kind permission of PSI/Madagascar, Copyright © 2016 PSI/Madagascar.

Reference

ACTwatch (2015). Madagascar [website]. Nairobi: ACTwatch http://www.actwatch.info/countries/
madagascar, accessed 30 March 2015.

Setting out degrees of participation

In February 2008, the National Institute for Health and Clinical Excellence (NICE) released guidance on community engagement. It argued that approaches which allow communities to work as equal partners, delegate some power to them, or give them total control may lead to more positive health outcomes (NICE, 2008). Box 10.3 sets out the guidance's four recommendations.

Whether you are applying a community development or social marketing approach, you need to set out explicitly the degree to which you will engage and empower your target audience. Arnstein's ladder of citizen engagement (1969) is a useful tool to help you be clear about the level of power and control being taken by communities. The ladder sets out a graded movement upwards through eight 'rungs'—from manipulation of citizens to total citizen control. It depicts participation as essentially a power struggle between citizens trying to move up the ladder and controlling organizations and institutions, intentionally or otherwise, attempting to limit their movement up the ladder and associated levels of increasing power and control. The metaphor of the ladder has become an enduring part of policy, academic enquiry, and practice. However, Mayo (2005) has put forward an alternative metaphor: that of a fruit tree as set out in Figure 10.2.

Mayo asserts that while most engagement strategy might be based on a core trunk of information provision and power transfer, there are in fact many legitimate and differing reasons for engagement, and differing processes that are relevant to them. These can be conceived as

Box 10.3 NICE recommendations for community engagement

1. Prerequisites for success

There is a need for:

- coordinated implementation of the relevant policy initiatives;
- a commitment to long-term investment;
- openness to organizational and cultural change;
- a willingness to share power; and
- the development of trust and respect among all those involved.

2. Infrastructure

Once the prerequisites have been met, it is easier to set up the infrastructure required to implement effective practice. There is also a need:

- to provide support for appropriate training and development of those working with the community—including members of that community; and
- for formal mechanisms which endorse partnership working and support for effective implementation of area-based initiatives.

3. Approaches

To support and increase levels of community engagement, 'agents of change' and a range of other approaches such as community workshops and resident consultancy can be used to encourage local communities to become involved in activities and area-based initiatives.

4. Evaluation

Finally, there is a need to invest in evaluation of community engagement programmes and processes in order to increase understanding of how community engagement and the different approaches used affect health and other social outcomes.

Source: data from NICE (National Institute for Health and Care Excellence). *Community engagement: improving health and wellbeing and reducing health inequalities: NICE Guidelines [NG44]*. London: NICE, Copyright © 2016 National Institute for Health and Care Excellence, https://www.nice.org.uk/guidance/ng44, accessed 01 May 2016.

separate branches that bear different fruits or desired outcomes. Each of these branches and their fruits have explicit levels of power transfer that have been set out at the beginning of the process.

The main point is that, regardless of what metaphor is used, it is important to be clear about why an organization is seeking to engage or partner with citizens, how much power is being transferred, and what are the most appropriate methods that relate to that process and the intended outcome. For example, if an organization is carrying out a consultation process then it should use consultative methodology and produce a report of the conclusions of the consultation.

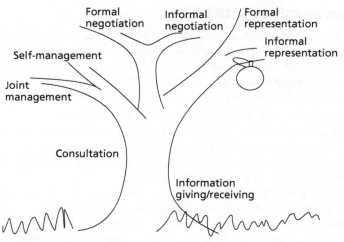

Figure 10.2 Mayo's fruit tree of participation.
Reproduced with permission from Mayo E. *A playlist for public services*. London: National Consumer Council, Copyright © 2005 Crown Copyright. Available at http://www.customerserviceexcellence.uk.com/UserFiles/File/Playlist_for_public_services(1).pdf, accessed 01 Apr. 2016.

How social marketing relates to and complements community empowerment and development

The links between community empowerment, community development, and social marketing need to be clearly articulated if we are to be able to develop more effective social programmes. Social marketing shares with community empowerment and development approaches to social development a focus on generating a deep understanding of individual and community beliefs, values, environmental and social factors, and how these can be harnessed to promote positive social improvement. Social marketing also shares the basic democratic principle of community development approaches that social and health goals need to be supported by the majority of the general population. However, social marketing differs from these approaches in that it focuses more on defining specific behavioural objectives and it applies a more methodical and systemic approach to project development, implementation, and evaluation. Community development and empowerment approaches tend to adopt a more reflexive approach to their implementation—one characterized by a willingness to shift more general social goals in response to expressed community needs.

Social marketing, as outlined in chapter one, is ultimately concerned with achieving measurable behavioural goals that relate to health and social improvement. Community development and empowerment programmes may have this outcome as a focus, but they may also be concerned with informing, educating, and creating attitudinal and belief change as end-points in themselves. Social marketing programmes often involve information and attitudinal change, but these are steps towards the ultimate goal of measurable behavioural objectives, and are not ends in themselves. So although it is desirable that social marketing programmes be informed by what is known about successful community empowerment and engagement programmes, and such programmes can gain much from an understanding of social marketing principles, the key imperative is to understand what the end-point of the intervention is and what approaches are best deployed to achieve this.

Building partnerships with NGOs

Voluntary organizations, foundations, and charities support, fund, and provide a huge rage and volume of local, national, and international social programmes. Many such organizations also sponsor and deliver a wide range of social marketing interventions. NGOs are increasingly well-managed and highly efficient organizations that can be effective partners in many social marketing programmes. As partners, therefore, they offer a range of advantages.

◆ NGOs are usually driven by strong ethical and humanitarian motives.
◆ They are fast on their feet and can often make decisions and take action more rapidly than some public sector or private sector organizations.
◆ They often have a very well-developed structure and delivery chain that can enable local initiatives to be developed and implemented quickly.
◆ They usually have good relationships and ready access to groups of the population that some businesses and public sector organizations might view as being 'hard to reach'.
◆ They often have strong brands and good reputations, so they can be very useful as the face and voice of social marketing initiatives rather than a government or government agency, whose branding or endorsement can sometimes limit the acceptability and or success of an intervention.
◆ NGOs that are foundations or research institutes often offer grants and funds to support social marketing initiatives and are a source of knowledge about what works and what does not.

For these reasons, when you are developing your low-cost social marketing partnership or coalition strategy you should consider as part of the early planning which NGOs may be able to assist you in developing, implementing, and evaluating the intervention.

How partners differ from stakeholders

In this chapter the term 'partners' and 'partnerships' is used to reflect the way different organizations can agree to come together around a shared commitment to a particular endeavour or cause. Some of the key differences between partners and stakeholders are set out in Box 10.4.

Box 10.4 How do partners differ from stakeholders?

Partners:

◆ are actively involved in the scoping, development, delivery, and evaluation of social marketing interventions;
◆ contribute resources, such as know-how, information, facilities, or finance; and
◆ make a commitment, usually in the form of a written agreement, to actively contribute.

Stakeholders:

◆ can be involved in a range of ways, from wishing to be informed through to some level of support;
◆ may not have an active interest in an initiative but would be offended if they were not informed or consulted; and
◆ are not subject to any form of written commitment to participate or deliver.

Partners bring different resources, skills, and expertise to a partnership to achieve things that they could not achieve alone. Although there tends to be a great deal of rhetoric about creating conditions where partners can come together 'as equals', the reality is rarely this straightforward, and acknowledging this from the start is an important factor if a partnership is going to work.

Stakeholders, in contrast ,are typically people or organizations who have an interest in the issue that the social marketing programme is seeking to influence but who are not formally engaged in developing or delivering the programme. For example, this interest may be because they are in a group affected by the issue, or because they are currently trying to do something about the issue from a different perspective. Stakeholders are typically identified and classified using a matrix with two parameters:

◆ their power and influence;
◆ their level of support for the initiative.

This is illustrated in Figure 10.3.

Stakeholders in each quadrant of this matrix require different management strategies, most of which involve setting out clear aims and objectives for each quadrant and sometimes for specific named stakeholders. The objectives depend on the characteristics of each stakeholder and can range from keeping them informed to attempts to get them to become partners. Action at the opposite extreme can include focusing on managing stakeholders who oppose the social marketing initiative either to reduce their impact or to encourage them to be positive in their attitudes. Typically, stakeholder management is evaluated by assessing how much progress has been made against each of the agreed objectives on a regular basis.

Although stakeholder management is a vital component of all social marketing initiatives, it will not deliver the impact that a fully engaged and well-managed partnership coalition can. Successful joint working with partners means moving away from a situation where a stakeholder may have a passive or reactive relationship with the social marketing programme to one that is active, evolving, long term, and mutually beneficial.

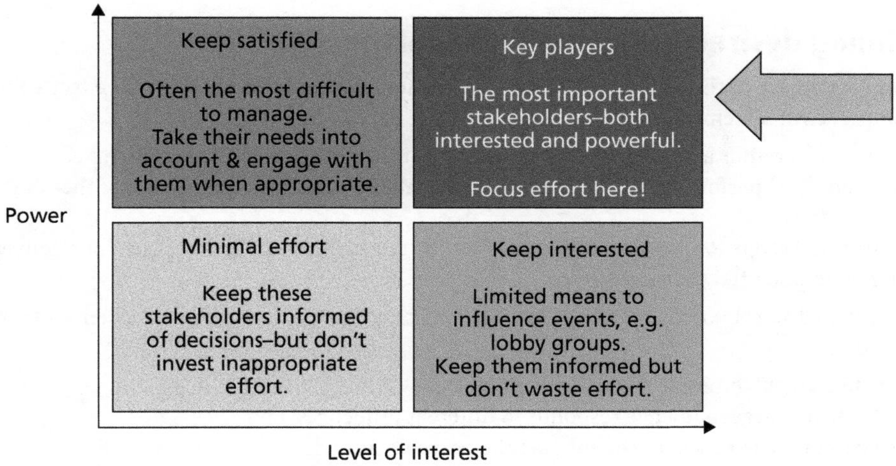

Figure 10.3 The power and matrix tool.
Reproduced with permission from Gardner JR, Rachlin R, and Sweeny HWA. *Handbook of strategic planning.* New York: John Wiley and Sons Inc., Copyright © 1986 John Wiley and Sons.

A true partnership approach:

- enables partners to work together to set objectives that are owned by all partners;
- recognizes that no one organization has all the answers;
- mobilizes partners to deliver appropriate, sustainable solutions;
- acknowledges that complex, sensitive issues require a long-term approach that works through cultural, rational, economic, environmental, and emotional influences;
- provides appropriate support to facilitate, maintain, and evaluate the partnership;
- listens, respects, forgives, and learns from mistakes.

How to find the right partners

Finding the right partner or partners is critical. When seeking partners, you will need to ask a series of questions.

- What are we trying to achieve?
- What is in it for the partner?
- What do we hope they can bring or help us with?
- What do we not need from them?
- What can they give or do?
- What can they not give or do?
- What can we give them?
- What can we not give them?

By answering these questions, you will ensure that the needs of partners are considered and contributions fully integrated from the planning stage. Investing the time and effort at the outset to bring the right organizations on board, and to create win–win outcomes for all partners, will help lay the foundations for a strong, mutually beneficial partnership.

Building a successful partnership takes time and effort. Be clear about the goals of your initiative and target group, as this will help you shortlist potential partner organizations. As discussed in chapter four, it is preferable to map out potential stakeholders during your initiative's scoping stage and to determine those who will become actual partners and what role they will play.

Defining desired outcomes from partnerships

A clear statement of the desired outcomes lays the foundation for developing an effective partnership. A clear statement of purpose should:

- include clear aims and objectives that put the citizen at the centre of the initiative;
- include key performance indicators, deliverables, and milestones from the citizen's perspective;
- outline the scope for partners to help deliver the outcomes as a starting point for a conversation with potential partners.

In assessing the role of an organization that you may want to partner, it is essential to keep in mind:

- the desired outcomes;
- the way the target audience responds to different influences; and
- the comprehensiveness of the support the partners provide to the target audience.

Ultimately, your choice of partners will be influenced by many factors. Table 10.1 shows some considerations that may help your prioritization.

Table 10.1 Assessing potential partners

Shortlisting criteria	Acceptance criteria
A good track record, sound management, and a stable financial position	Evidence from annual reports and accounts demonstrates organizational health and past good work in the area you are interested in.
Good standing with its own sector	The potential partner has a strong reputation as a for-profit or not-for-profit organization. It is recognized as a market leader. It has been a recipient of sector awards and other forms of recognition.
Access to the people you are seeking to help	User or customer profiles indicate that the potential partner is serving or seeking to serve the intended target audience. Evidence from the target audience indicates that the organization already influences and supports their lifestyle choices. The organization has established links to key social networks within the target audience or specific segments.
Access to relevant technical, research, or other facilities that will help with the social marketing programme	The forms of technical skills and insights and/or facilities sought exist within the organization. It has demonstrated a willingness to make these available.
Are they attractive partners? Are they like-minded? Are they reputable?	The organization has a good reputation within the target audience. More widely it seen as reputable and will withstand scrutiny for conflicts of interest.
Credibility: do the organization's brand, services, or products complement your brief?	The organization is known as an advocate and supporter of the issue and provides products and/or services that are compatible with the project focus and objectives.
An obvious role for the organization	There is a clear, well-defined opportunity and the partner has the necessary resources.
Capacity for partnering	There is support from senior managers and leaders. There are staff with good interpersonal skills and a willingness to partner. Sufficient time will be allocated to engage in active partnering.

The process of assessing the strengths and weaknesses of organizations as partners should help formulate a delivery matrix that maps out the roles of preferred partners. Such a matrix can be market tested with the target audience to validate the choices from their perspective. An active partnership should evolve and develop organically in response to the changing needs of the target audience. Different partners may have important roles at different times. It is essential that before a partnership begins everyone is clear about what is being offered, what is not or cannot be delivered, and how any conflicts that might arise will be settled.

Managing partnerships

The mechanisms for joint working with partners are outlined in Table 10.2. These are all tried and tested mechanisms but they should not be taken as the only acceptable solutions and should

Table 10.2 Proven mechanisms for joint working

Joint promotions	The for-profit organization will invest its resources in joint working with partners to raise awareness of the need for change (e.g. in promoting sensible drinking).
Joint marketing	The partner will invest its resources and lend its brand to support actions to bring about behaviour change. The partner's understanding of the target audience and its reach can be used to ensure that audiences are aware of and are supported to adopt recommended behaviours.
Provision of financial incentives	The partners will offer financial or other forms of incentives to encourage the desired behaviour being promoted by the coalition (e.g. free exchanges of energy-efficient light bulbs for older, less efficient ones in the cause of reducing energy use).
Provision of non-financial incentives	The partners will offer non-financial incentives, such as a healthy menu choices in support of a healthy eating programme.
Sponsorship	Rather than straight financial contributions, the partner will provide endorsements via the use of its logo, its outlets, staff time and effort, etc., to promote the programme's objectives—for example, use of locations to act as collection points for unused and unwanted or out-of-date medicines.
Financial sponsorship	The partner will donate cash to the partnership. The sponsor may reasonably expect cooperation, loyalty, and active public relations from the partnership. The cash may or may not be tied to a particular activity. It is essential that any finance is clearly accounted for, and care must be taken to ensure the sponsor has integrity—for example, tobacco sponsorship of a healthy eating programme may undermine its credibility.
Corporate volunteering and use of staff time	Many businesses now encourage skilled staff to help the NGO and public sectors. Partners can also offer to train their staff to assist with interventions by providing information or signposting, and to train other partners' staff in needed skills.
Socially responsible business practices	The corporation or NGO conducts its discretionary business practices and investments and/or fundraising activity in ways that support the partnership or the underlying cause.
Acting as an example of good practice	Being seen to 'walk the talk': the partner will ensure that the target audience receives consistent signals about making healthy choices and a positive message that change is possible. In addition, the workplace may be one of the few routes to reaching some members of the target audience. Employers can give support in a variety of ways ranging from providing information to supporting activities.
Advocacy	The partner will act as an advocate for the desired issue and may include references to the programme issue in its own marketing or service delivery. It may run informational campaigns to raise awareness about the issue as part of its contribution and work with other organizations and governments to bring about change.
Access to partner's promotions	The partner offers the use of existing promotions and channels to the partnership to support the programme—for example, allowing informational materials to be inserted into planned direct mail shots.
Funding research	The organization may sponsor research activity in support of the programme. It is important that any such research activity is independently monitored and evaluated, and is subject to strict governance.

not limit your imagination. In developing a partnership with any organization a focus on win–win outcomes is more important than precedent.

Developing a mutually beneficial and active partnership takes time, understanding, and respect for all parties' positions. The path to an agreement may be smoothed by introducing a participatory approach from the outset. Engaging partners early, ideally at the scoping stage, ensures there is time for:

- constructive discussion and negotiation with regards to the desired outcomes of the partnership, how they might best be achieved, and the contributions of the partners;
- thorough consideration of the implications of the partnership, the risks involved, and the attendant benefits;
- development of a shared, realistic vision based on common goals; and
- involvement in the planning and risk management processes.

Early engagement means that decision-makers can be fully briefed on the partnership and can include the resources required in the business planning process. Moving from the scoping phase to implementation means building the right active partnerships to deliver the desired outcomes. It is important to try and keep as many options for joint working open as possible at this stage.

In many circumstances, information, know-how, networks, branding, or facilities can be more important than money in achieving the partnership's objectives. There are many ways of matching these opportunities to preferred partners, or, where market research has revealed gaps, to finding new partners.

The core principles for partnerships are:

- be legal and above suspicion, e.g. by being non-exclusive and based on a formal contract;
- be fair and equitable;
- benefit society—be cost-effective and in accord with the available evidence;
- do not jeopardize the integrity and reputation of members of the partnership; and
- do not compromise the independence and impartiality of the partnership, e.g. through a real or perceived conflict of interest or the endorsement (actual or implicit) of an organization or its products and services.

Establishing a management framework

Successful partnerships are those with effective management frameworks, which are proportionate to the scale of the partnership, ensure all partners have a voice while providing overall leadership and accountability, and are efficient and non-bureaucratic. Every partnership should be founded on a written agreement that sets out the terms and conditions of the partnership and its objectives. You should set out clearly the expected duration of the partnership, the contribution of each partner, and any time scales for delivery. Agreements should ensure that there is a leadership and management structure for the partnership and that there are clear lines of accountability. Performance management mechanisms—including key success factors, performance indicators, monitoring arrangements, and evaluation criteria—all need to be set out. The partnership's first-year business plan should also ideally be included, setting out the source and application of resources, key milestones, and objectives to be delivered. At the very least, agreements should contain:

- details of the partners and responsible officers;
- a statement of intent: what is to be achieved, what each partner will do, and what partners will not be required to do;
- structures and procedures for managing the partnership, including roles and responsibilities, administrative arrangements, decision-making processes, and accountabilities;

- details of what resources are being committed by partners and what influence they and all partners have over these;
- a review and audit of the processes that will be put in place to monitor progress, the functioning of the partnership, and how adjustment will be made if necessary;
- caveats: these may include the use of intellectual property, use of copyright materials including logos, use of confidential information, and permissions that may be needed for the use of information or resources;
- legal status of the agreement and its implication; and
- the time frame for the partnership and the delivery of any specific areas of work or commitment.

The agreement should also be signed by an officer with the authority to represent the partner organization. It is a good idea to get the most senior person possible to sign the partnership agreement, as it is a public declaration of commitment that staff within the organization can refer to as the programme develops.

Conclusion

Partnerships developed to promote health have a long history within the public health movement. They sit at the heart of most of the big public health advances that have been achieved over the last hundred years. It is rare that one group, profession, or sector has all the answers, levers for change, or resources to promote health in a systemic way.

Partnerships that seek to sustain and support positive social and health development usually come about as a result of long-term commitment. It needs to be remembered that over the duration of the partnership the target audience will continually be exposed to new stimuli and influences. It is therefore essential that monitoring of such new developments and influences is continuous. Partnerships and coalitions also need to be evaluated on an ongoing basis. This is essential so that it can be ensured that any partnership can demonstrate that it continues to fulfil its purpose and is making a contribution to improving health that justifies the time and effort put into it.

Self-review questions

1. What are some of the reasons for establishing and managing partnerships as part of social marketing programmes?

2. What are the differences between partnerships with the for-profit sector, the not-for-profit sector, communities, and NGOs?

3. List some of the key things that need to be considered when managing stakeholders and partners in a social marketing programme.

4. When selecting organizations to partner with to deliver a social marketing programme, what are some of the most important issues to be considered?

Note

1. The UNITAID Private Sector RDT project is a partnership between PSI, Malaria Consortium, Foundation for Innovative Diagnostics, Johns Hopkins School of Public Health, and the World Health Organization, funded by UNITAID. For more information visit: http://www.unitaid.eu/en/creating-a-private-sector-market-for-quality-assured-rdts-in-malaria-endemic-countries

References

Arnstein, S. (1969). A ladder of citizen participation. *Journal of the American Institute of Planners* 35: 216–224.

Audit Commission (2005). *Governing partnerships: bridging the accountability gap*. London: Audit Commission.

Ban, Ki-Moon. (2008). *Keynote address to the Asian Forum on Corporate Social Responsibility*. http://www.unescap.org/speeches/keynote-address-asian-forum-corporate-social-responsibility, accessed 2 September 2016.

Bonnefoy, J., Morgan, A., Kelly, M.P., Butt, J., Bergman, V. (2007). *Constructing the evidence base on the social determinants of health*. Geneva: World Health Organization.

Crisp, N. (2007). *Global health partnerships: the UK contribution to health in developing countries*. London: COI. http://www.wales.nhs.uk/documents/DH_083510.pdf, accessed 11 July 2016.

Department of Health (2000). *Commercial sponsorship: ethical standards for the NHS*. London: Department of Health.

Economist Intelligence Unit (2008). *Corporate citizenship: profiting from a sustainable business*. London: Economist Intelligence Unit.

European Commission (2003). *Guidelines for successful public–private partnerships*. Brussels: European Commission Directorate-General Regional Policy.

Gillies, P. (1998). Effectiveness of alliances and partnerships for health promotion. *Health Promotion International* 13(2):99–120.

Kotler, P., Lee, N. (2006). *Corporate social responsibility: doing the most good for your company and your cause*. New York: John Wiley and Sons.

Mayo, E. (2005). *A playlist for public services*. London: National Consumer Council.

Ministry of Foreign Affairs of Denmark (2006). *Corporate social responsibility: support facilities in the public private partnership programme*. Copenhagen: Ministry of Foreign Affairs of Denmark.

Ministry of Health Planning (2003). *Prevention that works: a review of the evidence regarding the causation and prevention of chronic disease* [consultation draft]. Victoria, BC: Ministry of Health Planning.

National Institute for Public Health and the Environment (2006). *Report on the contributions to the Green Paper 'Promoting healthy diets and physical activity: a European dimension for the prevention of overweight, obesity and chronic diseases'*. Bilthoven: National Institute for Public Health and the Environment.

NHS Management Executive (1993). *Standards of business conduct for NHS staff. HSG(93)5*. London: Department of Health.

NHS Scotland (2003). *A common understanding: guidance on joint working between NHS Scotland and the pharmaceutical industry*. Edinburgh: NHS Scotland.

NICE (2008). *Community engagement: improving health and wellbeing and reducing health inequalities: NICE Guidelines [NG44]*. London: National Institute for Health and Care Excellence https://www.nice.org.uk/guidance/ng44, accessed 1 May 2016.

Putnam, R.D. (2000). *Bowling alone: the collapse and revival of American community*. New York: Simon and Schuster.

UNAIDS (2007). *AIDS is everybody's business: partnerships with the private sector—a collection of case studies from UNAIDS*. Geneva: UNAIDS.

United Nations (2003). *Report of the Secretary-General on enhanced cooperation between the United Nations and all relevant partners, in particular the private sector*. New York: United Nations.

Wallerstein, N. (2006). *What is the evidence on effectiveness of empowerment to improve health?* Copenhagen: WHO Regional Office for Europe http://www.euro.who.int/__data/assets/pdf_file/0010/74656/E88086.pdf, accessed 11 July 2016.

WHO (2000). *Guidelines on working with the private sector to achieve health outcomes: report by the Secretariat.* Geneva: World Health Organization http://apps.who.int/iris/bitstream/10665/78660/1/ee20.pdf, accessed 11 July 2016.

World Bank (2008). *What is empowerment?* Washington, DC: World Bank http://siteresources.worldbank.org/INTEMPOWERMENT/Resources/486312-1095094954594/draft2.pdf, accessed 21 February 2008.

World Economic Forum (2005). *Partnering for success: business perspectives on multi stakeholder partnerships.* Geneva: World Economic Forum.

Chapter 11

Ethical issues in social marketing

Lynne Eagle, Stephan Dahl, and David Low

A man without ethics is a wild beast loosed upon this world

Camus A, *The Plague*, tr. Stuart Gilbert, 1948

Learning points

This chapter:

◆ provides an overview of ethical challenges within social marketing, including:

  • targeting;

  • literacy challenges;

  • stigmatizing/victim blaming/generating fear, guilt, and shame;

  • coercion and nudging/limiting personal freedoms;

  • personal financial incentives;

◆ provides a review of competing ethical frameworks and discusses the implication of these for social marketing practice;

◆ discusses the role of social marketing ethical resources such as codes of ethics.

Social marketing's ethical dimensions

Before we discuss ethical issues in social marketing, we need to clarify what ethics means in this specific context. The scope of health-focused social marketing ethics is set out by Carter et al. (2012: 2):

> Ethics is the discipline devoted to moral reasoning about what we should do. It is traditionally divided into: meta-ethics, concerned with fundamental questions like 'what is good?' and 'what are convincing ethical arguments?'; normative ethics, focused on rules, frameworks or principles for evaluation; and practical ethics, concerned with the ethics of practices such as regulating, policing, teaching or medical care. Health promotion ethics is a form of practical ethics.

Whose values and whose mandate?

Some authors suggest that social marketing is value-neutral, given that the aims of activity are to change behaviours in ways that benefit individuals, communities, or wider society (Dann, 2007).

This is a minority view, countered by Rossi and Yudell (2012), who stress the value-ladenness aspect of social marketing activity. Values arise initially in relation to the issue of who defines what behaviour is desired, whether harm to others—not necessarily those targeted—may occur as a consequence of a social marketing intervention, and how this should be considered in the development of any intervention.

The question 'Who has the mandate to represent large and diverse populations for the purpose of informed consent, and how can this be implemented?' (Guttman and Salmon, 2004: 537) has been raised in relation to developing interventions. Additional questions then arise relating to how individual freedom of choice and individual rights can and should be balanced against benefits for society as a whole, and who should define or prioritize the benefits and decide when individual freedom should be restricted (see, for example, Lefebvre, 2011).

Further, the implications for interventions of levels of risk that may be acceptable to different segments of society but not to society as a whole need to be considered (Callahan and Jennings, 2002). There is a growing body of literature that documents wider ethical issues and unexpected impacts of interventions, including issues regarding targeting, segmentation, use of incentive schemes, the consequences of focusing on easy-to-reach or influence groups rather than those with the greatest need, and the needs of low-literacy groups and minority groups and cultures (Cho and Salmon, 2007; Eagle et al., 2013; Lynagh et al., 2013; Newton et al., 2013). These are now discussed in more detail.

Ethics of targeting

When resources are limited, which group or groups should be given priority over others? Is it ethical to target sectors of the population who are easiest to reach, or are likely to be the easiest to reach or the most receptive to an intervention (often called 'low-hanging fruit') rather than those who might benefit the most from changes to their behaviour? What are the implications for those who are not specifically targeted? It is suggested that non-inclusion of some groups is a form of discrimination (Braunack-Mayer and Louise, 2008). If an intervention is targeted at those most in need but it costs significantly more than interventions aimed at lower-priority groups, is it ethical to focus resources on one specific group at the expense of others? Is it ethical to target the behaviour of individuals without considering the socioeconomic or wider environmental factors that may act as significant barriers to the sustained adoption of the desired behaviour change (Eagle et al., 2013)? Where communities are involved in the development and implementation of an intervention but may lack expertise in making optimum decisions, what are the ethics of different courses of action? These are not simple questions to answer and the solutions will be situation-specific.

Ethics of literacy challenges

The problem of understanding and engaging with behaviour change issues is also closely related to functional literacy. The Organisation for Economic Co-operation and Development (Nutbeam, 2008) defines functional literacy in relation to whether a person is able to understand and employ printed information in daily life, at home, at work, and in their community. Varying definitions of literacy make cross-study comparisons difficult, but there appears to be agreement that some 20% of the population of most developed countries have severe literacy problems, and a further 20% have limited literacy (Adkins and Ozanne, 2005; Kemp and Eagle, 2008). Lack of numeracy skills is also linked to lower comprehension and low use of health information: 'Many patients cannot perform the basic numeracy tasks required to function in the current health care environment'(Peters et al., 2007: 742). Problems include understanding of risk magnitude, absolute versus relative risk, and medication compliance, with negative consequences for health outcomes (Reyna et al., 2009). There would appear to be an ethical obligation to provide written material in formats that are easily comprehended by target groups.

Ethics of stigmatizing/victim blaming/generating fear, guilt, and shame

It is possible for social marketing interventions to inadvertently stigmatize those they are trying to help, such as by focusing on encouraging individual weight loss without considering wider socioeconomic and community factors that may affect an individual's ability to lose weight and maintain a lower weight (Bombak, 2014). Carter et al. (2011) criticize some mass media interventions promoting weight loss as being coercive, promoting guilt, and portraying people with high body mass index levels in a negative way, potentially resulting in feelings of self-blame and lowered self-esteem. In contrast, Bayer (2008) suggests that stigma-based strategies can legitimately be used for some activities, such as reducing smoking rates.

As well as claims that the use of fear, guilt, and shame appeals constitute a form of coercion, it is also suggested that these types of appeal are overused and not universally effective (Hastings et al., 2004). Further, the use of extreme fear appeals may result in negative perceptions and loss of support from key stakeholders (see, for example, the analysis of the Australian White Ribbon Day campaign in Donovan et al., 2009).

Ethics of coercion and nudging/limiting personal freedoms

Coercion

Does social marketing involve coercion? A standard dictionary definition of coercion is: 'to compel or restrain by force or authority without regard to individual wishes or desires' (Harper Collins, 2001). The role of governments or their agencies in achieving behaviour change is contested, with some arguing that it is legitimate to influence behaviours to make people's lives healthier—i.e. 'paternalistic' concern—while others argue that individuals should have the freedom to make their own choices (Jones et al., 2011). In a seminal paper, Rothschild (1999) suggests that governments have both the right and the responsibility to protect free choice—but also to protect people from externalities caused by others, including costs as well as physical or emotional harm.

The three primary tools for behaviour change are identified as education, marketing (persuasion), and legislation. The situations in which each of these three alternatives may be used, individually or in combination, depends on people's motivations, opportunities, and abilities to change their behaviours (Rothschild, 1999).

According to Rothchild's conceptualization, if people are motivated to change behaviours, and have both the opportunity and ability to do so, then education may be all that is needed. However, while education informs, those using education alone assume behaviour change will follow, but the target(s) are then left to search for further information, such as the benefits from behaviour change and behavioural options. Thus, education alone may be insufficient for those who lack motivation, opportunity, or ability.

If people are motivated but do not have the opportunity to change their behaviours, multiple strategies may be needed to remove actual or perceived barriers and then to use a combination of education and marketing/persuasion to show that change can be achieved. Marketing activity presents choices and benefits, reinforcing incentives—or negative consequences of not changing behaviours—and inviting voluntary behaviour change. It is legislation that is perceived as a coercive force, as it requires specific behaviours.

When motivation does not exist, legislation may be needed, especially in situations (such as smoking in public places) where active resistance to behaviour change is evident. This may be coupled with marketing/persuasion if people do not believe they have the opportunity to undertake the desired behaviour—and a combination of education and marketing/persuasion if they also do not believe they have the ability to change.

Another key issue is the use of intervention strategies that restrict choice or limit personal freedom. While there are claims that coercion and paternalism may be justified to stop people harming others or to stop ill-informed actions (Carter et al., 2011), debate is needed over the circumstances under which coercion may or may not be an appropriate strategy.

Nudging

There are ongoing debates regarding whether all forms of persuasion are inherently unethical or whether there are boundaries within which these tactics are acceptable, such as when benefits outweigh risks (Rossi and Yudell, 2012). There is considerable debate, particularly in the UK, regarding behavioural economics and 'nudge' strategies—i.e. a range of non-legislatory interventions based on altering the physical situations or contexts in which behavioural decisions occur (commonly termed 'choice architecture'). Choice architecture is claimed to alter behaviours in predictable ways through the options intentionally made available or not, such as making healthy food more visible and accessible than less healthy options.

The issues are far from clear cut: the question 'Is it possible to interfere with individual decision-making while preserving freedom of choice?' has been asked (Ménard, 2010: 229). It has been suggested that acceptability is dependent on 'the right kind of nudge for specific circumstances' (Cohen, 2013: 10); this returns us to the original sections of this chapter—who has the mandate to determine what is 'right'? There appears to be no one right answer to the acceptability of nudge strategies as they appear to be context-dependent, incorporating the nature of the nudge and both the nudger and nudgee (Lucke, 2013). There are also many circumstances in which a 'nudge' is unlikely to be sufficient (French, 2011). See chapter six for a further analysis of these issues.

Limiting personal freedoms

Determining the balance between freedom and constraint is not a simple task, and polarized views are evident. There has long been evidence of philosophy-based concern regarding the role of government in health promotion, with opponents suggesting that 'health promotion is something the Nanny State (or the Welfare State) forces on us because it is good for us, such as a dose of nasty-tasting medicine that will make us grow big and strong and live longer' (Callahan, 2001: 83). Some commentators note that assertions of 'Nannyism' may be met with 'postures of reticence' on behalf of government, but 'in reality, complaints about Nannyism have negligible influence. There is virtually no resistance to the advance of government intrusion in lifestyle if it is deemed to be justified in terms of public health' (Fitzpatrick, 2004: 645).

This form of resistance is evident in other areas—for example, in spite of a considerable body of evidence that wearing motorcycle helmets reduces injury and death rates, compulsory helmet use has been seen by some as paternalism and thus a breach of individual freedom (Jones and Bayer, 2007).

Ethics of personal financial incentives

The provision of personal financial incentives to encourage behaviour change has been used in a number of areas, including smoking cessation, HIV prevention, exercise and screening programmes, and rubbish recycling (Lavack et al., 2007; Heise et al., 2013; Lynagh et al., 2013). Results have been mixed, although this is partially due to differences in evaluation methodologies and measurement tools, which make comparisons between interventions extremely difficult.

Supporters of the use of financial incentives to change behaviours hold that it makes sense both in financial terms and potential outcomes to pay to encourage behaviour change now, rather than to incur the costs of treating serious medical conditions at some future point in time. Criticisms of the use of such incentives are focused on two areas: efficacy and ethics. In terms of efficacy, there is very limited evidence of behaviour change being sustained once incentives are discontinued. For example, a recycling programme that achieved immediate, significant effects on recycling behaviours during the period financial incentives were in place showed no sustained behaviour change after they were stopped (Iyer and Kashyap, 2007).

There is also mixed evidence regarding whether positive rewards or penalties such as taxes on continued behaviour—for example, taxes on food deemed to be of low nutritional value (Laurance, 2009)—are more effective. These types of tax are always regressive, as those with the least financial resources are affected the most. Negative incentives such as taxes appear less effective than positive rewards (Mytton et al., 2007). The targeted behaviours must be seen within the context of the health systems in different countries: most research in this area originates from the USA or the UK and the findings may not be generalizable to other countries with very different health systems.

Further, questions arise as to whether personal financial incentives are equitable. The key argument here is whether the public should pay, through their taxes, to encourage some people to be to change their behaviours when others manage to do so without any financial reward (Lynagh et al., 2013). A second area of debate relates to claims that these types of incentive penalize people with poor health or disabilities, who may be willing but unable to change behaviours (Schmidt et al., 2012). Ethical dimensions are apparent in relation to the negative impact of personal financial incentives on intrinsic (internal) motivations, such as feelings of social responsibility, which are replaced by extrinsic (financial reward) factors. Personal financial incentives for blood donation have also raised concerns regarding the quality of blood donated, with some potential donors having chronic medical conditions that renders their blood unusable for transfusions. There also appears to be a negative impact in this area on people's willingness to donate in the future without such incentives (Mortimer et al., 2013).

Socioeconomic or environmental factors may also have an impact on equity issues owing to the limitations they place on possible behaviour change (Stephens, 2013). This might include the lack of exercise facilities—or lack of public transport to get people to those facilities—in some areas which may be targeted for fitness and weight reduction interventions or, as a more extreme example, the futility of encouraging handwashing or other personal hygiene actions in low socioeconomic areas such as slums, if they do not have adequate water supplies or other necessary infrastructure (Langford and Panter-Brick, 2013).

Unintended effects

While we have shown the extent of debate over several ethical issues, a dimension that is often overlooked is the consideration of unintended effects. We have known for decades that 'reactance' effects explain not only why some public health interventions may not be effective but also why they may produce effects contrary to those intended (Buller et al., 1998). Reactance occurs when direct or potential perceived threats to personal freedom—such as consumption of specific products or engaging in particular behaviours—are detected and resisted. The targeted groups may become motivated by the perceived threat itself, rather than the actual consequences of the threat, to assert their freedom and regain control of their own decision-making and thereby of their threatened freedom (Rains, 2013). Strategies such as nudging may thus lead to reactance effects if target groups perceive threats to their freedom of choice.

Engaging in the threatened behaviour is one means of re-establishing this freedom (Rummel et al., 2000). Reactance effects appear to be strongest when the threatened freedom is perceived as important and the affected individual perceives that their 'counterforce' efforts will achieve personal control. Conversely, if an individual does not perceive that their actions will be effective in countering the threat, reactance will be minimal (Quick and Stephenson, 2007).

If recognized as constituting a threat to personal freedom of choice, persuasive communication such as mass media public health intervention programmes may result in defiance and actions that resist or are the opposite of those intended. A further danger is that awareness of attempts to manipulate behaviour may result in the behaviour itself becoming more attractive—the 'forbidden fruit' problem that has been seen in interventions such as tobacco cessation programmes targeting adolescents (Sussman et al., 2010; Box 11.1).

Box 11.1 Case study: 'Thai Smoking Kid'

Encouraging people to quit smoking is a worldwide challenge. This case study from Thailand illustrates an innovative approach to the challenge. The Thai Health Promotion Foundation designed a low-budget (US$5,000) video-based intervention to be run online only. The intention was to increase the number of smokers calling a quitline for help. Research had indicated that smokers knew about the hazards of smoking, but disregarded their own health risks, believing that their health was under their control. The main barriers that prevented smokers from listening to warnings or taking action were the smokers themselves.

In the video, child actors with cigarettes in hand approached adult smokers in designated smoking areas and asked if the smokers could light their cigarettes. All adults refused the request and lectured the children on the dangers of smoking. The children then asked why the adults were still smoking and handed them a brochure with the message:

> You worry about me, but why not about yourself? Reminding yourself is the most effective warning to help you quit. Call the 1600 hotline to quit smoking.

The video was viewed more than a million times within the first three days after it was posted online, and more than five million times during the first ten days after posting. Media coverage, estimated at more than US$3 million in value, and social media commentaries (all overwhelmingly positive) extended well beyond Thailand.

The number of completed calls to the quitline went up by 62% in the first month after the video was released online, and averaged a 32% increase over pre-intervention levels for the following five months.

This intervention won a gold medal from the Warc Prize for Asian Strategy in 2013. The full case study is available on the Warc database (accessible via subscription).

Acknowledgements

This case study was created with grateful acknowledgement of the work of Warc (http://www.warc.com/) and the Thai Health Promotion Foundation (http://en.thaihealth.or.th/).

Adapted with permission from Eagle L and Dahl S. *Marketing ethics and society*. London: Sage Publications Ltd., Copyright © 2015 Lynne Eagle and Stephan Dahl.

Source: data from Warc. *THPF: The Smoking Kid - A personal message to the smokers (Jay Chiat Strategic Excellence Awards, Gold, October 2013)*. Copyright © 2013 American Association of Advertising Agencies.

Competing theoretical foundations and frameworks

Several competing ethical frameworks are available, each with different values (Carter et al., 2011). The frameworks most commonly cited focus either on intentions (often termed 'deontology', from the Greek word for duty) or on consequences or outcomes (often termed 'teleology', from the Greek word for ends, but also referred to in the literature as 'consequentialism'). Teleology is also frequently broken down into 'utilitarianism' and 'egoism' options (Andreasen, 2001; Eagle et al., 2013), although the latter is not used in the business context. A summary of common ethical frameworks is provided in Table 11.1.

The selection of an ethical decision-making framework will have an impact on the development of behaviour change intervention strategies. For example, a social marketing intervention that was driven by good intentions without potential negative consequences being considered would be acceptable under deontological reasoning but not under teleological reasoning. A further problem is the lack of clear and unambiguous interpretation of the frameworks. For example, fear-based interventions would be acceptable under deontological reasoning, given their positive intentions. If they caused distress, however, teleological principles would render the approaches unacceptable. Indeed, as several social advertisers have found to their cost, marketing communication regulators in many countries appear to operate under teleological principles, resulting in the advertising component of an intervention being withdrawn from the media entirely, or requiring modification before being able to be rescheduled (see, for example, Eagle et al., 2013; Eagle and Dahl, 2015). Interventions that have raised ethical issues relating to the implicit use of specific ethical frameworks include the UK Department of Health's Fishhook Smoking Cessation activity, parts of which were modified due to concerns regarding distress caused by some images (for more details refer to Self-review question 2); the Australian White Ribbon Day activity noted earlier (Donovan et al., 2009); and the American Road Crew Drink-Driving activity (Rothschild et al., 2006).

The challenge for social marketers is in choosing which frameworks and other factors to apply in ethical decision-making. This problem becomes more complex when working in developing rather than developed countries, such as where folk beliefs hold that illness is caused by sorcery (Eagle et al., 2014).

Universal moral values

We noted earlier the challenges of designing effective and ethical social marketing interventions in developing countries. Ethical perceptions differ between diverse cultural groups such as those traditionally seen as 'eastern' and 'western' countries, but the extent of these differences is unclear (Vitell et al., 2013). While writers based in western countries tend to minimize

Table 11.1 Overview of common ethical frameworks

Key provisions	Comments
Deontology (based on the work of 18th-century philosopher Immanuel Kant)—focuses on intentions	
Holds that there are ethical 'absolutes' that are universally applicable, with the focus on means or intentions	Deontology accepts that actions intended to do good may have unintended negative consequences, such as creating fear or distress. This is contrary to beliefs that interventions should do no harm, particularly to vulnerable groups who may not be the target of the intervention. The principle of 'do no harm' is difficult to enact when there is little control over who is exposed to an intervention, such as through mass media or Internet-based resources (Donovan et al., 2009).
Teleology/consequentialism—focuses on the outcomes or effects of actions	
Usually divided into: a) utilitarianism, in which behaviour is ethical if it results in the greatest good for the greatest number; b) egoism, in which the benefits to the individual undertaking action are stressed and the impact on other people is de-emphasized—this is not a viable option for social marketing other than being suggested as a means of signalling the ability or competence to deliver results (Malloy and Agarwal, 2010)	Utilitarianism presents challenges when comparing alternative courses of action with different levels of potential impact—for example, a programme that provides minor benefits to all versus one that provides major benefits to many but has no, or a negative, impact on others. The earlier discussion regarding the consequences of focusing on easy-to-reach or influence groups rather than those with the greatest need is relevant here, together with the suggestion that utilitarianism could also be interpreted as the least harm for the greatest number of those affected (Payne and Pressley, 2013). As previously noted, while stigmatizing some groups would be unacceptable for many, Bayer (2008) suggests it can legitimately be used for activities such as reducing smoking rates.
Relativism	
No universal set of ethical principles: individual cultures, societies, or social groups having their own ethical frameworks; no set of principles considered superior to others and no group empowered to judge the ethical standards of other groups	Relativism ignores the possibilities that: a) a group's principles are based on incorrect information; and b) the implications of a group's principles are repugnant to other groups (e.g. sexism or racism).
Social contract theory	
Implicit contract existing between the state and/or organizations and individuals or groups regarding rights and responsibilities as a member of society *Distributive justice* Assignments of benefits and burdens according to some standard of fairness	Given that contracts and justice mechanisms are implied rather than stated explicitly, there is no shared understanding of what rights and responsibilities and fairness measures apply to the various parties. For example, the Charter of the United Nations makes reference to basic assumptions about the right of all citizens to health (Easley et al., 2001). Interventions that include the objective of reducing disparities between different population segments would draw on these two frameworks.

Source: data from Ferrell OC and Fraedrich JB, *Business ethics: ethical decision making and cases*, Second Edition. Boston, MA: Houghton Mifflin, Copyright © 1994 Houghton Mifflin.

the importance of cultural differences, writers from within non-western cultures suggest that the relative importance of beliefs on behaviours may vary significantly (Enderle and Niu, 2012; Mohiuddin and Haque, 2012). The literature is silent on the potential implications of differences between western and eastern norms and ethical perspectives within business, let alone within social marketing.

Social marketing thought and practice is claimed to have 'evolved differently in the developing and developed world' (Lefebvre, 2011: 54), making calls for the development of a common social marketing language (Quinn et al., 2010) challenging. There is agreement that ethics resources and support for social marketing practitioners is desirable, and the issue is being debated within the various social marketing organizations—a movement with parallels in related areas such as public health. An ambitious recent call for a 'transcendental code of ethics' for all marketing professionals has been made (Payne and Pressley, 2013) but these authors merely list broad principles in an authoritarian way; for example: 'the inability of the marketing decision maker to understand that there may be ethical components to a decision being made must be overcome' (p. 69). This type of simplistic approach does not consider what ethical resources and support might be most needed and used by practitioners, or what outcomes might be achieved as a result.

The potential role of a code of ethics

Codes are not panaceas. There is substantial evidence that the existence of a code of ethics (CoE) will not of itself prevent unethical behaviour (Messikomer and Cirka, 2010); nor will it change behaviours in the in the broad health care sector (Eriksson et al., 2007). As the then-president of Harvard University observed in the 1970s, 'no instruction can suffice to turn a scoundrel into a virtuous human being' (Bok, 1974: 7).

There are numerous potential benefits from CoEs: together with support from professional associations, possibly including specific ethics training, CoEs may help educate inexperienced practitioners and sensitize them to issues they may face in the future, as well as aiding in the development of evaluation tools and in the commissioning of future interventions (Eagle, 2008; Kaptein and Schwartz, 2008). They may also enable individuals to make ethical decisions through being able to apply principles, processes, and decision-making models to ethical issues (Sonenshein, 2007), clarifying expectations around decision-making and encouraging discussion of ethical dilemmas and potential actions (Helin et al., 2011). While the issue has not been specifically examined in the social marketing context, examination of the wider business ethics literature indicates clear differences between the characteristics of ineffective and potentially effective codes. These are summarized in Table 11.2.

Code quality and implementation

The quality of code content and the way in which codes are implemented, in terms of usefulness to practitioners, will have an impact on ethical performance (Erwin, 2011). For a code to be 'living', it needs to be more than a collection of bland statements of good intent but rather needs to 'get its hands dirty'—to be relevant to the real-world ethical issues specific to the social marketing profession and offer guidance in the evaluation of potential courses of action to resolve dilemmas (Smythe, 2012: 48). In order to have value both as an educational and as a decision-making support tool, the process of consultation within the social marketing community regarding its development will require 'thoughtful debate' (Skubik and Stening, 2009: 515). The processes involved will be lengthy, but wide consultation and co-creation of a code will

Table 11.2 Business code characteristics

Ineffective codes	Characteristics of potentially effective codes
◆ Codes are based on strategic legitimacy where there is an appearance, but not an embedded alignment, of organizational and societal/stakeholder interests and only token support from senior management. ◆ Collectivist cultures may result in weak support for ethical guidance if this is at variance with observed practices. ◆ Codes are used as a means of coercion and control, decreasing the ability to manage ethical ambiguities. ◆ Codes do not reflect actual organizational culture (see, for example, Helin et al., 2011; Long and Driscoll, 2008).	◆ Codes contain high educational value, are non-authoritarian, provide a clear rationale for ethical behaviour, and are empowering for actual decision-making. ◆ Codes clearly state principles and shared values, including what behaviours are desirable versus prohibited. ◆ Commitment to codes is embedded within all aspects of associations' and organizations' activity and explicitly endorsed by leaders. ◆ Codes are communicated through effective communication channels in readable terms, using positive tones and demonstrating relevance to real-world practice. ◆ Discussions of values are open and difficult dilemmas are debated. ◆ Violations are seen to be addressed and repercussions are communicated. Failure to do this results in frustration, anger, and cynicism (see, for example, Schwartz, 2005; Stevens, 2008).

Reproduced with permission from Eagle L and Dahl S. *Marketing ethics and society.* London: Sage Publications Ltd., Copyright © 2015 Lynne Eagle and Stephan Dahl.

Source: data from Schwartz MS. Universal moral values for corporate codes of ethics. *Journal of Business Ethics*, Volume 59, pp. 27–44, Copyright © 2005 Springer; Long BS and Driscoll C. Codes of ethics and the pursuit of organizational legitimacy: theoretical and eWmpirical contributions. *Journal of Business Ethics*, Volume 77, pp. 173–189, Copyright © 2008 Springer; Stevens B. Corporate ethical codes: effective instruments for influencing behavior. *Journal of Business Ethics*, Volume 78, pp. 601–609, Copyright © 2008 Springer; Helin S, Jensen T, Sandström J, and Clegg SR. On the dark side of codes: domination not enlightenment. *Scandinavian Journal of Management*, Volume 27, pp. 24–33, Copyright © 2011 Elsevier B.V.

increase acceptance of the resource, with subsequent resultant benefits for practitioners. If, however, a CoE or other form of ethical guidance is developed without adequate consultation and results only in a list of broad general principles, it will, in common with codes in other areas, unfortunately only 'occupy the role of platitude' (Malloy et al., 2009: 381).

Relationship of a social marketing CoE to corporate and other professional codes

A social marketing CoE would not operate in isolation—we have noted that there are developments within the public health field, with practitioners working in both sectors. Social marketers work for a range of organizations, many of which have their own CoEs; professional codes may also apply, such as in broad health sectors where responsibility boundaries across different professions may be unclear (Carter et al., 2011). Any new social marketing CoE should not conflict with these codes. In addition, there is the influence of the organization in which a social marketer works—thus, there will always be an organizational dimension to code adherence (Malloy et al., 2009). Research within the accounting profession indicates that professional CoEs have less influence than organizational environments (Somers, 2001). Whether and how professional associations connect professionalism and organizations has been studied in the medical context (Noordegraaf, 2011), but not within social marketing.

Code enforcement

A challenge to the implementation of a CoE is that membership of a social marketing association is voluntary, unlike membership of established, recognized professions such as medicine or law, which is a requirement for practice registration. Those governed by professional associations could lose the right to practice in their profession if found guilty by their peers of a significant transgression of professional ethics, but the same does not apply to social marketing (Eagle, 2008). Social marketers—nd, indeed, commercial marketers—are not subject to the same level of peer control; there is no requirement that they be licensed, and membership of sector organizations is voluntary. Overarching codified legislation and thus the ability to enforce standards or codes in the way that established professional groups are able to do is thus missing (Hunt and Vitell, 2006).

Indirect sanctions are, however, possible and appear to exist already in consultancy areas such as among those undertaking social science research on behalf of the UK Government, where a range of specific ethical expectations are signalled. These include not just standard research ethical procedures such as obtaining 'valid, informed consent' from research participants but also the requirement to take 'reasonable steps to identify and remove barriers to participation' and to avoid 'personal and social harm' (Government Social Research Unit, 2005: 8). Sanctions and redress are noted in this document but are specifically not spelled out. A reasonable implicit conclusion is that consultants who breach the Government Social Research Unit's provisions would not be considered for future commissions from government sources. This strategy could readily be extended both to social marketing intervention activity commissioned by similar organizations in other countries, and could also include funding from all direct and indirect government sources for this type of activity.

A second indirect compliance measure currently being debated involves the formal accreditation of members of social marketing organizations. Accreditation has been found to affect positively both quality of work and ethical conduct within clinical health (Braithwaite et al., 2010) and counselling (Even and Robinson, 2013), and it would seem reasonable to assume that similar effects would be found in social marketing. The major social marketing associations have begun to explore options for potential accreditation processes, having already agreed on a set of competency standards which will guide education and training, but full accreditation mechanisms are still some way in the future.

Conclusion

Ethical issues are far more prevalent within social marketing than is generally realized, with issues covering all aspects of intervention planning and implementation. Overarching issues include the choice of values to be applied to a specific behaviours and who has the mandate to plan interventions that will have an impact on others. More specific issues arise in relation to targeting and to the strategies and tactics selected for a specific intervention, together with the recognition of possible unintended effects and the level of risk that might be acceptable to different stakeholders. Competing ethical frameworks that may result in different decisions and outcomes present a challenge, as does the implicit use of specific frameworks by communications regulators. While codes of ethics offer some valuable guidance they are not panaceas, and code enforcement mechanisms are under-developed compared to those of more established professions, but progress is being made to develop appropriate resources.

Self-review questions

1. Find a recent social marketing intervention and critique it from the perspective of deontological reasoning, then repeat it from a teleological perspective. How might the intervention be viewed by the developers and by communication regulators under these two perspectives?

2. Review prior decisions by communications regulators such as the Advertising Standards Authority regarding social marketing interventions. See, for example, the adjudication regarding the 'Fishhook' smoking cessation intervention (see the BBC report on the campaign at http://news.bbc.co.uk/1/hi/uk/6658335.stm and the Campaign report at http://www.campaignlive.co.uk/article/657521/watchdog-bans-doh-fish-hook-ads). What ethical framework appears to have been used in making their decisions? What are the implications for future intervention development?

References

Adkins, N.R., Ozanne, J.L. (2005). The low literate consumer. *Journal of Consumer Research* **32**: 93–105.

Andreasen, A.R. (2001). *Ethics in social marketing*. Washington DC: Georgetown University Press.

Bayer, R. (2008). Stigma and the ethics of public health: not can we but should we. *Social Science & Medicine* **67**: 463–472.

Bok, D. (1974). Can higher education foster higher morals? *Business and Society Review* **66**: 4–12.

Bombak, A.E. (2014). The contribution of applied social sciences to obesity stigma-related public health approaches. *Journal of Obesity* Article 267286.

Braithwaite, J., Greenfield, D., Westbrook, J., Pawsey, M., Westbrook, M., Gibberd, R., et al. (2010). Health service accreditation as a predictor of clinical and organisational performance: a blinded, random, stratified study. *Quality and Safety in Health Care* **19**: 14–21.

Braunack-Mayer, A., Louise, J. (2008). The ethics of community empowerment: tensions in health promotion theory and practice. *Promotion & Education* **15**: 5–8.

Buller, D.B., Borland, R., Burgon, M. (1998). Impact of behavioral intention on effectiveness of message features: evidence from the Family Sun Safety project. *Human Communication Research* **24**: 433–453.

Callahan, D. (2001). Promoting healthy behavior: how much freedom? Whose responsibility? *American Journal of Preventive Medicine* **20**: 83.

Callahan, D., Jennings, B. (2002). Ethics and public health: forging a strong relationship. *American Journal of Public Health* **92**: 169–176.

Carter, S.M., Cribb, A., Allegrante, J.P. (2012). How to think about health promotion ethics. *Public Health Reviews* **34**: 1–24.

Carter, S.M., Rychetnik, L., Lloyd, B., Kerridge, I.H., Baur, L., Bauman, A., et al. (2011). Evidence, ethics, and values: a framework for health promotion. *American Journal of Public Health* **101**(3), 465–472.

Cho, H., Salmon, C.T. (2007). Unintended effects of health communication campaigns. *Journal of Communication* **57**: 293–317.

Cohen, S. (2013). Nudging and informed consent. *The American Journal of Bioethics* **13**: 3–11.

Dann, S. (2007). Reaffirming the neutrality of the social marketing tool kit: social marketing as a hammer, and social marketers as hired guns. *Social Marketing Quarterly* **13**: 54–62.

Donovan, R.J., Jalleh, G., Fielder, L., Ouschan, R. (2009). Ethical issues in pro-social advertising: the Australian 2006 White Ribbon Day campaign. *Journal of Public Affairs* **9**: 5–19.

Eagle, L. (2008). *Social marketing ethics: report for National Social Marketing Centre*. London: National Social Marketing Centre.

Eagle, L., Dahl, S. (2015). *Marketing, ethics and society*. London: Sage.

Eagle, L., Dahl, S., Hill, S., Bird, S., Spotswood, F., Tapp, A. (2013). *Social marketing*. Harlow: Pearson.

Eagle, L., Low, D., Dahl, S. (2014). Can social marketing combat sorcery? *International Social Marketing Conference Proceedings*. Melbourne: Monash University http://www.aasm.org.au/international-social-marketing-conference-2014/proceedings/by-paper-number/.

Easley, C.E., Marks, S.P., Morgan, R.B. Jr (2001). The challenge and place of international human rights in public health. *American Journal of Public Health* 91: 1922–1925.

Enderle, G., Niu, Q. (2012). Discerning ethical challenges for marketing in China. *Asian Journal of Business Ethics* 1: 143–162.

Eriksson, S., Helgesson, G., Höglund A.T. (2007). Being, doing, and knowing: developing ethical competence in health care. *Journal of Academic Ethics* 5: 207–216.

Erwin, P.M. (2011). Corporate codes of conduct: the effects of code content and quality on ethical performance. *Journal of Business Ethics* 99: 535–548.

Even, T.A., Robinson, C.R. (2013). The impact of CACREP accreditation: a multiway frequency analysis of ethics violations and sanctions. *Journal of Counseling & Development* 91: 26–34.

Ferrell, O.C., Fraedrich, J.B. (1994). *Business ethics: ethical decision making and cases, 2nd edition*. Boston, MA: Houghton Mifflin.

Fitzpatrick, M. (2004). From 'nanny state' to 'therapeutic state'. *British Journal of General Practice* 54: 645.

French, J. (2011). Why nudging is not enough. *Journal of Social Marketing* 1: 154–162.

Government Social Research Unit (2005). *GSR professional guidance: ethical assurance for social research in government*. London: HM Treasury.

Guttman, N., Salmon, C.T. (2004). Guilt, fear, stigma and knowledge gaps: ethical issues in public health communication interventions. *Bioethics* 18: 531–552.

Harper Collins (2001). *Collins concise dictionary*. Aylesbury: Harper Collins Publishers.

Hastings, G., Stead, M., Webb, J. (2004). Fear appeals in social marketing strategic and ethical reasons for concern. *Psychology & Marketing* 21: 961–986.

Heise, L., Lutz, B., Ranganathan, M., Watts, C. (2013). Cash transfers for HIV prevention: considering their potential. *Journal of the International AIDS Society* 16.

Helin, S., Jensen, T., Sandström, J., Clegg, S.R. (2011). On the dark side of codes: domination not enlightenment. *Scandinavian Journal of Management* 27: 24–33.

Hunt, S.D., Vitell, S.J. (2006). The general theory of marketing ethics: a revision and three questions. *Journal of Macromarketing* 26: 143–153.

Iyer, E.S., Kashyap, R.K. (2007).Consumer recycling: role of incentives, information, and social class. *Journal of Consumer Behaviour* 6: 32–47.

Jones, M.M., Bayer. R. (2007). Paternalism and its discontents: motorcycle helmet laws, libertarian values, and public health. *American Journal of Public Health* 97: 208.

Jones, R., Pykett, J., Whitehead, M. (2011). The geographies of soft paternalism in the UK: the rise of the avuncular state and changing behaviour after neoliberalism. *Geography Compass* 5: 50–62.

Kaptein, M., Schwartz, M.S. (2008). The effectiveness of business codes: a critical examination of existing studies and the development of an integrated research model. *Journal of Business Ethics* 77: 111–127.

Kemp, G., Eagle, L. (2008). Shared meanings or missed opportunities? The implications of functional health literacy for social marketing interventions. *International Review on Public and Nonprofit Marketing* 5: 117–128.

Langford, R., Panter-Brick, C. (2013). A health equity critique of social marketing: where interventions have impact but insufficient reach. *Social Science & Medicine* 83: 133–141.

Laurance, J. (2009). Time for a fat tax? *The Lancet* **373**: 1597.

Lavack, A.M., Watson, L., Markwart, J. (2007). Quit and win contests: a social marketing success story. *Social Marketing Quarterly* **13**: 31–52.

Lefebvre, R.C. (2011). An integrative model for social marketing. *Journal of Social Marketing* **1**: 54–72.

Long, B.S., Driscoll, C. (2008). Codes of ethics and the pursuit of organizational legitimacy: theoretical and empirical contributions. *Journal of Business Ethics* **77**: 173–189.

Lucke, J. (2013). Context is all important in investigating attitudes: acceptability depends on the nature of the nudge, who nudges, and who is nudged. *The American Journal of Bioethics* **13**: 24–25.

Lynagh, M.C., Sanson-Fisher, R.W., Bonevski, B. (2013). What's good for the goose is good for the gander. Guiding principles for the use of financial incentives in health behaviour change. *International Journal of Behavioral Medicine* **20**: 114–120.

Malloy, D., Agarwal, J. (2010). Ethical climate in government and nonprofit sectors: public policy implications for service delivery. *Journal of Business Ethics* **94**: 3–21.

Malloy, D., Sevigny, P., Hadjistavropoulos, T., Jeyaraj, M., McCarthy, E.F., Murakami, M., et al. (2009). Perceptions of the effectiveness of ethical guidelines: an international study of physicians. *Medicine, Health Care and Philosophy* **12**: 373–383.

Ménard, J-F. (2010). A 'nudge' for public health ethics: libertarian paternalism as a framework for ethical analysis of public health interventions? *Public Health Ethics* **3**: 229–238.

Messikomer, C.M., Cirka, C.C. (2010). Constructing a code of ethics: an experiential case of a national professional organization. *Journal of Business Ethics* **95**: 55–71.

Mohiuddin, M.D.M.G., Haque, M.S. (2012). Behaving ethically: an essence of Islamic marketing system. *European Journal of Business and Management* **4**: 34–44.

Mortimer, D., Ghijben, P., Harris, A., Hollingsworth, B. (2013). Incentive-based and non-incentive-based interventions for increasing blood donation. *The Cochrane Database of Systematic Reviews* **1**: Article CD010295.

Mytton, O., Gray, A., Rayner, M., Rutter, H. (2007). Could targeted food taxes improve health? *Journal of Epidemiology and Community Health* **61**: 689–694.

Newton, J.D., Newton, F.J., Turk, T., Ewing, MT. (2013). Ethical evaluation of audience segmentation in social marketing. *European Journal of Marketing* **47**: 1421–1438.

Noordegraaf, M. (2011). Remaking professionals? How associations and professional education connect professionalism and organizations. *Current Sociology* **59**: 465–488.

Nutbeam, D. (2008). The evolving concept of health literacy. *Social Science & Medicine* **67**: 2072–2078.

Payne, D., Pressley, M. (2013). A transcendent code of ethics for marketing professionals. *International Journal of Law and Management* **55**: 55–73.

Peters, E., Hibbard, J., Slovic, P., Dieckmann, N. (2007). Numeracy skill and the communication, comprehension, and use of risk-benefit information. *Health Affairs* **26**: 741–748.

Quick, B.L., Stephenson, M.T. (2007). The reactance restoration scale (RRS): a measure of direct and indirect restoration. *Communication Research Reports* **24**: 131–138.

Quinn, G.P., Ellery, J., Thomas, K.B., Marshall, R. (2010). Developing a common language for using social marketing: an analysis of public health literature. *Health marketing quarterly* **27**: 334–353.

Rains, S.A. (2013). The nature of psychological reactance revisited: a meta-analytic review. *Human Communication Research* **39**: 47–73.

Reyna, V.F., Nelson, W.L., Han, P.K., Dieckmann, N. (2009). How numeracy influences risk comprehension and medical decision making. *Psychological Bulletin* **135**: 943–973.

Rossi, J., Yudell, M. (2012). Value-ladenness and rationality in health communication. *The American Journal of Bioethics* **12**: 20–22.

Rothschild, M.L. (1999). Carrots, sticks, and promises: a conceptual framework for the management of public health and social issue behaviors. *Journal of Marketing* **63**: 24–37.

Rothschild, M.L., Mastin, B., Miller, T.W. (2006). Reducing alcohol-impaired driving crashes through the use of social marketing. *Accident Analysis & Prevention* **38**: 1218–1230.

Rummel, A., Howard, J., Swinton, J.M., Seymour, D.B. (2000). You can't have that! A Study of reactance effects and children's consumer behavior. *Journal of Marketing Theory and Practice* **8**: 38–44.

Schmidt, H., Asch, D.A., Halpern, S.D. (2012). Fairness and wellness incentives: what is the relevance of the process-outcome distinction? *Preventive Medicine* **55**: S118–S123.

Schwartz, M.S. (2005). Universal moral values for corporate codes of ethics. *Journal of Business Ethics* **59**: 27–44.

Skubik, D.W., Stening, B.W. (2009). What's in a credo? A critique of the academy of management's code of ethical conduct and code of ethics. *Journal of Business Ethics* **85**: 515–525.

Smythe, V. (2012). Codes of ethics. In: P. Bowden (ed). *Applied ethics: strengthening ethical practices.* Prahran, VIC: Tilde University Press.

Somers, M.J. (2001). Ethical codes of conduct and organizational context: a study of the relationship between codes of conduct, employee behavior and organizational values. *Journal of Business Ethics* **30**: 185–195.

Sonenshein, S. (2007). The role of construction, intuition, and justification in responding to ethical issues at work: the sensemaking-intuition model. *Academy of Management Review* **32**: 1022–1040.

Stephens, C. (2013). Paying the piper: additional considerations of the theoretical, ethical and moral basis of financial incentives for health behaviour change. *International Journal of Behavioral Medicine*: 1–4.

Stevens, B. (2008). Corporate ethical codes: effective instruments for influencing behavior. *Journal of Business Ethics* **78**: 601–609.

Sussman, S., Grana, R., Pokhrel, P., Rohrbach, L.A., Sun, P. (2010). Forbidden fruit and the prediction of cigarette smoking. *Substance Use & Misuse* **45**: 1683–1693.

Vitell, S.J., Nwachukwu, S.L., Barnes, J.H. (2013). The effects of culture on ethical decision-making: an application of Hofstede's typology. In: A.C. Michalos, D.C. Poff (eds). *Citation classics from the Journal of Business Ethics.* Heidelberg: Springer, 119–129.

Chapter 12

Using digital and social media platforms for social marketing

Melissa K. Blair

I grew up in a physical world, and I speak English. The next generation is growing up in a digital world, and they speak social.

Angela Ahrendts, Senior Vice-President for Retail, Apple

Learning points

This chapter:

- helps readers identify the benefits of using digital and social media platforms for social marketing behaviour change interventions;
- outlines how to identify the individual and macro behaviour change principles that can be applied through digital media;
- develops consideration of how social media networks can facilitate behaviour change;
- assists readers with understanding the role of social currency for social media implementation.

Introduction to using digital and social media platforms for social marketing

Social marketing in the 21st century means that practitioners and academics must learn to keep up with the ever-mobile multidevice consumer, across new technologies, platforms, and behaviours. We now have the ability to research, create, test, and evaluate innovative, sustainable digital tools, which will create healthier lifestyles and positive societal change.

Digital communication has changed the way big brands and organizations deliver information to the end-user. Messages have gone from being one-directional to interactive, from telling to helping, and from linear to multiple directions. Message formats have gone from fixed to mobile and, thanks to advances in digital analytics, actual behaviour is monitored and analysed in comparison to only declared behaviour. Gone are the days when a big campaign would leave marketers waiting weeks, months, or years even to see results. Digital communication has created an environment where practitioners and academics can consistently test, refine, and evolve interventions.

The idea of social support from online interactions has been around since the inception of the Internet (White and Dorman, 2001). However, social media networking sites such as Facebook have taken this dynamic communication to another level and allow people to extend their offline friendships into an online environment (Centola, 2013). People are able to share information and updates with others, comment on other people's activities, and send and receive private messages, creating a world where perceived social norms and influence play an integral role.

This chapter will explore how these advances in digital communication and social networks mean that practitioners and academics can utilize the principles of social marketing to develop social programmes where people can be supported both individually and collectively through addiction, weight loss, and depression, among many other behaviour problems and wicked problems (social or cultural problems that are difficult to solve because of incomplete, contradictory, and changing requirements). In this sense, digital interventions are not meant to be a stand-alone activity, but are rather a supporting mechanism that can complement a variety of other tools and strategies from the social marketing mix.

The benefits of using digital media for social marketing

By now, many organizations have long recognized the necessity and benefits of using digital channels for marketing. The vast suite of digital tools available has created an opportunity for social marketers to transform the way we can change behaviour. Digital media provide a platform where social behavioural interventions can be delivered by applying effective principles of individual behaviour change. The benefits to using digital interventions for social marketing include:

- access: the ubiquity of smartphones and computers;
- hyper-targeting: segmentation and personalization;
- context: timeliness and appropriateness to individuals' behaviour change journeys— individuals can more easily change routines and environment;
- ease: step by step, chunking;
- social support: communities and social norming;
- cost-effectiveness: smaller budgets with greater reach;
- ongoing monitoring and feedback: consistent refinements.

These interventions can be disseminated through multichannel digital campaigns and embedded into websites, social media, mobile apps, and wearable technology. The ease of access provides simple ways for individuals to maximize their capabilities to regulate their own behaviour, and the use of digital measurement tools has provided the opportunity to craft personalized plans and programmes for change. Another great advantage of digital media is that experimenting with communication techniques and messages is much less resource-intensive and potentially less risky than investing money in other expensive tactics such as traditional television adverts (Box 12.1).

Measuring behaviour with digital tools

Increasing levels of public participation in a diverse range of social and digital media have created a population of subjects whose natural, everyday engagement with social behaviours can be monitored and explored with a rapidly expanding repertoire of social technologies. Traditional health-related activities such as shopping for health and beauty products, signing up for gym memberships, and contacting doctors to make appointments have all become increasingly routine online activities, and these digital traces of everyday life provide direct observations of the

Box 12.1 Case study: using WhatsApp for BBC Media Action's response to the Ebola crisis

Trushar Barot and Yvonne Macpherson

The outbreak of Ebola virus disease in West Africa was the worst of its kind in history. The overall response to the epidemic, and the criticisms made of it, have been well documented by many organizations, not least by reviews set up by the World Health Organization. The communication response to the crisis was an important contributor to the containment of the epidemic.

BBC Media Action, the BBC's international development charity, mounted one of the first and largest communication responses to the epidemic. The challenge became getting information out as quickly as possible.

At the commencement of the growing crisis, the BBC had already started special public health programming on Ebola for its World Service radio and global TV audiences. This not only gave up-to-date information on the spread of the virus but also provided valuable and potentially life-saving information for those in the region on how to reduce the risk of catching the disease, on understanding the symptoms, and on where to get help. However, the

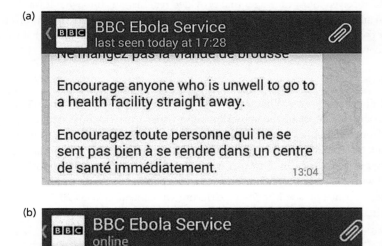

Figure 12.1 Examples of the BBC's Ebola WhatsApp information service.
Reproduced from *BBC Online. How BBC Ebola WhatsApp service is battling virus and finding great stories*, http://www.bbc.co.uk/blogs/collegeofjournalism/entries/0f944ab7-9f96-4091-a927-db826630d997, accessed 01 Oct. 2015, Copyright © 2015 BBC.

BBC wanted to do more and saw a significant opportunity to reach people on their mobile phones. Without the time to develop an app—and considering the expense that would be incurred to develop and promote it—the idea of using WhatsApp emerged (Figure 12.1).

In mid September 2014, the BBC's Ebola WhatsApp information service was born—the first 'lifeline' humanitarian service to be launched inside the app—as a dual-language offering, in English and French. The content included text messages, pictures/visuals, and short audio clips in order to cover the different user preferences for understanding the information. Video clips were avoided, as they could be too big for many subscribers' data limits. In an effort not to spam users, the BBC posted a maximum of three items a day.

Editorially, the BBC established quite narrow parameters: the content had to be public service information or significant news developments that directly affected people in the region. It had to be short and to the point and be conveyed in simple and easy-to-understand terms. There were no links back to the website—the point was to get the content that people needed delivered straight to them.

WhatsApp is primarily an interactive platform, so there was a need to monitor the messages they got back from subscribers carefully and follow up with them where needed. The BBC quickly realized that a lot of the questions users were sending in via that platform were practical concerns that they hadn't really understood in the broader coverage of the story.

The BBC received many messages that provided real insights into what it was like living in the region and the difficulties and challenges people faced. There were tip-offs on stories that were later covered on main outlets. They found compelling personal stories that were used to enhance coverage across TV, radio, and online channels.

Results

The BBC Ebola service on WhatsApp went direct to people's mobile phones, with 22,000 direct subscribers. Most of the subscribers (80–90%) were from West Africa, which was detected from the mobile phone numbers. The biggest subscriber group was in Sierra Leone, followed by Nigeria and Ghana, with a number of subscribers also in Liberia, Guinea, Mali, and further across Africa in Tanzania, Kenya, and Uganda. The BBC's World Service was honoured with a George Foster Peabody award for public service for its Ebola service.

For more information see: http://www.elrha.org/wp-content/uploads/2015/10/humanitarian-broadcasting-in-emergencies-2015-report.pdf

health-related behaviours that people engage in (Centola, 2013). The use of digital measurement tools has provided the opportunity to craft personalized plans based on users' past behaviour online.

To develop this type of user-centric behavioural intervention, the approach needs to involve quantitative and qualitative research with the target user population, right through from development to deployment stages of the digital interventions. This methodology extends traditional usability testing or user-centred design by incorporating psychological concepts such as empathy, and through this process it goes beyond just asking about behaviours and also looks at motivations and feelings regarding the intervention (Lathia et al., 2013).

One of the main challenges with creating these measurable digital interventions is that a portion of behavioural outcomes often relies on self-reporting (e.g. meal reporting, alcohol consumption) (Centola, 2013). The natural concern about studies of self-reported behaviour is that this data is not an accurate representation of people's real activities. However, the increasing trend towards digital integration of offline activities, such as the use of health sensors, provides some promising new directions that mitigate this concern. For instance, the use of health sensors in handheld communication devices provides new tools for real-time data collection of health behaviours using digital technologies (Berke et al., 2011). Further research is needed to make sure the data can be relied on, bearing in mind the possibility of misreporting and missing data.

Applying individual behaviour change principles in digital media

Through this user-centric design, digital social programmes that are developed should make the behaviour change journey easier and more relevant for users. The selection of behavioural change principles plays a significant role when designing social marketing digital interventions. These principles provide the opportunity for social marketers to increase the benefits of changing by maximizing self-regulation support, which in turn builds self-efficacy and confidence to change (Bandura, 1983; 1986). Self-regulated learning processes involve goal-directed activities that users instigate, modify, and sustain (Zimmerman, 1989). These activities include attending to instruction, processing and integrating knowledge, rehearsing information to be remembered, and developing and maintaining positive beliefs about learning capabilities and anticipated outcomes of actions (Schunk and Rice, 1989). Digital interventions provide an optimal platform to support these types of activities.

Examples of individual behaviour change principles that can be directly applied and executed through digital interventions include:

- skill development, where users can develop the relevant skills needed to achieve success (e.g. goal setting);
- repetition through a consistent structure that encourages individuals to practise and put their skills to work;
- strengthening motivation to engage in the desired behaviour by rewarding change and helping individuals to develop appropriate beliefs;
- chunking that can include step-by-step lessons with personalized tools to complete each task;
- prompts and reminder messages that are triggered to keep people motivated;
- ongoing monitoring and immediate feedback to provide positive reinforcement to encourage progress;
- message framing, which is personalized, based on responses to feedback.

How smart are smartphones?

When it comes to delivering a behavioural intervention on a digital platform, smartphones have become an ideal medium to provide timely messaging and capture automated recording of behavioural data. There are new algorithms for merging large volumes of information from mobile sensing applications and online social network websites for a quantitative understanding of human behaviour (Lathia et al., 2013). Recent research has aimed to answer the question of whether we can accurately, efficiently, and unobtrusively measure what mobile phone users are doing and feeling, and use this effectively to support behaviour change.

The functionality and access of smartphones allows individuals to interact seamlessly offline and online, blurring the distinction between the two worlds, which offers researchers a high-fidelity record of subjects' everyday interactions. Figure 12.2 illustrates the three key components of digital behaviour interventions using smartphones: monitor behaviour, learn and infer behavioural patterns, and deliver targeted behaviour change (Lathia et al., 2013; Box 12.2 and Box 12.3).

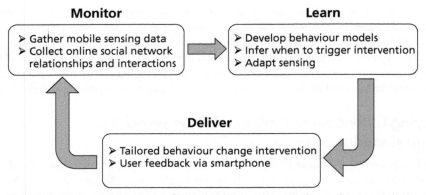

Figure 12.2 The three key components of digital behaviour interventions using smartphones. Reproduced with permission from *Lathia N, Pejovic V, Rachuri K, Mascolo C, Musolesi M* and *Rentfrow PJ*. Smartphones for large-scale behavior change interventions, *Pervasive Computing*, Volume 12, Issue 3, pp. 66–73, Copyright © 2013 IEEE.

Applying macro behaviour change principles in digital media

Social influencers are a primary factor in the adoption of healthy behaviours (Centola, 2013). Many people are willing to start new behaviour changes but find it hard to maintain or comply with them. The compliance and success rate of behaviour change can depend on having contact with family, friends, or even strangers or celebrities who also engage in these behaviours (Centola, 2013). Social norming helps people to develop positive feelings about changing and reduces motivation to continue with the undesired behaviour (Abraham et al., 2009).

Box 12.2 Example weight management digital programme

The scenarios below demonstrate an example of a weight management digital programme that is designed to detect the smartphone user's likely current behaviour and mood in order to provide timely, personalized messages to support them on the programme.

Scenario A

User behaviour: Lonely, bored, and at home
Programme response: The smartphone has detected that the user is at home in the middle of the day, with no movement or co-location. The programme reads this behaviour as 'low mood': it triggers a message pop-up with a link to a virtual social support community and prompts the user's preferred physical activities.

Scenario B

User behaviour: Out for the evening with friends
Program response: The smartphone has detected that the user is in town in the evening with consistent movement and a co-location. The programme reads this behaviour as 'good mood' and triggers a message pop-up with planned reminders of acceptable ways to refuse or substitute fattening foods/drinks and links to calorie guides for foods.

Box 12.3 Case study A: Impromy Weight Loss Programme—creating a personalized weight loss experience

Developed in collaboration with the Commonwealth Scientific and Industrial Research Organisation, the Impromy programme focuses on improving health through weight loss and good nutrition. It comprises meal replacements along with high protein meals and ongoing support by trained pharmacy staff.

A mobile app was developed (Figure 12.3) as part of the programme to provide users with feedback on their progress and offer virtual support between visits to the in-person consultant. During the initial Impromy consultation at the pharmacy, participants receive a personalized meal programme and a membership number that they can enter into the app to create a tailored personal programme.

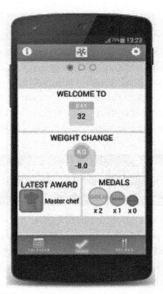

Figure 12.3 The Impromy mobile app.
Reproduced with permission from *Impromy Program*, http://impromy.com/app/, accessed 01 May 2016, Copyright © 2016 Probiotec Ltd.

The app aims to help participants track weight loss, access nutritious recipes, receive motivational messages, and get helpful, periodic reminders for weigh-ins and to complete meal diary entries. Users can achieve medals and unlock awards as a motivational mechanism to reward weight loss progress and increase programme compliance.

One of the most powerful elements of digital media is the influence of online communities. The use of social networking sites makes it easier than ever to satisfy the need to belong (Baumeister and Leary, 1995). These macro behaviour change principles that can be applied through digital interventions include:

◆ social influencers, where individuals can see people that they look up to also engaging in the same behaviour;

◆ model behaviour, where individuals receive approval from others;

◆ power of community, where individuals can elicit social support from others.

This approach to using digital media entails a shift in focus from the interpersonal dimensions of behaviour to the community-wide effects of social network structure on the spread of behaviours through online populations.

The role of social media networking sites in developing supportive networks

Peer-to-peer interaction in the health sector has a long history, starting with the creation of support groups for alcohol and tobacco abstention, weight control, long-term treatment, and grief and trauma counselling (Kiesler, 1985). The value of these peer-counselling organizations is mainly derived from personal and empathetic interaction (Kaplan et al., 1977). The rapid growth of social media communities provides an optimal venue to support long-term behaviour change in a similar manner. An imperative factor in facilitating these types of groups is the need for 24-hour moderation. When designing an intervention with a digital community network, this should be highly considered, as moderation can be issue-sensitive and resource-intensive (Box 12.4).

Box 12.4 Case study B: Impromy Weight Loss Programme—creating a personalized weight loss experience

Back to the Impromy weight loss programme. Earlier in the chapter we explained how Impromy had developed an app that customizes the participant's personal weight loss journey. The support is also coupled with access to a private Facebook groups. This group, called 'Impromy—weight loss support group', states that its mission is 'to give the users of Impromy a place to chat and give each other moral support as well as share recipes'.

Once participants have been accepted into the group, they gain access to a growing community of Australians, all on a similar journey to lose weight and improve their health. People within the community post inspiring quotes, ask for advice on how to approach weight loss with friends and family, share recipe ideas, post pictures of themselves before and after Impromy, proudly share their stories, and engage in discussions about the programme and their goals.

The Facebook group offers members a safe, inclusive circle of people who are facing the same challenges as them. Members can gain strength from the support of a community and really fulfil that sense of belonging.

From an organizational perspective, not only is this group fostering brand advocates for Impromy who are more likely to encourage others to try the programme, it is also helping Impromy to achieve its organizational goals by strengthening its customers' confidence and capacity to achieve personal weight loss goals.

Reproduced by kind permission of Probiotec Limted, Copyright © 2015 http://impromy.com

Using social media to achieve campaign objectives

Social media platforms have become a high-priority channel for organizations to disseminate behaviour change communications. The effectiveness of a social media campaign can be
positively affected by the use of traditional media, but this is not a necessary driver of success
(UTalkMarketing.com, 2009). When a social media campaign is highly novel or creative, it can
generate a tremendous amount of earned news media coverage that further boosts the campaign
(Hamill et al., 2013).

It is increasingly important for organizations to decide strategically on the right platforms
suited to their target audience and behaviour change objectives. Similar to offline outreach tactics, it is not necessary to use every single platform. Including a variety of social media channels
can increase participant involvement in a campaign, with the proviso that running a campaign
well across the most appropriately suited social media channels makes more sense than trying to
include networks that will not enable your target audience to take the action that your campaign
is seeking. Box 12.5 outlines four key components it is necessary to consider before deciding to
create a presence on social media platform. It should be noted that these should be reviewed for
each social media channel being considered.

Value creation in social media

For most social media marketers, the burning question remains how best to reach out to social
media users and what types of messages cut through the online clutter. Social marketing practice has shifted from the core focus of offering motivational exchanges to consumers to the
creation of value (Grönroos and Voima, 2013). This applies more than ever in the social media
environment. The majority of social media users have subscribed to a channel with the intention
of following and connecting with family and friends. With the increasing presence of organizations and brands on social media platforms, users can make a conscious choice whether or not
to follow them. They ultimately decide if they are willing to let a campaign into their lives; in
order to do that, it must provide value to them. Successful social media campaigns help users to
feel like members of a community and establish identity by allowing participants to express part
of themselves to others (Vivaldi Partners Group, 2010).

Social currency describes the resources and abilities that are created and accessible through
presence in online networks and communities (Ralphs, 2011). The social currency wheel is used

Box 12.5 Considerations when developing a social media presence

When developing a social media presence on a platform it is important to consider the following components.

+ **Character/persona**—who does your brand sound like? If you picture your social brand
  as a person, what is that character (e.g. inspiring, friendly, professional, authoritative)?

+ **Tone**—what is the general vibe of your brand (e.g. scientific, clinical, honest, personal)?

+ **Language**—what kind of words do you use in your social media conversations (e.g. fun,
  jargon-filled, insider)?

+ **Purpose**—why are you on this social media channel in the first place? What is your
  social currency?

to explain how users' social processes and behaviours drive their online conversions, as shown in Figure 12.4. An organization with relevant social currency will encourage further social encounters with their target audience.

Social media engagement

The organizations that find the most success in their social media communities are those that can develop highly relevant content. Examples of high-value social media content are those that provide the following:

- tips and tricks (life hacks) (e.g. top 10 ways to refresh your skin);
- practical and easy applications for everyday life (e.g. 5-minute healthy omelettes);
- myth-busting factual information (e.g. nut milk vs. regular milk);
- inspiration (e.g. I can do that);
- aspiration (e.g. I want to do that/I want to be like that);
- entertainment and evoking emotion.

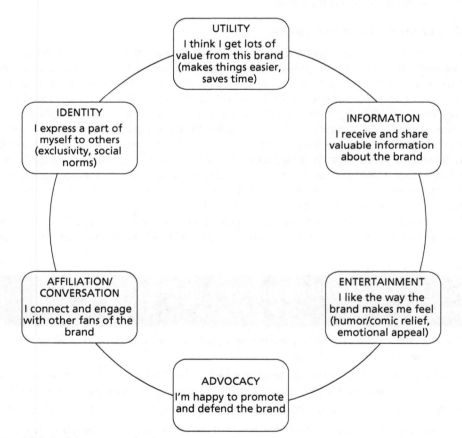

Figure 12.4 Social currency wheel.
Adapted with permission from *Vivaldi Group. Social currency 2012: how brands and businesses can prosper in a digitally connected world.* London: Vivaldi Group, Copyright © 2012 Vivaldi Inc.

A case study review conducted by Freeman et al. (2015) analysed social media campaigns to identify how best to develop effective online social marketing campaigns. This review found that key success factors for campaign engagement included the following:

- using functions that social media users are already familiar with, such as photo tagging and re-tweeting—complex third-party tools or the need for participants to register or provide personal details can severely dissuade participation and engagement;
- click-through ads on social media sites, which may work better if users are directed within the social media site's pages, as opposed to being forced offsite to an external website;
- clear and achievable calls to action;
- campaigns that can be spread from friend to friend through the automated sharing process of existing social network page feeds, and not require onerous further action of participants;
- recruiting large numbers of motivated volunteer 'seeders' who can leverage their personal social media connections with others, which appears to be more likely to generate action than impersonalized advertisements.

Social media measurement

Using existing in-built social media tools, analytics, and metrics can easily be captured to assess how successfully campaigns have engaged with participants and audiences. Typical social media analytics include the number of 'views', 'shares', 'comments', and 'likes', but it takes very little effort to like a campaign on Facebook, and there may be no direct link between the number of likes and the likelihood of behaviour change (Freeman et al., 2015). Therefore, large numbers of followers or participants may actually mean very little in terms of how important or meaningful a campaign truly is (Obar et al., 2012).

Deeper engagement would be considered to be people sharing content as a form of advocating the organization, with the capacity to influence others. However, for academics and practitioners it is essential to establish if there is a connection between engagement and behaviour change. Measuring actual participation offline as a result of some exposure to a social media campaign should be a measurement objective (such as making an appointment for cancer screening). Suggested methods for this include analysing the content of any online comments and interactions for evidence of behaviour change, and conducting surveys and interviews with campaign participants to ask about their behaviour directly (Freeman et al., 2015).

Social media advertising

Although developing a successful social media campaign may be at lower cost than a mass media campaign, many social media platforms are moving towards being a monetary-based channel for brands and organizations. It has become a 'pay to play' environment in order to reach fans and followers. The availability of social media advertising should be considered when deciding which channels are best suited for a target audience. Additional budget consideration should take into account that social media campaigns can be time- and human resource-intensive owing to the requirement of ongoing content generation and interaction with users (Gold et al., 2012; Box 12.6).

Conclusion

This chapter has focused on the benefits for academics and social marketers that are keenly experimenting with using digital and social media as tools for both information sharing and

Box 12.6 Case study: The Line campaign

'The Line' is an Australian long-term, evidence-based social marketing campaign that encourages healthy, equal, and respectful relationships by challenging and changing attitudes and behaviours that support violence against women. Its core target audience is young people aged 12 to 20, but it also aims to support parents, caregivers, teachers, and other influencers. The objectives of the campaign are as follows.

- It defines crossing-the-line behaviours.
- It supports the development of healthy, equal, and respectful relationships.
- It challenges social norms around rigid gender roles, gender inequality, and sexism.
- It aims to redefine a 'strong' man as someone who never hurts a woman.
- It encourages young people to break the cycle of violence.

Role of social media

The role of social media is absolutely central to the whole relationship 'game' for young people. Research conducted for The Line indicated that the 'flirting game' has shifted to a significant degree to social media: from the first indications of being singled out, flirty talk, moving things on to more sexual flirting, and then the official declaration of a 'relationship' on Facebook to the drama of the 'coupling' and 'break-up' phases.

There is also a sense that social media lowers the bar, and that previously unacceptable behaviours (in real life) become easier to do online. The potential is that this erodes, rather than promotes, good relationship norms.

The Line campaign has developed a Facebook page with over 90,000 followers. The page was created to foster a space to discuss respectful relationships among the community. There is a high level of engagement from members both with each other and back to The Line directly. Due to the high sensitivity of the issue, the page is moderated full-time to provide members with access and answers to correct information and support. Through the use of direct messaging, members can receive personal answers with confidentiality.

The majority of content is image-based posts such as 'memes' or culturally relevant images with the purpose of evoking conversation or increasing knowledge on what respectful relationships are. The content is not always branded and is delivered in a voice and conversational tone that is relevant and relatable to the target audience.

behaviour change. Both individual and macro behaviour change principles can be successfully applied in a digital environment and advances in analytics and sensor technology reveal that digital interventions can be highly effective in motivating participants through relevant and timely support. As more behaviours are recorded and inevitably connected with social technologies, the variety of designs available for exploring the effects of social interactions on behaviour outcomes will continue to increase.

Furthermore, the combination of network theory and social media has shown that strategically structured online communities can create social environments that promote behaviour change. By developing social media content that provides values to its users, digital campaigns can be highly effective in raising brand awareness, recruiting participants, and motivating them to take small, concrete actions.

Academics and practitioners that are looking to implement digital interventions need to consider their objectives, invest the appropriate time and resources, and take a 'test and learn' approach.

There are only a few research studies that have examined the success of social media in influencing real behaviour change. Therefore, to truly understand the possible impact—moving beyond measuring awareness and developing outcome measurement frameworks—further research is needed to advance the knowledge and skill in the field of digitally supported behavioural interventions.

Self-review questions

1. Describe the benefits of using digital interventions for behaviour change.
2. What are the individual behaviour change principles that can be applied in a digital intervention? What are the macro behaviour change principles?
3. List the dimensions of the social currency wheel and explain why they are important when developing content for a social media campaign.
4. Discuss the risks and considerations that are associated with setting up digital and social media communities.

References

Abraham, C., Kelly, M.P., West, R., Michie, S. (2009). The UK National Institute for Health and Clinical Excellence (NICE) public health guidance on behaviour change: a brief introduction. *Psychology, Health and Medicine* **14**: 1–8.

Bandura, A., Cervone, D. (1983). Self-evaluative and self-efficacy mechanisms governing the motivational effects of goal systems. *Journal of Personality and Social Psychology* **45**(5): 1017–1028.

Bandura, A., Cervone, D. (1986). Differential engagement of self-reactive influences in cognitive motivation. *Organizational Behavior and Human Decision Processes* **38**: 92–113.

Baumeister, R.F., Leary, M.R. (1995). The need to belong: desire for interpersonal attachments as a fundamental human motivation. *Psychological Bulletin* **117**(3): 497–529.

Berke, E.M., Choudhury, T., Ali, S., Rabbi, M. (2011). Objective sensing of activity and sociability: mobile sensing in the community. *The Annals of Family Medicine* **9**(4): 344–350.

Centola, D. (2013). Social media and the science of health behavior. *Journal of the American Heart Association* **127**(21): 2135–2144.

Freeman, B., Potente, S., Rock, V., McIver, J. (2015). Social media campaigns that make a difference: what can public health learn from the corporate sector and other social change marketers? *Public Health Research and Practice* **25**(2): e2521517.

Gold, J., Pedrana, A.E., Stoove, M.A., Chang, S., Howard, S., Asselin, J., et al. (2012). Developing health promotion interventions on social networking sites: recommendations from the FaceSpace Project. *Journal of Medical Internet Research* **14** (1): e30.

Grönroos, C., Voima, P. (2013). Critical service logic: making sense of value creation and co-creation. *Journal of the Academy of Marketing Science* **41**(2): 133–150.

Hamill, S., Turk, T., Murukutla, N., Ghamrawy, M., Mullin, S. (2013). I 'like' MPOWER: using Facebook, online ads and new media to mobilise tobacco control communities in low-income and middle-income countries. *Tobacco Control E-publication 23*(3): 306–312.

Kaplan, B.H., Cassel, J.C., Gore, S. (1977). Social support and health. *Medical Care* 15(suppl 5): 47–58.

Kiesler, C.A. (1985). Policy implications of research on social support and health. In: S. Cohen, S.L. Syme (eds). *Social support and health*. San Diego, CA: Academic Press: 347–364.

Lathia, N., Pejovic, V., Rachuri, K., Mascolo, C., Musolesi, M., Rentfrow, P.J. (2013). Smartphones for large-scale behavior change interventions. *Pervasive Computing 13*: 66–73.

Obar, J., Zube, P., Lampe, C. (2012). Advocacy 2.0: an analysis of how advocacy groups in the United States perceive and use social media as tools for facilitating civic engagement and collective action. *Journal of Information Policy* 2:1–25.

Ralphs, M. (2011). Built in or bolt on: why social currency is essential to social media marketing. *Journal of Direct, Data and Digital Marketing Practice 12*(3): 211–215.

Schunk, D.H., Rice, J.M. (1989). Learning goals and children's reading comprehension. *Journal of Reading Behavior 21*(3): 279–293.

UTalkMarketing.com (2009). *Cadbury Creme Egg social media campaign*. London: The Knowledge Engineers http://www.utalkmarketing.com/pages/article.aspx?articleid=14167&title=cadbury_creme_egg_social_media_campaign, accessed 20 October 2015.

Vivaldi Partners Group (2010). What is social currency? [website]. New York: Vivaldi Partners Group. http://www.vivaldipartners.com/vpsocialcurrency/about, accessed 15 October 2015.

White, M., Dorman, S.M. (2001). Receiving social support online: implications for health education. *Health Education Research 16*(6): 693–707.

Zimmerman, B.J. (1989). Models of self-regulated learning and academic achievement. In: B.J. Zimmerman, D.H. Schunk (eds). *Self-regulated learning and academic achievement: theory, research, and practice*. New York: Springer-Verlag: 1–25.

Chapter 13

Social franchising: strengthening health systems through private sector approaches

Julie McBride, Kim Longfield, Dana Sievers, and Dominic Montagu

Nearly every problem has been solved by someone, somewhere. The challenge of the 21st century is to find out what works and scale it up.

Bill Clinton

Learning points

This chapter:

- ◆ introduces the concept and practice of social franchising as an approach to delivering high-quality prevention, care, and treatment services in developing countries;

- ◆ explains and illustrates how social franchising can be used in the health context to improve access to health services and to prevent and treat disease;

- ◆ explores some of the different types of social franchising models and how they can be established and integrated with existing services;

- ◆ sets out some of the major lessons learned about how to establish, maintain, and promote effective and efficient social franchises that focus on health.

Introduction to social franchising

Franchising is a method of expanding a business and distributing goods and services. Franchisors grant a license to third parties (franchisees) for conducting business under a trademark (International Franchise Association, 2015). Franchisors specify the products and services that will be offered by franchisees and provide them with an operating system, brand, and support, including the elements listed in Box 13.1 (Burand and Koch, 2010).

Box 13.1 Elements of franchising

- Standardized business systems
- Strong brand identity
- Valuable know-how and experience
- Financing assistance
- Training and start-up support
- Reliable supply channels
- Marketing services
- Research and development
- Continuous support
- Peer learning opportunities

Source: data from Burand D and Koch DW. Microfranchising: a business approach to fighting poverty. *Franchise Law Journal*, Volume 30, Issue 1, pp. 24–34, Copyright © 2010 American Bar Association.

What is social franchising?

Social franchising is the application of commercial franchising concepts to achieve socially beneficial ends rather than profit. Social franchising has been used in health and other development areas, and has created opportunities for local entrepreneurs to deliver socially beneficial products and services in underserved communities worldwide (Social Sector Task Force, 2013).

How is social franchising related to social marketing?

Social franchising for health care arose from the need to create a distribution channel for socially marketed ethical drugs (e.g. injectable contraceptives) and devices (e.g. intrauterine devices) that require a skilled health care provider to prescribe or administer. Unlike over-the-counter products, consumers' use of ethical products is dependent upon health care providers' willingness and ability to diagnose, prescribe, and administer treatment to them. When the supply of such providers is low, social franchising can be used to expand it and thus create a distribution network for the products being socially marketed. Most low- and middle-income countries lack sufficient public health services. As a result, the majority of the population seeks care from the private sector (Bloom et al., 2008; Shah et al., 2011). While there is a perception that the private sector provides a higher quality of services than the public sector, standards for service delivery are often lacking, and when they exist there is little enforcement (Montagu et al., 2011; Patouillard et al., 2007; Shah et al., 2011; Berendes et al., 2011; Bennett et al., 2005; Hanson and Berman, 1998). Also problematic is that clients pay for the majority of private services out of pocket, which means that access can be restricted, especially for poorer clients (Tung and Bennett, 2014). These challenges are compounded, for family planning and other preventive services of high public health priority, because patient volumes are often small and prices and profit margins low. As a result, private providers can be reluctant to offer such services.

Clinical social franchising aims to strengthen the health system through the private sector. The franchisor—typically an implementing non-governmental organization (NGO): either a local agency or an international agency with an in-country presence—supports network members by branding private clinics and purchasing drugs in bulk at wholesale prices (Montagu, 2002; Ruster et al., 2003). This franchise model is designed to deliver three essential outputs for a health system (Montagu, 2002; Hillstrom, 2008):

1. maintain quality standards
2. achieve scale
3. generate economies of scale.

Maintaining quality standards

If care is not delivered in accordance with minimum accepted quality standards, it will not improve health outcomes. Quality can suffer as networks grow in size. As such, standards, and processes for supporting and enforcing them, must be developed and systemized. Franchise networks maintain standards by:

- providing franchisees with simple-to-follow clinical guidelines and business systems that work when used as intended;
- training and continuously supporting franchisees in using the franchise guidelines and systems;
- supplying franchisees with quality medicines and equipment; and
- aligning the incentives of franchisees with the aims of franchisors.

Franchisees often perceive a personal value and reputational incentive for adhering to network standards: they want to deliver good care, which the franchise can support, or they want to be affiliated with a reputable brand. When franchisees fail to comply with network standards they can lose their franchise. As long as the value of the franchise is greater than the value of breaking the rules, franchisees tend to comply, and standards are maintained across large networks.

Achieving scale

While a health care network will necessarily start small, it must be capable of growing into one that comprises hundreds or thousands of access points in a relatively short period of time—all the while, maintaining standards. If a network does not achieve scale, it will not be able to serve the population at a national level. Franchise networks scale better than many other models because they grow exponentially as the brand gains equity and demand for new franchise opportunities increases.

Generating economies of scale

The cost to serve each client should decrease as the network grows; otherwise, the system will be too expensive to sustain. Franchise networks generate economies of scale because costs associated with starting and operating new businesses are shared by franchisees, and costs associated with maintaining the network stay relatively stable even as the franchise grows, reducing the cost per client served (Box 13.2).

The evolution of social franchising

The application of franchising to the health sector started in the 1990s and has since grown in scale, scope, and sophistication. The Greenstar network established by Population Services International in Pakistan and the Sangini network established by the Nepal Contraceptive Retail Sales Company were early pioneers in the field (Center for Social Innovation, 2013; Viswanathan et al., 2014). Each brought small private sector providers under a common brand that offered

Box 13.2 Case study: the Sun Quality Health Network in Myanmar

Han Win Htat and Daniell Crapper

Aims

Myanmar (Burma) has historically experienced minimal government investment in its health system, and out-of-pocket expenditures on health are over 90% (World Bank Group, 2012a; 2012b). People in Myanmar typically receive services from unregulated private sector providers. In 2001, Population Services International launched the Sun Quality Health (SQH) social franchise network of private practitioners to improve the quality of services offered to those most in need and deliver cost-effective care at scale.

Behavioural objectives and target group

For providers, SQH establishes and implements franchise protocols to achieve minimum service delivery standards, and encourages the correct use of prescription medication through pre-packaged drugs. SQH positions itself as a trusted professional network of general practitioners offering high-quality services. Through SQH membership, providers can simultaneously build a business and reputation, while fulfilling a desire to earn merit[1] through a positive contribution to the community.

For clients, SQH is the friendly neighbourhood clinic where quality-assured and affordable health care is consistently available. The Sun brand gives them confidence that they are choosing the best medical services to meet their families' health needs (O'Connell et al., 2011).

Customer orientation

Evidence-based campaigns that use a mix of media and interpersonal communication support SQH interventions. Sun signboards on each clinic ensure easy identification (Figure 13.1). In 2008, Population Services International developed Sun Primary Health, a complementary village health worker network, offering primary health care services to harder-to-reach rural communities. Sun Primary Health providers refer clients to SQH clinics when necessary; together, they are the Sun network.

The social offering

Population Services International/Myanmar sets affordable prices and uses performance-based incentives to reduce the cost of care. A strong sense of social responsibility among providers ensures subsidies are targeted to the poor (Huntington et al., 2012). For example, the network offers low-income clients who are suspected of having tuberculosis transportation to clinics as an incentive to complete diagnosis and start treatment.

Target audience engagement and exchange

Population Services International conducts geo-mapping of health facilities before expanding to an area. Motivated providers with established private clinics that meet minimum infrastructural and other standards are invited to join the network. Population Services

Figure 13.1 A Sun Quality Health clinic in Myanmar.
Reproduced by kind permission of PSI/Myanmar, Copyright © 2004 Moe Thein Swe.

International conducts training, regular supportive supervision, and quality assurance visits; holds providers accountable against service delivery standards; and provides access to internationally procured commodities.

Audience insight and segmentation

Private providers are an essential entry point for health care and clients place a high level of trust in them. Providers were, however, outside the formal health system for decades; there was no continued education after medical school and minimal quality assurance. Providing a reliable business model could support providers to offer affordable health services and increase client flow.

Integrated intervention mix

The Sun network maximizes service integration when possible. Services now include HIV prevention and treatment, reproductive and sexual health, tuberculosis, malaria, cervical cancer, and maternal and child care services.

Co-creation through social markets

Given its scale, the Sun network supports the Myanmar Government's vision for a stronger health system and universal coverage by 2030. Population Services International enables meaningful and cost-effective engagement with the private sector at scale. Such a model can also reduce out-of-pocket expenses for clients.

Systematic planning

Population Services International capitalizes on lessons learned from other social franchises and on business model development. Burden of disease data and consumer and provider preferences determine how and where services should be delivered.

Results and learning

The University of California, San Francisco, and Johns Hopkins University conducted a series of evaluations to measure programme performance, which found that Sun increased health impact, quality, equity, and cost-effectiveness (Aung et al., 2012; 2014; Bishai et al., 2013; Montagu et al., 2013). In 2013 the Sun network provided 3.4 million total consultations (Viswanathan et al., 2014). By January 2015 over 1,400 franchised practitioners were serving in 219 of Myanmar's 326 townships.

Population Services International has learned that rapid scale-up is achievable: the number of Sun providers has grown by a factor of three over the past ten years. This has, however, put pressure on support functions. It takes considerable resources to supervise low-performing clinics, and the scale of the network has made systems more bureaucratic, which can reduce the speed of innovation.

Integrating new services increases the data collection burden on providers and Population Services International staff. These 'opportunity costs' of belonging to the network may offset some of the value providers see in the network. There are opportunities to increase the use of technology around treatment algorithms, supervision, training, data collection, and referrals. Population Services International must also focus on rationalizing the size of the network, exploring how clients value the network, and ensuring that the model constantly evolves.

References

Aung, T., Montagu, D., Schlein, K., Khine, T.M., McFarland, W. (2012). Validation of a new method for testing provider clinical quality in rural settings in low and middle-income countries: the observed simulated patient. *PLoS One* 7(1): e30196.

Aung, T., Montagu, D., Su Su Khin, H., Win, Z., San, A.K., McFarland, W. (2014). Impact of a social franchising program on uptake of oral rehydration solution plus zinc for childhood diarrhea in Myanmar: a community-level randomized controlled trial. *Journal of Tropical Pediatrics* 60(3):189–197.

Bishai, D., Sachathep, K., LeFevre, A. (2013). Determining the cost-effectiveness of managing acute diarrhea through social franchising of ORASEL: a randomized controlled trial. *Lancet* 381(2): S17.

Huntington, D., Mundy, G., Hom, N.M., Li, Q., Aung, T. (2012). Physicians in private practice: reasons for being a social franchise member. *Health Research Policy and Systems* 10(25).

Montagu, D., Sudhinaraset, M., Lwin, T., Onozaki, I., Win, Z., Aung, T. (2013). Equity and the Sun Quality Health private provider social franchise: comparative analysis of patient survey data and a nationally representative TB prevalence survey. *International Journal for Equity in Health* 12(5).

O'Connell, K., Hom, M., Aung, T., Theuss, M., Huntington, D. (2011). Using and joining a franchised private sector provider network in Myanmar. *PLoS ONE* 6(12): e28364.

Pundarika Foundation (2012). Accumulation of merit: preparing the heart for Bodhicitta. Crestone, CO: Pundarika Foundation http://www.tsoknyirinpoche.org/2579/accumulation-of-merit-preparing-the-heart-for-bodhicitta/, accessed 30 March 2015.

Viswanathan, R., Schatzkin, E., Sprockett, A. (2014). *Clinical social franchising compendium: an annual survey of programs: findings from 2013.* San Francisco, CA: Global Health Group, Global Health Sciences, University of California, San Francisco.

World Bank Group (2012a). Health expenditure, total. Washington, DC: World Bank http://data.worldbank.org/indicator/SH.XPD.TOTL.ZS, accessed 30 March 2015.

World Bank Group (2012b). Out-of-pocket health expenditure. Washington, DC: World Bank http://data.worldbank.org/indicator/SH.XPD.OOPC.ZS?page=1, accessed 30 March 2015.

quality and affordable family planning products and services. Their models were so successful in attracting franchisees and serving clients that the networks have since expanded to include thousands of providers in urban and rural areas.

The early success of social franchising made it increasingly popular in the development community as a means of improving access to quality health care in low- and middle-income countries. The industry has grown from just a handful of franchises in 2000 to what is now estimated to be more than 90 franchises in 40 countries around the globe (Figure 13.2). Many countries are home to more than one franchise, while other programmes span regions.

In addition to growth in scale, social franchising has grown in the scope of services offered (Figure 13.3). Early franchises focused on a few services within one health area, such as family planning and other reproductive health services, or HIV testing and counselling. Today, services have become more comprehensive and diverse, and most franchises cover at least two health areas, including maternal and child health, reproductive health, malaria, and tuberculosis.

Common models of social franchising for health care

Experience gained over the years has led to increasingly sophisticated applications of social franchising. The success of the models used depends on a number of factors, including the market conditions of the country—such as availability of health insurance, donor support, or other sources of funding—and the supply of health care providers.

The most commonly used model is the fractional model. Population Services International and Marie Stopes International are the largest fractional franchisors globally. Most NGO-sponsored networks have been designed as fractional franchises because they can leverage the existing infrastructure of clinics and expand rapidly. Within these existing clinics, fractional franchising adds services or improves those already offered. More comprehensive versions of the fractional model are appearing as social franchising evolves and franchisees offer a broader range of health areas and services.

Business format franchising, where the entire business operating system is standardized and franchised, is most effectively used with providers who wish to start their own practice but do not have the skills or capital to do so on their own. The HealthStore Foundation's® Child and Family Wellness (CFW) shops in Kenya (Box 13.3) and the Unjani Clinic in South Africa are examples of business format franchises (Imperial Health Sciences, 2015).

Holding franchisors accountable for achieving results

Over time, professionalization within the franchising community has increased, and there has been a growing desire to measure performance as well as to understand social franchising's effectiveness for delivering health care. While franchisors had been measuring their

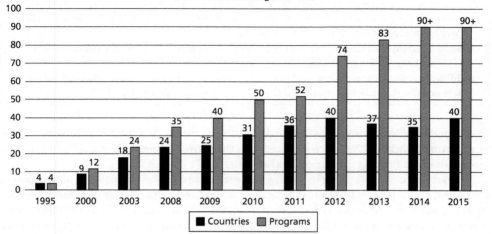

Figure 13.2 The growth of social franchising in selected countries, 1995–2015.
Source: data from *The Global Health Group. Clinical Social Franchising: An annual survey of programs, 2009*. San Francisco, CA: The Global Health Group, University of California, San Francisco, Copyright © 2009 The Global Health Group; *The Global Health Group. Clinical Social Franchising Compendium: An annual survey of programs, 2010 (May 2010)*. San Francisco, CA: The Global Health Group, University of California, San Francisco, Copyright © 2010 The Global Health Group; *The Global Health Group. Clinical Social Franchising Compendium: An annual survey of programs, 2011 (May 2011)*. San Francisco, CA: The Global Health Group, University of California, San Francisco, Copyright © 2011 The Global Health Group; *The Global Health Group. Clinical Social Franchising Compendium: An annual survey of programs, 2012 (May 2012)*. San Francisco, CA: The Global Health Group, University of California, San Francisco, Copyright © 2012 The Global Health Group; *The Global Health Group. Clinical Social Franchising Compendium: An annual survey of programs: findings from 2012 (May 2013)*. San Francisco, CA: The Global Health Group, University of California, San Francisco, Copyright © 2013 The Global Health Group; *The Global Health Group. Clinical Social Franchising Compendium: An annual survey of programs: findings from 2013 (June 2014)*. San Francisco, CA: The Global Health Group, University of California, San Francisco, Copyright © 2014 The Global Health Group; *The Global Health Group. Clinical Social Franchising Compendium: An annual survey of programs: findings from 2014*. San Francisco, CA: The Global Health Group, University of California, San Francisco, Copyright © 2015 The Global Health Group; *The Global Health Group. Clinical Social Franchising Compendium: An annual survey of programs: findings from 2015*. San Francisco, CA: The Global Health Group, University of California, San Francisco, Copyright © 2016 The Global Health Group.

performance, there were no standard metrics and none were tied to a common set of goals, especially at the health systems level. The right evidence would allow franchisors to benchmark their performance over time, report on system-level change to donors, and compare their performance against other franchisors.

In 2009, a group of measurement experts and stakeholders created the Social Franchising Metrics Working Group (SFMWG), an interagency group that standardizes metrics for performance, advocates their adoption, and develops materials to support franchisors to measure and report metrics. By 2014 the group represented 13 organizations, including franchisors, academics, donors, and professional networks (GHG, 2015).

The SFMWG identified five common goals for social franchising at the health systems level, which would be measurable and comparable (Viswanathan et al., 2014):

1. health impact
2. cost-effectiveness
3. economic equity
4. increased use
5. quality.

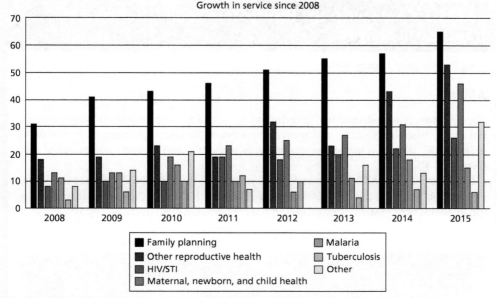

Figure 13.3 Health areas covered by social franchising 2008–2015.

Source: data from *The Global Health Group. Clinical Social Franchising: An annual survey of programs, 2009*. San Francisco, CA: The Global Health Group, University of California, San Francisco, Copyright © 2009 The Global Health Group; *The Global Health Group. Clinical Social Franchising Compendium: An annual survey of programs, 2010 (May 2010)*. San Francisco, CA: The Global Health Group, University of California, San Francisco, Copyright © 2010 The Global Health Group; *The Global Health Group. Clinical Social Franchising Compendium: An annual survey of programs, 2011 (May 2011)*. San Francisco, CA: The Global Health Group, University of California, San Francisco, Copyright © 2011 The Global Health Group; *The Global Health Group. Clinical Social Franchising Compendium: An annual survey of programs, 2012 (May 2012)*. San Francisco, CA: The Global Health Group, University of California, San Francisco, Copyright © 2012 The Global Health Group; *The Global Health Group. Clinical Social Franchising Compendium: An annual survey of programs: findings from 2012 (May 2013)*. San Francisco, CA: The Global Health Group, University of California, San Francisco, Copyright © 2013 The Global Health Group; *The Global Health Group. Clinical Social Franchising Compendium: An annual survey of programs: findings from 2013 (June 2014)*. San Francisco, CA: The Global Health Group, University of California, San Francisco, Copyright © 2014 The Global Health Group; *The Global Health Group. Clinical Social Franchising Compendium: An annual survey of programs: findings from 2014*. San Francisco, CA: The Global Health Group, University of California, San Francisco, Copyright © 2015 The Global Health Group; *The Global Health Group. Clinical Social Franchising Compendium: An annual survey of programs: findings from 2015*. San Francisco, CA: The Global Health Group, University of California, San Francisco, Copyright © 2016 The Global Health Group.

The power of the SFMWG is that it is a self-governed community that holds franchisors accountable for achieving results. Shared commitment to evidence and a belief in the benefit of alignment around a core set of metrics has allowed franchisors to standardize and share performance, and potentially to increase the impact of social franchising at the health system level.

At the last publication in 2016, the compendium (see Figure 13.6) reported on three core metrics: disability-adjusted life-years (DALYs) averted (health impact), cost/DALY (cost-effectiveness), and the distribution of clients across wealth quintiles (economic equity).

The other metrics—quality and increased use—have been less straightforward and the group continues to work on finding comprehensive approaches for measuring those. In 2014, the SFMWG added sustainability to the list of goals and will work with stakeholders to agree upon a definition and corresponding metric.

Box 13.3 Case study: the HealthStore Foundation's® CFW franchise in Kenya

Greg Starbird and Lauren Beek

Aims

The HealthStore Foundation® was founded in 1997 with a mission to improve access to essential drugs, basic health care, and prevention services for poor communities in the developing world. Its model maintains standards, is replicable, and achieves economies of scale (Figure 13.4).

In Kenya, where 106,000 children die each year before their fifth birthday, the HealthStore Foundation® founded the CFW franchise in 2000, which use a business format franchising model to distribute essential medicines in remote communities (UNICEF, 2015).

Figure 13.4 Children running in front of a CFW clinic in Kenya.
Reproduced by kind permission of The HealthStore Foundation®, Copyright © 2012 Blue Marble Media.

Behavioural objectives and target group

The CFW franchise is designed to incentivize health care providers to establish practices in underserved communities and hold them to a standard of care for effective treatment. It also works to increase coverage and draw new clients to CFW clinics and drug shops.

Customer orientation

Kenya's regulatory environment struggles to enforce quality in health care. Perverse incentives can encourage providers to deliver substandard or even harmful services. For example, some providers buy cheap counterfeit drugs to maximize profits, causing the children who receive those drugs to suffer from easily treated diseases.

The HealthStore Foundation® believes that to transform health care, it must be more profitable for providers to follow good practices than not. Its model applies incentives that motivate providers to maintain quality standards across all CFW clinics.

The social offering

CFW clinics offer essential treatment for malaria, diarrheal diseases, and skin, eye, and ear infections. CFW nurses provide quick diagnoses using rapid diagnostic tests; prevention products like mosquito nets, hand soap, and condoms; and education on health topics, like clean water, HIV transmission, and proper use of mosquito nets.

Target audience engagement and exchange

CFW clinics target potential clients through outreach, educational events, and local community groups. The CFW brand offers a promise of quality and the franchise uses its brand to create awareness and motivate clients to try its services. CFW franchisees are trained to convert trial into usage by delivering services that meet or exceed client expectations.

The network engages new franchisees by promising economic opportunity and ongoing support, education, and recognition for good service. The HealthStore Foundation® advertises franchise opportunities in locations based on its cluster-based expansion strategy. Once a potential franchisee has signalled interest, the CFW franchise supports the provider through the start-up process: accreditation, training, site selection, and financing.

Competition analysis

Kenya's tiered government distribution system is meant to serve clients at the base of the economic pyramid (BoP), but facilities are often understaffed, lacking resources, and ineffective at controlling quality (PSP4H, 2014). The private sector is split between high-level providers who do not serve BoP consumers for lack of profits, as well as fragmented providers nearer the BoP who deliver inconsistent or low-quality care and regularly sell counterfeit drugs.

The CFW franchise is designed to outcompete the counterfeit drug sellers and unregulated retail clinics serving the BoP by introducing an option for care that is more effective, but equally accessible.

Audience insight and segmentation

The CFW franchise gathers audience insight through market research, routine reports, and feedback from franchisees. Market research showing that people who live near a CFW outlet are significantly more likely to seek treatment has informed the placement of new clinics. Through random distribution of coupons to patients across wealth quintiles, the franchise learned that customers are more likely to value incentives that offer products (e.g. gift with purchase) than less tangible benefits (e.g. a percentage discount). Insight about the target population's health needs, care seeking, and product use helps the CFW franchise to improve its offering and marketing strategies.

Integrated intervention mix

The HealthStore Foundation® licenses the CFW outlet operation to franchisees—from menu mix, to drug handling, to recordkeeping—and provides ongoing support. It helps franchisees secure financing and high-quality products, receive regular training, select and prepare new sites, and coordinate efforts with national governments. The Foundation's compliance programme, executed through routine and random visits, ensures that drug, hygiene, financial, and other operating standards are consistently maintained throughout the network (Figure 13.5).

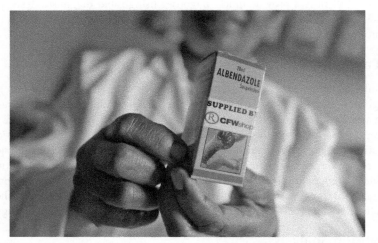

Figure 13.5 A CFW franchisee in Kenya holds a product from CFW's approved supply chain.
Reproduced by kind permission of The HealthStore Foundation®, Copyright © 2010 Riccardo Gangale.

Network standards for outreach have allowed the CFW franchise to reach hundreds of thousands of Kenyans per year with educational and promotional messages. Each franchisee agrees to conduct at least two outreach events per month— typically a CFW nurse presenting a health issue to 15–20 people from a community group.

Co-creation through social markets

Clients expect value for money, convenience, and trustworthiness from their health care providers. The CFW franchise's model aligns incentives between franchisor, franchisees, and third-party payers in a way that ensures clients' expectations are met.

CFW units are profitable, so franchisees want to own and operate them, driving scale. Because owning a CFW clinic is a source of both livelihood and pride, franchisees are also incentivized to adhere to the rules and maintain quality standards to protect their business.

Donor funds are currently used to subsidize clinic inputs, but the franchise is restructuring the flow of funds by creating third-party payer options that will reimburse franchisees for outputs, like services rendered to clients at the BoP. In this way, funds will create health markets that work for the poor. The CFW franchise's broad reach and reputation for quality will stimulate the market for demand-side health care financing products that increase consumer purchasing power.

Systematic planning

The CFW franchise began by creating a menu of services and drugs that would address communities' most pressing health needs and projecting how one franchised unit would operate. The team used market estimations to model a single unit's profitability and then applied the model to show how the network could scale to hundreds of units. Once funds were secured to establish it as a franchisor in Kenya, the team developed marketing and operations plans and began recruiting franchisees. The franchise continually collects and analyses data to adjust and improve its marketing and operations.

Results and learning

The CFW network has grown to 64 clinics and has served more than 5 million people in Kenya. The largest barrier to further growth has been suboptimal use of subsidies in the system. The current use of funds for clinic inputs helps attract clients and deliver care, but as long as franchisees serve the poor—which they must to remain a part of the CFW network—their earning potential will be low because their clients' purchasing power is low.

When subsidies are administered directly to franchisees for services provided instead of for clinic inputs, franchisees will have a greater incentive to deliver quality care to the poor. Franchisees can profit while at the same time achieving health impact, and the CFW network will also be able to grow and recover operating costs.

References

PSP4H (2014). *Health spending behaviour among low income consumers in Kenya: the myth that 'the poor can't pay'*. Nairobi: Private Sector Innovation Programme for Health.

UNICEF (2015). *State of the world's children 2015: executive summary*. New York: United Nations Children's Fund.

Key lessons learned

There are many lessons that industry experts have learned about social franchising in health care over the past 20 years. Here are the top ten.

1. **Be selective with franchisees—long-term success of the franchise depends on mutually beneficial partnerships.** A thorough recruitment and selection process with evidence-based selection criteria should be used to identify strong franchisee candidates. Franchisee selection should be made very carefully and with the understanding that both parties are entering into a long-term partnership. Due diligence is required to ensure that a potential franchisee is the right fit for a network. Conversely, the franchisor must accurately represent itself and its offering so that franchisees can make informed decisions about membership based on realistic expectations.

2. **Create value—consistency in network standards can only be achieved when the cost of deviation is too high to risk non-compliance.** For a franchise to succeed, the benefits of affiliation must outweigh the costs of membership requirements. If franchisees do not

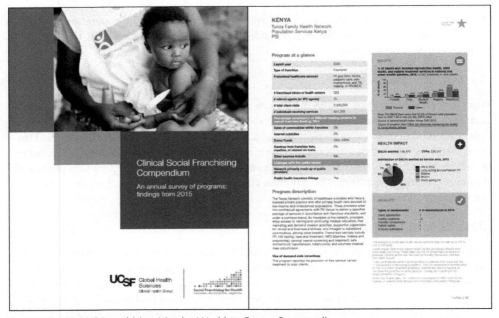

Figure 13.6 Social Franchising Metrics Working Group Compendium
Reproduced with permission from *Viswanathan, R., Behl, R.,* and *Seefeld, C.A.* Clinical social franchising compendium: an annual survey of programs: findings from 2015. San Francisco, CA: The Global Health Group, Global Health Sciences, University of California, San Francisco. Copyright © 2016 The Global Health Group.

experience sufficient tangible benefits with membership, they will be unwilling, or even unable, to maintain standards.

3. **Align incentives—franchising works best when franchisor and franchisee performance incentives are aligned.** Franchisees become successful as they provide more goods and services to clients, thereby fulfilling the franchisor's mission of health impact. If a franchisor does not adequately perform for franchisees, they can withdraw their business and the franchisor loses the contribution that the franchisee makes to its mission. In this way, franchisors and franchisees are in a symbiotic relationship where each is incentivized to do its best for the other.

4. **Standardize business systems—standardization leads to greater scalability.** Standardizing policies, procedures, forms, and customer service enables the franchisor to replicate more easily a successful medical clinic model across many locations. It is also easier to build the business acumen of health care personnel when business training is focused on very specific operational tasks that have been standardized, such as managing clinic finances.

5. **Strictly enforce clinical quality standards—a franchise can grow while maintaining standards if, and only if, standards are consistently enforced**. Franchisors must have very clear policies about the consequences of non-compliance with clinical quality standards. Those policies must also be enforced—for example, by revoking membership—so that franchisees take them seriously. Maintaining and enforcing clinical standards across networks is essential because it ensures that clients receive the appropriate quality of care and it protects franchises' brand image.

6. **Stay relevant—the franchise offering should continuously evolve to meet the needs of franchisees.** The first iteration of a franchise system is an essential part of a start-up plan,

but it will evolve over time, based on operating experience and changing market conditions. Franchisors must continually communicate with franchisees to understand their needs and support them accordingly.

7. **Integrate services—franchisees' service offerings should be relevant to the basic needs of the communities they serve.** Franchised offerings should be responsive to disease burden and the services most needed in the communities they serve. Donor funding for fractional franchises has traditionally been 'vertical' and supported one franchised service at a time, which has made integrating multiple services through this model difficult. While there are examples of fractional franchise networks integrating 'packages' of services, like gestational diabetes screening with reproductive health services, there remains potential to do much more integration across health areas (PSI, 2014).

8. **Measure performance—the social franchising community stands out as one that holds itself accountable for results.** The complexity of delivering clinical services across hundreds, sometimes thousands, of delivery points requires a high degree of acuity and professional attention to operational details. In response to this challenge, the social franchising community of practice has become a leader in self-assessment and in developing and adopting common performance measures to improve operations, management, systems, and outcomes.

9. **Use subsidies efficiently—subsidies will yield the highest returns when used to pay for clinic outputs rather than inputs.** When subsidies are administered directly to franchisees for clinic outputs (e.g. health impact) instead of for clinic inputs (e.g. training and supplies), then franchisees will have a greater incentive to deliver care to those most in need and do so in a manner that meets franchise standards.

10. **Keep costs down and revenues up—franchisors should work towards reducing reliance on donors for top-down funding to support franchise operations.** The majority of franchises receive donor funding to support service delivery; only three programmes rely on revenue from sales/services. In 2013 approximately 65% of franchises reported the same five donors as their primary funding source (Viswanathan et al., 2014). Franchisors should consider revenue-generating activities when possible. Possible strategies include product sales, cross-subsidization, training and marketing fees, franchise dues, and franchise royalties. In some contexts, it is appropriate for governments to include franchises in health financing and universal health care schemes, like insurance. Doing so makes it possible for franchisees to profit from serving clients who would otherwise be unable to pay for services.

Conclusion

Because of its ability to maintain standards at scale while also achieving economies of scale, the social franchise model has tremendous potential to strengthen health systems in the developing world. Costs associated with starting and maintaining social franchise operations have historically been covered through large donor grants. As the funding environment changes, it is possible that such donor funding will decrease. This will challenge donors and franchisors to operate differently (Beyeler et al., 2014).

At the very least, franchisors will need to demonstrate the added value of social franchising and how responsive it is to the goals of impact, cost-effectiveness, quality, equity, and improved 'total markets' for health. Alignment around the common set of metrics will help ensure that all franchisors can more accurately report their contributions to the health system.

Franchisors will also be challenged to find alternative ways to start and sustain operations. They will need to experiment with cost recovery mechanisms and more efficient and integrated business models. Some franchises are being designed with a goal of complete cost recovery, while still trying to address longstanding barriers to health care, such as low consumer purchasing power and shortages of health care professionals.

Guaranteeing that financial sustainability does not come at the cost of serving those most in need will remain a challenge, however. Franchisors operating under more traditional models, with health impact and equity as primary goals, will need to ensure that no one is left behind as they expand the total market for health and work with national stakeholders to strengthen health systems. All parties—governments, donors, and franchisors—will need to work together and remain realistic about what it will take to achieve universal health care when traditional funding sources are unavailable.

New types of franchise implementers, such as for-profit businesses and local entrepreneurs, are entering the social franchising space because they see the potential of the model to transform their health care businesses into more profitable and impactful enterprises. This is an exciting development: their experience will add greatly to the growing body of knowledge in social franchising. New sources of capital are also becoming available for health care franchising (GHG, 2014). Because of social franchising's potential to deliver high social returns and eventual financial returns, impact investors are already exploring the possibilities of investing in franchise start-ups. Going forward, it will be important to combine the desire for health and social impact with these business models, and to ensure that they too are in line with universal health coverage goals.

Social franchising for health care via the private sector will no doubt continue to attract capital in one form or another because it brings both socially beneficial products and services to clients at the base of the economic pyramid, and scalable business opportunities to micro-entrepreneurs. Those social returns, combined with the potential for long-term financial returns, make it a very attractive investment for anyone with money to donate, lend, or invest. The challenge for the social franchising community—donors and implementers alike—is to use those funds and each other wisely so that rapid advances in the industry can be made and more people will have access to the health services they need, at a price they can afford.

Self-review questions

1. What other private sector interventions could strengthen national health systems?
2. How can the social franchising community coordinate more effectively with the commercial franchise community to share best practices and lessons learned?
3. What are some alternative funding sources that could sustain and scale up franchise networks?
4. What are the trade-offs between sustainability and the larger social goals of health impact and equity?
5. How can the private sector help national stakeholders reach their universal health care goals?

Recommended reading

Clinical social franchising compendium (editions published 2009–2014). San Francisco, CA: Global Health Group, Global Health Sciences, University of California, San Francisco http://sf4health.org/research-evidence/reports-and-case-studies

For more on social franchising:

- ◆ **Center for Health Market Innovations** (2015). Social franchising [website]. Washington, DC: Center for Health Market Innovations http://healthmarketinnovations.org/ approaches/social-franchising, accessed 30 March 2015.
- ◆ **International Franchise Association's Social Sector Task Force** (2015). Washington, DC http://www.socialsectorfranchising.org
- ◆ **Social Franchising for Health** (2015). Social Franchising for Health [website]. San Francisco, CA: Social Franchising for Health http://sf4health.org/, accessed 30 March 2015.
- ◆ **Montagu, D.** (2002). Franchising of health services in low-income countries. *Health Policy and Planning* 17(2): 121–130.

For more on key players in social franchising:

- ◆ **Marie Stopes International** (2015). Social franchising [website]. London: Marie Stopes International http://mariestopes.org/what-we-do/social-franchising, accessed 30 March 2015.
- ◆ **PSI** (2015). Franchising for health [website]. Washington, DC: Population Services International http://www.psi.org/approach/social-franchising/, accessed 30 March 2015.

For more on metrics and accountability:

- ◆ **GHG** (2015). Metrics working group [website]. San Francisco, CA: Social Franchising for Health http://sf4health.org/measuring-performance/metrics-working-group, accessed 30 March 2015.

For more on sustainability:

- ◆ **Beyeler, N., Briegleb, C., Sieverding, M.** (2014). *Financial sustainability in social franchising: promising approaches and emerging questions.* San Francisco, CA: Global Health Group, Global Health Sciences, University of California, San Francisco http://sf4health.org/sites/ sf4health.org/files/wysiwyg/Financial-Sustainability-in-Social-Franchise-Programs.pdf

For more on the featured case studies:

- ◆ CFW/Kenya:
  - **HealthStore Foundation®** (2003). Our mission [website]. Minneapolis, MN: HealthStore Foundation® http://www.cfwshops.org/index.html, accessed 30 March 2015.
  - **Rangan, V.K., Lee, K.** (2011). CFW clinics in Kenya: to profit or not for profit. *Harvard Business Review* https://hbr.org/product/cfw-clinics-in-kenya-to-profit-or-not-for-profit/an/ 512006-PDF-ENG

- ◆ Suraj SF network:
  - **Marie Stopes Society** (2014). Reproductive health franchise project [website]. Karachi: Marie Stopes Society http://mss-rhf.org/, accessed 30 March 2015.
  - **Saeed, R., Khan, F.K.** (2010). *Case study: 'Suraj'—a private provider partnership.* Karachi: Marie Stopes Society http://www.sf4health.org/sites/sf4health.org/files/reports/Suraj-Case-Study-Final-2010.pdf

- ◆ SQH/Myanmar:
  - **PSI** (2015). Myanmar [website]. Washington, DC: Population Services International http://www.psi.org/country/myanmar/, accessed 30 March 2015.
  - **Montagu, D., Longfield, K., Briegleb, C., Aung, T.** (2013). *Private sector healthcare in Myanmar: evidence from the 'Sun' social franchise.* Washington, DC: Population Services International and Global Health Group, Global Health Sciences, University of California San Francisco http://www.psi.org/wp-content/uploads/2014/10/Private_Sector_Healthcare_ Myanmar_Evidence_from_Sun_Social_Franchise1.pdf

Note

1. Merit is an important concept in Buddhism and is based on the idea that good deeds accumulate throughout a lifetime and subsequent incarnations, bringing a person closer to the goal of enlightenment (Pundarika Foundation, 2012).

References

Bennett, S., Hanson, K., Kadama, P., Montagu, D. (2005). *Working with the non-state sector to achieve public health goals: making health systems work, working paper no. 2.* Geneva: World Health Organization.

Berendes, S., Heywood, P., Oliver, S., Garner, P. (2011). Quality of private and public ambulatory health care in low and middle income countries: systematic review of comparative studies. *PLoS Medicine* 8: e1000433.

Beyeler, N., Briegleb, C., Sieverding, M. (2014). *Financial sustainability in social franchising: promising approaches and emerging questions.* San Francisco, CA: Global Health Group, Global Health Sciences, University of California, San Francisco.

Bloom, G., Standing, H., Lloyd, R. (2008). Markets, information asymmetry and health care: towards new social contracts. *Social Science and Medicine* 66: 2076–2087.

Bloom, G., Standing, H., Lucas, H., Bhuiya, A., Oladepo, O., Peters, D.H. (2011). Making health markets work better for poor people: the case of informal providers. *Health Policy and Planning* 26: i45–i52.

Burand, D., Koch, D.W. (2010). Microfranchising: a business approach to fighting poverty. *Franchise Law Journal* 30(1): 24–34.

Center for Social Innovation (2013). *PSI: taking a service model to scale.* Stanford, CA: Stanford Graduate School of Business.

GHG (2014). *Second Global Conference on Social Franchising for Health, 22–24 October 2014, Cebu, Philippines.* San Francisco, CA: Global Health Group, Global Health Sciences, University of California, San Francisco http://sf4health.org/sites/sf4health.org/files/wysiwyg/2014SF%20 Conference%20Report_FINAL.pdf, accessed 30 March 2015.

GHG (2015). Metrics working group [website]. San Francisco, CA: Social Franchising for Health http:// sf4health.org/measuring-performance/metrics-working-group, accessed 24 March 2015.

Hanson, K., Berman, P. (1998). Private health care provision in developing countries: a preliminary analysis of levels and composition. *Health Policy and Planning* 13(3): 195–211.

Hillstrom, S. (2008). *Increasing access to life-saving medicines through business format franchising.* Minneapolis, MN: HealthStore Foundation®.

Imperial Health Sciences (2015). Unjani clinic pilot [website]. Centurion: Imperial Health Sciences http://www.ihs.za.com/content/unjani-clinic-pilot, accessed 30 March 2015.

International Franchise Association (2015). What is a franchise? [website]. Washington, DC: International Franchise Association http://www.franchise.org/what-is-a-franchise, accessed 24 March 2015.

Montagu, D. (2002). Franchising of health services in low-income countries. *Health Policy and Planning* 17(2): 121–130.

Montagu, D., Anglemyer, A., Tiwari, M., Drasser, K., Rutherford, G.W., Horvath, T., et al. (2011). *Private versus public strategies for health service provision for improving health outcomes in resource-limited settings.* San Francisco, CA: Global Health Sciences, University of California, San Francisco.

Patouillard, E., Goodman, C.A., Hanson, K.G., Mills, A.J. (2007). Can working with the private for-profit sector improve utilization of quality health services by the poor? A systematic review of the literature. *International Journal for Equity in Health* 6:17.

PSI (2014). *PSI/pasmo gestational diabetes mellitus.* Washington, DC: Population Services International.

Ruster, J., Yamamoto, C., Rogo, K. (2003). *Franchising in health: emerging models, experiences, and challenges in primary care.* Washington, DC: World Bank Group.

Shah, N., Wenjuan, W., Bishai, D.M. (2011). Comparing private sector family planning services to government and NGO services in Ethiopia and Pakistan: how do social franchises compare across quality, equity and cost? *Health Policy and Planning* **26**: i63–i71.

Social Sector Task Force (2013). About social sector franchising [website]. Washington, DC: International Franchise Association http://www.socialsectorfranchising.org/about.html, accessed 24 March 2015.

Tung, E., Bennett, S. (2014). Private sector, for-profit health providers in low and middle income countries: can they reach the poor at scale? *Globalization and Health* **10**: 52.

Viswanathan, R., Schatzkin, E., Sprockett, A. (2014). *Clinical social franchising compendium: an annual survey of programs: findings from 2013.* San Francisco, CA: Global Health Group, Global Health Sciences, University of California, San Francisco.

Index

Date Due
